CHARACTERISTICS OF CONGRESS:

Patterns in Congressional Behavior

W9-BCF-556

GLENN R. PARKER

Florida State University

PRENTICE HALL, Englewood Cliffs, New Jersey 07632

Library of Congress Cataloging-in-Publication Data
Parker, Glenn R.
Characteristics of Congress: patterns in congressional behavior/
Glenn R. Parker.

P. cm.
Bibliography: p.
Includes index.
ISBN 0-13-126111-8
1. United States. Congress. 2. Legislators—United States.
I. Title.
JK1061.P27   1989
328.73'073—dc19
            88-17050
                CIP

**To Chris, in the hope that he will also
be seduced into studying Congress**

Editorial/production supervision
  and interior design: Mary Kathryn Leclercq
Cover design: Photo Plus Art
Manufacturing buyer: Peter Havens

© 1989 by Prentice-Hall, Inc.
A Division of Simon & Schuster
Englewood Cliffs, New Jersey 07632

Printed in the United States of America
10 9 8 7 6 5 4 3 2 1

ISBN   0-13-126111-8

Prentice-Hall International (UK) Limited, *London*
Prentice-Hall of Australia Pty. Limited, *Sydney*
Prentice-Hall Canada Inc., *Toronto*
Prentice-Hall Hispanoamericana, S.A., *Mexico*
Prentice-Hall of India Private Limited, *New Delhi*
Prentice-Hall of Japan, Inc., *Tokyo*
Simon & Schuster Asia Pte. Ltd., *Singapore*
Editora Prentice-Hall do Brasil, Ltda., *Rio de Janeiro*

CONTENTS

LIST OF FIGURES AND TABLES   xi

Figures vi
Tables vii

PREFACE   xiii

Acknowledgments xvii

Chapter One
INDEPENDENT CONGRESSMEN   1

Evidence of Independence 4
Accounting for the Independence of Congressmen 10
Policy Consequences 17
Summary 18

Chapter Two
ATTENTIVE HOME STYLES   21

Evidence of Attentive Home Styles 26
Why Congressmen Adopt Attentive Home Styles 34
Policy Consequences 40
Summary 41

Chapter Three
POPULAR CONGRESSMEN AND AN UNPOPULAR CONGRESS   45

Evidence of the Popularity of Congressmen and the
  Unpopularity of Congress 46
Why We Love Our Congressmen but Not the Congress 54
Policy Consequences 61
Summary 62

Chapter Four
STABILITY IN THE MEMBERSHIP OF CONGRESS   65

Historical Trends in Turnover 66
Turnover in the Contemporary Congress 70
Conditions Promoting Stability in the Membership of Congress 81
Policy Consequences 89
Summary 92

Chapter Five
CAREER PATHS IN CONGRESS   95

Patterns in Congressional Careers 96
The Institutionalization of Congressional Careers 109
Policy Consequences 112
Summary 115

Chapter Six
BARGAINING PROCESSES   117

Where and How Bargains Are Made in Congress 119
Factors Promoting Bargaining 129
Policy Consequences 133
Summary 135

Chapter Seven
DECENTRALIZATION: THE FRAGMENTATION
OF CONGRESSIONAL POWER   137

Committees 138
Political Parties 151
Factors Promoting the Fragmentation of Power 157
Policy Consequences 160
Summary 162

Chapter Eight
CONSTITUENCY REPRESENTATION   165

Arenas of Constituency Representation 166
Factors Promoting Constituency Representation 173
Policy Consequences 179
Summary 181

Chapter Nine
LACK OF PARTY DISCIPLINE 184

Evidence of Lack of Party Discipline 185
Why Is Party Discipline So Weak? 194
Some Policy Effects of Weak Party Discipline 196
Summary 197

Chapter Ten
COZY TRIANGLES 199

How to Spot Cozy Triangles 204
Why Cozy Triangles Survive and Thrive 209
Policy Consequences 212
Summary 214

Chapter Eleven
PUTTING THE PIECES TOGETHER 216

Interrelationships Among Characteristics 217
Simulating Major Characteristics of Congress 219
Legislative Actors 221
Congressional Committees 228
Prefloor Congressional Procedures 230
Evaluating Legislative Success in the Simulation 234
Additional Suggestions 234
Characteristics of a Simulated Congress 235

APPENDIX 238

REFERENCES 240

INDEX 249

LIST OF FIGURES
AND TABLES

FIGURES

1-1 Ticket-Splitting in Presidential Elections 1900–1980, 13

1-2 Reelection Rates of House and Senate Incumbents 1946–1986, 15

2-1 Percentage of Electorate Writing to Their Congressman 1947–1984, 28

2-2 Time Spent in the Constituency 1959–1980, 30

2-3 Time Spent in Session: U.S. Congress 1789–1984, 31

2-4 Days in Recess: U.S. Congress 1943–1984, 39

3-1 Confidence in Leaders of National Institutions 1966–1981, 47

3-2 Constituent Trust 1978–1984, 49

3-3 Congressional Unpopularity 1939–1984, 50

3-4 Perceived Responsiveness of Congressmen 1964–1980, 54

3-5 Criteria Used in Evaluating Congress, 55

3-6 Perceived Importance and Time Spent on Congressional Activities, 57

4-1 Percentage of First-Term Members in House of Representatives 1789–1986, 66

4-2 House and Senate Retirements 1948–1986, 76

4-3 Senate Elections Won by 60 Percent of the Vote 1944–1984, 78

4-4 Partisan Defections to House and Senate Incumbents 1956–1982, 83

5-1 Time Spent in the District and Committee Responsibilities, 108

7-1 Organization of the House of Representatives, 152

7-2 Organization of the Senate, 153

9-1 Party Voting in the House of Representatives 1886–1984, 190

11-1 Hypothesized Relationships Among Characteristics of Congress, 217

TABLES

2-1 Voter Likes and Dislikes of Their Representative: 1978–1984, 32

2-2 Increases in House Perquisites: 1945–1975, 36

3-1 Whom People Would Turn to for Help if Faced with Specific Personal Problems, 53

4-1 Percentage of First-Term Members in Specified Congresses to Members Serving Additional Terms in Subsequent Congresses, 72

4-2 Membership of Classes in the House and the Entering Classes from Which They Principally Derive, 74

4-3 Safe Democratic and Republican Senate Seats in Northern States: 1946–1980, 79

5-1 Index of House Committee Prestige and Corresponding Rank: 80th–96th Congresses, 104

5-2 Mean Number of Days Spent in the District Per Congress by House Committee Chairs: 1963–1980, 107

5-3 Selection of Senate Committee Chairmen from 1784 to 1846, 110

7-1 Cleavages within House Committees: 1973–1980, 145

7-2 Party Committees in the Senate and House, 150

7-3 Informal Groups in Congress, 155

8-1 Representatives' Views of Functions Expected of Them, 174

9-1 Regional Fragmentation in the U.S. House of Representatives, 191

10-1 Subgovernment Importance, Cooperation, and Conflict in Six Policy Areas, 201

PREFACE

This book addresses several important questions relating to the study of congressional behavior. What are the major characteristics of Congress and its members? How have these characteristics shaped legislative politics and the behavior of congressmen? Why do these characteristics persist, and how do they influence legislative policy making? The "characteristics of Congress" examined in this book are descriptive statements about salient and persisting patterns in congressional behavior. The purposes of this study are: to identify persisting patterns in congressional behavior by drawing upon empirical research on diverse topics in the study of Congress; to offer explanations for why these patterns persist by synthesizing past empirical findings and conclusions, and by suggesting hypotheses; and to discuss the impact of these patterns in legislative behavior on the nature of congressional policy making.

This book is designed to appeal to undergraduates interested in understanding Congress and to legislative scholars in search of hypotheses, data, and generalizations for explaining congressional behavior. For undergraduates, the book acquaints students with extensive empirical research on Congress and simplifies the effort involved in comprehending, organizing, and retaining this information. For legislative scholars, the book identifies generalizations about Congress that have received broad empirical support and, therefore, can serve as assumptions for constructing models of legislative behavior; the book also aids scholars engaged in legislative research by describing important over-time trends in congressional behavior and by offering hypotheses to explain these salient patterns in legislative behavior. What makes these characteristics of Congress so important to understanding or analyzing congressional behavior is that they go a long way in defining the operations of Congress and the behavior of its members.

While it is often difficult to pinpoint the exact event or circumstance that served as the genesis for a book, I have no difficulty in identifying the stimuli for this book: my undergraduate students. Every year I am besieged by students in my undergraduate course on Congress to simplify their task of understanding Congress and legislative behavior. The message is always the same: The complexity of Congress, and the sophisticated analyses associated with legislative research, create obstacles to their understanding of congressional politics. The solution is also invariant: I am implored to simplify the tasks of organizing and comprehending the wealth of facts about Congress. This book is my response to that challenge. It represents my attempt to simplify the understanding of Congress while presenting a broad array of information about congressmen and the legislative process.

Characteristics of Congress enhances the understanding and retention of information about congressional politics by easing the storage and organization of that information. How well the book accomplishes this aim will depend upon the extent to which information about Congress is retained, the diversity of the information retained, and the gain in the breadth of the reader's understanding of congressional politics. Traditional topics of concern to congressional scholars like legislative elections, floor voting, and party leadership are not examined as specific topics but are discussed in terms of their relationship to 10 characteristics of Congress. This approach is not a mere reshuffling of traditional topics of legislative research into different categories: Past empirical findings are cast in a different light with respect to many of these topics as they are reexamined in terms of the persisting attributes of Congress and congressmen. This approach facilitates the integration of findings and generalizations from diverse areas of legislative research that might otherwise remain unconnected because of the traditional compartmentalization of congressional politics into the study of committees, party leaders, congressional elections and recruitment, interest groups and political parties, legislative oversight, floor voting, and constituency behavior.

Another factor that spurred the writing of this book was the cognizance of how similar in nature were the findings drawn from empirical works on diverse topics in the study of Congress. The widespread empirical replication of these findings, and the persistence of these patterns in legislative behavior over long periods of time, set these derivative generalizations apart from others. While some of these generalizations about patterns in legislative behavior may seem so commonplace as to be termed "truisms," this should not obscure their value in linking together findings drawn from diverse studies of legislative behavior. Nor should the simplicity of these descriptive statements be regarded as void of analytic value. I have tried to demonstrate that these generalizations account for some of the essential aspects of legislative policy making and define many of the basic features of Congress. Since these patterns are basic to the operations of Congress and the behavior of its members, and have received widespread empirical support, the characteristics of Congress can serve as important assumptions in creating deductive models of congressional behavior.

Assumptions serve as the foundation upon which theories are constructed. One example is the assumption common to many rational choice models of congressional behavior—namely, that incumbents are driven by the desire to be reelected (Mayhew, 1974a; Fiorina, 1977). Once introduced into an analysis, other behavioral propositions consistent with these assumptions can be derived deductively. Therefore, assumptions are extremely powerful devices for constructing rather elaborate theories, despite their apparent simplicity. Assumptions are rarely tested and only infrequently challenged; they are often justified on the grounds that they are essential for theoretical predictions, or they are defended on the basis of a "causal story"—a logical, hypothetical set of conditions that is purported to lend credibility to the validity of an assumption. Differentiating between useful and not so useful assumptions is normally based on the significance of the results of an analysis based on the assumptions, or on the degree to which the results theoretically fit predictions. An even stronger case can be made for introducing an assumption into an analysis if it is empirically valid. Since theories and models are expected to speak ultimately to the empirical world, they should be constructed upon a basis that can be justified empirically. Hopefully, some of the patterns in legislative behavior that I identify—the characteristics of Congress—can function as assumptions in deducing hypotheses and propositions about Congress.

The characteristics of Congress combine attributes of congressmen and attributes of the legislative process. The characteristics of congressmen are their political independence, lack of turnover, attention to constituents, popularity among voters, career orientations, and representation of constituent interests. The characteristics of the legislative process examined in this book are bargaining in legislative decision making, decentralization of power, lack of party discipline, and the existence of "cozy triangles" between agencies, congressional committees, and constituency groups. Each of these characteristics, in turn, influences the formation of policy in Congress.

Congressmen are characterized as independent political actors who exercise considerable freedom in how they behave in Washington and in the personal goals they pursue. Despite this freedom of action, congressmen devote considerable attention to their constituency responsibilities. This is one reason why congressmen are normally popular with their constituents. Congressmen, like most political actors, are goal-oriented; they seek the satisfaction that results from pursuing careers in

Congress that lead to the exercise of power, influence over a policy or program, and electoral security. In addition to realizing their own career objectives, congressmen make a concerted effort to represent the interests of their districts and states in major policy-making arenas.

Congress is characterized as an institution with little change (turnover) in its membership where bargaining processes dictate legislative outcomes. One obvious characteristic of the legislative process is the high degree of decentralization of power: Power and influence is widely dispersed over a large number of structural units, like committees and subcommittees, and a wide range of legislative actors such as informal groups and factions within the parties. The present-day Congress is distinguished from earlier ones by the general lack of party discipline; party members evidently prefer their freedom to maneuver to the constraints imposed by party discipline. Finally, the existence of mutually beneficial relations between committees, groups, and agencies structures a large number of the decisions made within Congress and the federal bureaucracy.

These 10 characteristics were selected for study because they are important forces in shaping legislative behavior and therefore enter into many explanations of the operations of Congress and the behavior of its members. In addition, they represent persisting features of Congress and congressmen, many of which have left and continue to leave an indelible mark on Congress. Finally, these characteristics were selected because they reflect salient attributes of Congress and its members. This is not to deny that some of these characteristics may be less stable or persisting than others; where changes in the persistence of a characteristic have occurred, I have noted them. On the whole, the characteristics selected for study are persistent ones, though not immutable.

One final point: There are some interesting interrelationships among these 10 characteristics. In the final chapter, I speculate about these interrelationships, suggesting some hypothetical linkages among them. In addition, I describe how these characteristics might be used within a laboratory or classroom setting to structure a simulation of the legislative process.

The simplicity of these characteristics and their limited number should not mislead the reader into feeling that he or she has missed "something" important about Congress. These 10 characteristics represent major generalizations about congressional behavior that have accumulated over the years, and the simplicity of these generalizations should not obscure their analytic value for understanding congressional behavior. Many of these characteristics occupy prominent positions in theories of legislative behavior or deal with central questions in the study of Congress. This is not to argue that this book gives an exhaustive treatment of every topic; like all books, this one also leaves some topics untouched. Hopefully, these exclusions will not impair the readers' understanding of Congress.

Each chapter in the book follows the same outline. The first section defines and describes a particular characteristic of Congress. Next, the empirical evidence of the existence of the characteristic is synthesized and summarized; the reader's attention is focused on how the characteristic manifests itself in various aspects of congressional behavior. In the third part of each chapter, some hypotheses and theories that explain the existence and persistence of a characteristic are critically examined. Finally, some of the theories and hypotheses that link a specific characteristic to the nature of legislative policy making are explicated in the concluding section of each chapter.

I have tried to concentrate on what I believe to be the most important aspects of Congress and congressional behavior in writing this book. If some topics are neglected, it is only the natural (and unfortunate) result of the need to limit one's study. I am certain that legislative scholars will think of other characteristics that could be added to this inquiry. If this book has stimulated such thinking, then it has accomplished more than I had ever expected. Some may argue that the emphasis on patterns in legislative behavior ignores, for the most part, deviations from these patterns. My approach falls prey to this criticism. I would only counter that such anomalies are so much easier to detect once we have defined the patterns from which these deviations occur.

ACKNOWLEDGMENTS

I would like to acknowledge the support of the Florida State University, which granted me a sabbatical to complete this book. I would also like to express my appreciation to several legislative scholars whose research has stimulated my interest in Congress over the years: Roger H. Davidson, Richard F. Fenno, Morris P. Fiorina, David Brady, Joseph Cooper, Charles S. Bullock III, Larry Dodd, John Kingdon, and Nelson Polsby. These scholars have left an indelible mark on my understanding of Congress; my intellectual debts to them should be evident throughout this book. This book has also benefited from the advice and comments of several scholars who read earlier versions: Professor Roger Davidson, University of Maryland; Professor Charles S. Bullock, III, University of Georgia; and Professor Richard Champagne, University of Wisconsin–Madison. Their suggestions helped to improve the book and I will always be in their debt. In addition, I would like to thank Karen Horton and Katy Leclercq of Prentice Hall for the assistance and advice they provided during the writing and editing of the manuscript. My deepest debt is owed to my wife Suzanne Parker for enduring endless discussions about characteristics of Congress; without her patience and encouragement, the ideas behind this book would have remained just that—ideas.

Chapter One
INDEPENDENT CONGRESSMEN

A major characteristic of congressmen is that they exercise considerable latitude and freedom in the pursuit of personal goals within Congress. They pursue these goals generally unfettered by electoral reprisal on the part of constituents or punishment at the hands of party leaders. This is not to deny that there are costs associated with voting against one's constituents or party. Voting persistently with the opposition party, for instance, may incur the wrath of other party members as well as leaders, resulting in an informal ostracism from the party; a string of "wrong" votes may stir a significant segment of a member's constituency coalition to defect at the next election.

Members are not ignorant of these costs when they make their decisions, but they seem willing to endure them nonetheless. One reason members seem "prepared" to incur these costs is because they rarely have to endure them. Only occasionally is a member reprimanded for voting against the party, and only a chemical trace of the policy decisions taken by congressmen ever emerges on the consciousness of their constituents. In sum, incumbents seek to realize personal goals such as reelection, "pet" policies, and power, and they exercise significant freedom from the constraints imposed by political parties, constituents, and leaders in the pursuit of these individual goals.

Even institutional norms that once constrained expressions of independence appear to be on the wane. In his 1960 study, Donald Matthews observed that "the first rule of Senate behavior, and the one most widely recognized off the Hill, is that new members are expected to serve a proper apprenticeship" (p. 92). In its simplest terms, the apprenticeship norm restrained junior senators from participating fully in the work of the Senate; they were expected to serve a rather lengthy period as novice legislators learning the traditions and ways of the Senate. Speaking of the House of Representatives, Richard Fenno (1965) described the apprenticeship norm in similar terms:

> Every new member of the House is expected to observe an apprenticeship—to work hard, tend to his constituency, learn his committee work, specialize in an area of public policy, appear often but speak very seldom on the floor, and cooperate with the leaders of his committee and of his party. (p. 71)

The apprenticeship norm set effective limits on the extent to which members could express their independence and individuality within the Senate or the House, but declining adherence to this norm removed an effective constraint on the independence of incumbents.

The experience of former Representative John Brademas (D-Ind.) captures the nature of the times in earlier congresses. He recalled standing at the back of the House floor with the late Albert Thomas (D-Tex.), a senior member who firmly believed that "going along was the best way of getting along." The occasion was the third speech in the same week by a newly elected freshman. This prompted Brademas to comment to Thomas that he had been in Congress for three years and had not yet spoken that much on the floor of the House. Thomas turned to him, and said, "yes, John. And you've got a lot of friends because of it." This constraint on the activism of freshmen has all but disappeared, according to Charles Clapp (1963):

> The old admonition that new members should observe but not participate in debate was swept aside long ago. Apprenticeship may still precede full partnership, but the increased volume and complexity of the problems with which the Congress is compelled to cope dictate more efficient use of the membership. (pp. 12–13)

The empirical evidence for the decline of the apprenticeship norm is indeed impressive. For example, Herbert Asher's study of the learning of legislative norms in the House of Representatives finds that support for apprenticeship among freshmen eroded during their first five months in office. Perhaps of greater importance is his finding that almost two-thirds of the nonfreshmen members that he interviewed denied the necessity of apprenticeship altogether (Asher, 1973). In a similar vein, David Rohde and his colleagues (1985) report that the apprenticeship norm has virtually disappeared in the Senate. "The evidence from our interviews is clear, unequivocal, and overwhelming: the norm is simply gone" (p. 175). Freshmen are not expected to remain on the sidelines nor is their participation in committee or on the floor subject to rigid constraints (Sinclair, 1986). In fact, individualistic behavior that might have been restricted by the apprenticeship norm is now being encouraged, even by senior senators. The experience of former Senator William Buckley (1973), unusual in earlier eras, is far more commonplace today:

> The ancient tradition that stated that freshman senators were to be seen and not heard has disappeared. Somewhat to my surprise, on my initial rounds I was encouraged by the most senior members to speak out when I felt I had learned the ropes and had something to say . . . (p. 147)

Congress is quite tolerant of individualistic behavior, even rather offensive displays of independence. Legislative deviance may not be encouraged as a role model for others to follow, as Ralph Huitt (1960) contended in his analysis of Senator William Proxmire's legislative style,[1] but few would deny that deviant behavior is tolerated in Congress. And Congress has had its share of iconoclasts. The flamboyance of such legislators as Adam Clayton Powell (D-N.Y.), who disregarded House rules by using public funds for personal expenses,[2] and Bella Abzug (D-N.Y.), who intentionally stirred the ire of her colleagues on a daily basis by insisting upon wearing a hat (with a plumed feather) on the floor of the House, may be institutional anomalies, but the aberrant behavior they displayed was more or less tolerated by their colleagues.

When thinking of independent legislators, attention normally turns to the Senate, since individuality appears to be a guiding rule in its organization and operation. "The contemporary Senate accords its members very wide latitude; maximum accommodation of the individual members has become the overriding expectation" (Sinclair, 1987, p. 25). For example, a lot of business in the Senate is conducted by unanimous consent agreements, which ensure that each senator has a say in determining the legislative schedule; any decision rule that requires unanimous approval guarantees that no one will be disadvantaged (unless they agree to be disadvantaged). Moreover, the potential for unlimited debate, the infamous Senate filibuster, grants every senator a potential veto over decisions favored even by a large majority of senators. The House of Representatives, like the Senate, is also supportive of individualistic pursuits:

> Regardless of the goals a member pursues, or in what combination, their achievement by most is not enhanced through the integration of committee power, strong party organizations, or parliamentary procedures that limit a member's floor opportunities to debate, amend, and otherwise influence legislation. Reelection, internal power, and good public policy are, within the framework of congressional politics, highly individualistic pursuits. (Woll, 1985, p. 63)

The independence and individuality of representatives and senators find expression within Congress in a number of ways.

EVIDENCE OF INDEPENDENCE

Independence and individuality are exhibited in making policy decisions, in creating personal electoral coalitions, and in pursuing individual legislative goals through committee assignments. Congressmen leave their personal imprint on each of these activities. Legislative outcomes often reflect the efforts of dozens of congressmen pursuing some individual objective, rather than the results of cohesive and coordinated partisan majorities. Electoral coalitions, too, have an individualistic flavor: Incumbents often encourage their supporters to affix their loyalties to the "man and not the party." By reducing their dependence on political parties for electoral support, the existence of personalized electoral coalitions strengthens the bargaining positions of incumbents in their dealings with party leaders. Finally, the committee system provides mechanisms for realizing personal legislative goals, and committee assignments reflect personal ambitions. All of these displays of independence tell the same story: Congressmen exercise considerable latitude within Congress.

Policy Making.   Most of the policy-making behavior of congressmen involves individualistic pursuits. Members operate as individual policy entrepreneurs in a variety of ways: casting votes, drafting bills and amendments, sponsoring legislative measures, participating in floor and committee debate, and engaging in committee and subcommittee deliberations (hearings, mark ups, investigations, preparation of reports accompanying legislation). Obviously, a congressman cannot be involved in each and every activity, nor can he perform all of the necessary work involved in each task. Congressional services such as the Congressional Research Service, Office of Technology Assessment, Congressional Budget Office, General Accounting Office, and committee and personal staff help congressmen to keep abreast of legislative actions and aid in developing legislation. But it is the congressman himself who orchestrates the interplay of these resources: He decides his areas of interest, and the policy alternatives that should be embodied into law; legislative recommendations are frequently accepted or rejected by the congressman depending upon the extent to which the solutions are consistent with his goals and attitudes. In short, congressmen are actively involved in individualized pursuits, although they may seek and receive assistance from other legislative actors.

Members generally promote policy issues on a unilateral basis. That is, they formulate their legislative measures without much attention to the legislative efforts or initiatives of their colleagues or party leaders. The large number of identical bills introduced each year are expressions of this unilateral promotion of legislative issues; the variation in these measures is slight, at best. While some duplication of effort can be attributed to the members' desire to gain visibility or to demonstrate legislative effort, the inclination (if not the preference) of congressmen for a unilateral approach to most issues seems equally relevant.

This penchant of congressmen to ply their policy-entrepreneurial talents within the legislative arena often runs counter to the designs of party leaders. "Too many leaders can spoil the policy" might be the refrain that is most frequently voiced by legislative leaders. They correctly perceive that congressmen pursue disjointed policies (unconnected policy outcomes) in the absence of centralized sources for coordinating policies. The weaknesses of party leaders inhibits their ability to provide direction and to encourage comprehensive policy agendas. In fact, leaders often find it necessary to tolerate the individualistic policy pursuits of their members in the hope of building support for current or future party policies. The old caricatures of leaders pressuring members and "twisting" arms to gain votes have been replaced by new leadership strategies that permit members greater involvement in the formation of party policy (Sinclair, 1983). Further, recalcitrant members are not usually punished for failing to support party leaders, and leaders themselves seem willing to accept most excuses for party defections. Leaders are more willing to bargain and compromise with their colleagues over policy matters of interest to the party; persuasion has replaced command as the operative mode for conducting leader–follower relations in the present-day Congress.

Congressmen also exhibit their independence in policy making through their voting in Congress. The extent to which congressmen vote their own attitudes and beliefs, rather than constituency opinion or the party line, might go unnoticed given the significance of party and constituency in legislative decision making. Many studies have found that political parties exercise a profound influence on the voting behavior of congressmen, with the impact of constituency opinion not far behind (Turner, 1951; Truman, 1959; Clausen, 1973). This finding has been repeated with such frequency that one political scientist was moved to remark, "a fortune awaits the person who can exact a toll of twenty-five cents for every time a political scientist repeats the tiresome truism: Party is the best single predictor of voting in the United States Congress" (Clausen, 1973, p. 91). To contest the importance of party and constituency in legislative voting seems futile in light of the evidence supporting the claim. The only reservation expressed here is that this explanation leaves very little room for the influence of the congressman's own values, beliefs, and attitudes.

That congressmen express their independence in floor voting is often ignored in accounting for their behavior, but there is substantial evidence that the individual member is, even if overlooked, a significant variable.

For instance, Warren Miller and Donald Stokes (1966) demonstrate that representatives express their own attitudes and perceptions in roll-call voting: the "evidence shows that the Representative's roll call behavior is strongly influenced by his own policy preferences and by his perception of preferences held by the constituency" (p. 56).

Studies of legislative turnover and voting behavior generally reach the same conclusion about the influence of individual attitudes in congressional decision making: New members promote policy changes because they exhibit voting patterns that differ from their predecessors (Brady and Lynn, 1973; Asher and Weisberg, 1978). Thus, replacing one representative with another makes a difference both to parties and to constituents since different policy perspectives are likely to result from such a change. This fact is evident in Lewis Froman's study (1962) of House votes on reciprocal trade issues between 1948 and 1958. Froman reasoned that if a congressman's own attitude influenced his vote, apart from the effects of party and constituency, representatives replacing incumbents in one-party districts (those solidly in the control of one political party or the other) would nevertheless vote differently from the representatives they replaced. He tested this hypothesis and found that those one-party districts that failed to elect the same incumbent during the 10-year period exhibited the greatest over-time shifts between support and opposition to reciprocal trade legislation. Thus, districts that changed representatives experienced a different brand of representation, even though the constituency and party characteristics of the district remained stable.

Perhaps the clearest expression of the impact that a member's attitudes can have on his vote is the influence of ideology in House and Senate voting. The common liberal-conservative ideological continuum can account for a substantial proportion of the variation in the voting behavior of congressmen. For example, in separate studies, Keith Poole and R. Steven Daniels (1985) and Herbert Kritzer (1978) found a clear unidimensional organization to major House and Senate votes that reflected a liberal-conservative continuum. There is also evidence that sizable voting blocs on the floor of Congress (Brady and Bullock, 1980) and in committees (Parker and Parker, 1985) organize on the basis of similarities in ideological outlook. The conservative coalition of Republicans and conservative (mostly southern) Democrats, a loosely formed voting bloc of like-minded congressmen, emerged in the 1930s as an alliance to thwart federal support for organized labor. The coalition continues to appear on floor votes in the contemporary Congress although less frequently in recent years (*Congressional Quarterly Weekly Report*, 1987). In House committees, liberal and conservative factions (voting blocs) can be identified, and successful coalitions within these committees have a distinct ideological flavor (Parker and Parker, 1985). Thus the existence of ideological voting in Congress is evidence of the importance of individual attitudes and values in legislative decision making,[3] and is one way in which the independence of congressmen affects policy making.

One final expression of the independence of members in policy making is the willingness of members to impose a trustee perspective on their legislative responsibilities. Trustees tend to see their representational obligations as requiring them to exercise their own best judgment in deciding legislative policy; delegates, on the other hand, see their responsibilities as requiring them to follow the dictates of their constituents rather than their conscience in casting roll-call votes. Practicality aside, most constituents prescribe the delegate role for their representative (Parker, 1986b). Congressmen, however, seem to prefer the more independent position associated with the trustee role: More than 60 percent of the congressmen interviewed in 1977 believed that they should follow their own conscience rather than the dictates of their constituents when the two clash (Parker, 1986b).

The trustee role is, of course, a general orientation toward legislative responsibilities, and particular issues or votes may stimulate members to assume delegate roles no matter how committed they are to exercising their own independence. Unusually controversial votes where constituent sentiment is intense may provide just the type of conditions that quickly turn die-hard trustees into delegates. Such conditions aside, congressmen seem to envision their legislative responsibilities as requiring them to exercise their own independence, giving free rein to the influence of their own attitudes, values, beliefs, and perceptions in making policy decisions.

Elections. A salient feature of current congressional elections is the development of personal electoral followings. While political party remains a potent predictor of congressional as well as mass voting behavior, congressmen and senators in the present Congress have been quite adept at attracting large voter followings who owe their allegiance to the officeholder rather than the political party. Electoral coalitions are, of course, primarily composed of partisans, and the personal electoral followings created by representatives and senators are no exception. Incumbents do not eschew the support of partisans; in fact, the incumbent's party affiliation probably serves as an initial inducement for the organization of his or her electoral coalition. Nor do incumbents attempt to destroy these party attachments; rather, congressmen attempt to wean their followers from an exclusive dedication to the party. They try to establish a "higher authority"—the incumbent—among their electoral supporters; they want coalition members to follow their lead whether or not their policy positions coincide with those of the political party. Fidelity to the party is only a secondary consideration to congressmen, and they try to establish the same priorities among their supporters. The result is the development of electoral coalitions within districts and states that are loyal to individual congressmen.

These personal electoral organizations free members from reliance upon their political parties for cadres of election workers and supporters. With their own electoral organizations in place and operating on a full-time basis, congressmen see little need to make party a major theme in their campaigns or in their presentations to constituents. After all, emphasizing partisanship may produce electoral defections: People who have defected to the incumbent's side may return to the fold if partisanship emerges as a critical issue in an election. Therefore, it behooves most incumbents to deemphasize partisan considerations and to emphasize his or her own record. This may explain why constituent perceptions of their representative rarely contain a trace of partisanship: Most constituents see their member in highly personal terms, not partisan ones (Parker and Davidson, 1979).

Without an electoral basis for influencing the commitments of congressmen to their political parties, leaders must depend upon the willingness of members to support the party's position in constructing legislative majorities. And the willingness of congressmen to back the party is likely to depend upon the extent to which the policy interests and goals of individual members can be realized by following party leaders. When party and individual goals are identical, party causes and individual ones lead to the same legislative decision: Support the party. The general lack of party voting in Congress suggests that such circumstances arise somewhat infrequently.

Committee Assignments.   A major vehicle for realizing personal goals is the committee system. Committees provide members with forums to espouse national causes and to legitimate claims of policy expertise. In addition, committees place their members in a network of specialists that ensures them contact with important policy actors, such as interest groups and administration officials; such contacts can enhance a member's prestige and further constituency interests. Some committee assignments would seem to be especially beneficial in motivating constituent support. Committees like Public Works and Interior, for example, provide the type of legislative outcomes that divert federal monies to districts and states. Water projects, dams, federal land acquisitions and devolutions, are just a few of the legislative benefits that these committees can provide to individual constituencies. Assignment to committees like these may ingratiate voters to the incumbent and result in satisfying (and safe) reelection victories.

On the other hand, independent congressmen can be expected to ignore the reelection benefits stemming from a particular committee assignment if it means the subordination of preferred goals. Motivations to realize legislative goals, rather than electoral ones, guide many preferences for committee assignments. For instance, Charles Bullock (1972b) analyzed the committee assignments of House freshmen between 1947 and 1967 and found that committee assignments rarely helped the narrowly elected survive reelection:

> Most congressmen may be free to make committee requests on the basis of subject-matter interests, political ambitions, desires for power, and other goals which may or may not be perceived to improve their standing with their constituents. Congressmen may be able to pay proper homage to the Madisonian ideal of constituency interest representation by processing casework, visiting the district, expressing concern for district problems, and making a display of their attempts to resolve such problems. (p. 1006)

(For a similar conclusion, see Fowler, Douglas, and Clark, 1980.)

Even if electorally beneficial committee assignments do not deliver safe reelections, do incumbents nevertheless seek such assignments? The answer appears to be "no." For example, freshmen congressmen in the 92nd Congress (Bullock, 1976) were largely motivated to select their committee assignments on the basis of policy concerns, and in the 97th Congress, policy motivations rivaled electoral ones (Smith and Deering, 1983); in both Congresses, about 80 percent of the freshmen congressmen expressed an interest in a policy-oriented committee assignment. These preferences occurred despite the obvious need of these politically insecure members to strengthen their electoral holds on their districts! Reelection may be an important consideration to every member—after all, it is the penultimate objective that must be realized before other goals can be pursued—but it does not consume all of their attention or energies. The same conclusion emerges from an analysis of the committee requests made by Democratic senators between 1953 and 1971: 21 percent of the requests mentioned the senator's interest in a policy domain as the rationale for requesting the assignment, while about one-third of the senators' requests cited reelection reasons (Bullock, 1985).

Thus, the independence of representatives and senators results in the pursuit of committee assignments that reflect their own individual policy interests. This is not to say that the interests of constituents play no role whatsoever in the selection of committee assignments. As I discuss later, some assignments are requested to maintain a constituency "stake" on a committee or because the existing geographical distributions in federal spending warrants assignment to a particular committee.

Does this mean that congressmen forsake entirely the electoral benefits that can be attained by assignment to certain committees? Not really. One of the marks of the contemporary Congress is the expansion of the number of committees to which a congressman is assigned (Parker, 1986b). As a consequence, the potential conflict between maximizing reelection or other legislative goals never really materializes. Incumbents can pursue several goals simultaneously—reelection, policy, and power—because they can serve on committees that aid their reelection while also holding committee assignments that enhance the attainment of other personal goals. It might seem that incumbents would be overburdened by such multiple obligations, forcing them to let some obligations slip in order to realize other ones. Fortunately, "trade-offs" of this nature rarely arise since committee and personal staff keep an incumbent abreast of the activities in all of his committees. Hence, congressmen are able to pursue multiple goals without the fear that doing so would irreparably harm the attainment of any single goal or drastically reduce the probability of realizing any of them.

ACCOUNTING FOR THE INDEPENDENCE OF CONGRESSMEN

The independence of congressmen in the present Congress is bolstered by institutional and electoral conditions, home styles, and membership changes. Institutional conditions, such as existing levels of government subsidies for office perquisites, enable most incumbents to withstand the pressures from their party leaders by preventing party leaders from reprimanding their colleagues by denying them either their office resources or their positions on committees. Office resources and committee assignments are critical for the realization of personal legislative goals: Office resources help members to build and maintain voter coalitions and to develop policy proposals for legislative action; committee assignments provide forums for pursuing policy interests, power, or reelection.

Electoral conditions have weakened the inclination of members to rally around the party's position on legislation. The declining attachments of constituents to the political parties and the considerable electoral safety exhibited by most legislators make incumbents less dependent upon the parties for their survival at election time. Without electoral incentives for supporting the party, the rationale for exercising one's independence within Congress becomes even more compelling.

The home styles of representatives and senators—the ways in which incumbents cultivate their constituencies—provide them with a means through which the information reaching constituents can be structured ("packaged") to promote certain objectives, such as reelection. Frequently incumbents structure the information reaching their constituents to gain their trust and, therefore, some latitude in Washington. Finally, membership changes—younger and more ambitious members entering Congress (Payne, 1980)—may have gradually changed the complexion of the institution by creating an environment that is more conducive to legislative independence and individuality. Clearly, these four factors do not exhaust the explanations or causal variables linked to the independence of congressmen, but they seem necessary, if not sufficient, for the maintenance of this characteristic of Congress.

Institutional Conditions. Two institutional conditions have bolstered the independence of congressmen by virtually prohibiting the intervention of party leaders in the affairs of their colleagues: the seniority system and the automatic allocation of office resources. The seniority system is a tradition within Congress that has the force of written law—rarely is the principle that longevity counts ignored by party leaders or other members. While it is not mentioned in the rules of either the House of Representatives or the Senate, the notion that consecutive terms in Congress should serve as a decision rule for allocating a variety of legislative benefits has been adhered to quite faithfully. The benefits may range from office space—the Rayburn House Office Building is a more prestigious and better furnished location for an office than either the Longworth or Cannon Office Buildings—to committee assignments—Government Operations is a more prestigious committee assignment than is Veteran Affairs.

The seniority rule provides an automatic way of allocating these benefits that is largely immune to the influence of party leaders. Members receive the same allocation of office resources, and their positions on committees are guaranteed, as long as there is not a significant change in the ratio of Democrats to Republicans within the institution (House or Senate). Changes in the ratio of Democrats to Republicans in the institution would result in members with the least seniority being removed from committees. Aside from interparty turnover, however, seniority ensures members a claim to a committee position by virtue of having been assigned to that committee in the past. It turns turf into property.

Since party leaders violate the seniority rule only at risk to their own power, seniority offers members protection against the discretionary behavior of their party leaders. Seniority has been, and remains, an important basis for selecting committee chairmen; it also serves as a deterrent to leadership actions to reprimand recalcitrant members by removing them from their "pet" committees. Once assigned to a committee, only shifts in party ratios or unusual political circumstances can provide adequate rationale for removing a member from a committee. For example, two southern Democratic congressmen were stripped of their seniority for supporting Barry Goldwater's 1964 presidential candidacy. By protecting members from the type of actions that can shatter goal pursuits, such as being removed from a committee, the seniority system has strengthened the independence of congressmen.

Committee assignments are a relished commodity in Congress because they provide mechanisms for translating legislative goals into reality. For instance, incumbents with interest in particular policy issues may find assignment to a committee with jurisdiction over these issues essential for realizing this goal. After the committee assignment is made, the need to curry the favor of party leaders declines since the seniority system protects members against being removed from committees. Party leaders still have a say if members want to transfer from one committee to another; here, considerations of party loyalty may figure into the decision to grant a transfer to a requesting member (Rohde and Shepsle, 1973). The ability of most congressmen to receive their preferred committee assignment early in their congressional careers (Gertzog, 1976), however, limits their motivations to transfer; hence, party leaders can only influence their colleagues over the short haul.

By removing the leadership threat to the realization of personal goals attained through committee assignments, members have gained a measure of freedom from their parties and leaders. In fact, one major cause of the emergence of the seniority system can be traced to the institutional protections that it afforded members against the discretionary actions of party leaders. The evolution of the seniority system owes a great deal, according to Nelson Polsby and his colleagues (1969), to the membership revolt against then "czarist" House Speaker Joseph Gurney Cannon (1903–1911).[4] Until this revolt by "insurgent" Republicans and Democrats, the Speaker held the formal power to name the membership of committees from top to bottom, majority and minority. Speaker Cannon's arbitrary use of this appointment power led to a revolt on the part of House members that wrested this authority and vested the power of appointment in party committees on committees. Once the threat of arbitrary action in the designation of committee assignments was neutralized, members could give fuller expression to the types of individualistic behaviors that might have led to the loss of a committee position in earlier times.

Office perquisites also help incumbents to realize policy and reelection goals. Financial support for constituent mailings and expenses incurred in travel between the district (or state) and Washington are just two examples of federally subsidized resources available to congressmen that appear to enhance the satisfaction of the reelection goal. For instance, incumbents who mailed "baby books" to their constituents as a gift for the new father and mother increased their reelection margins (Cover and Brumberg, 1982), and increased office allowances in the House and Senate helped to strengthen the electoral safety of incumbents who represented areas that were politically atypical of their own party loyalties and ideologies (Parker, 1986b). Office "perks" are allocated on a universal basis, and the inability of party leaders to control this resource reduces their influence over their members.

The staffs of congressmen—another subsidized resource—also enhance the realization of both policy and reelection goals. Personal staff serve as the basic components in the "political" machine that members assemble to run their offices, and they function as a full-time election apparatus between and during elections. Many congressional challengers, and those interested in election reform, often assail the ability of incumbents to exploit their office resources in their reelection campaigns despite legislative restrictions to the contrary. Personal staff help members realize their policy goals by performing much of the research and "legwork" that goes into the making of policy. Staff handle legislative issues by drafting bills, preparing statements for debate or for insertion into the *Congressional Record*, and organizing congressional hearings; in many instances, they operate as the incumbent's contact with constituent groups and policy experts. These functions are performed, of course, in addition to the basic clerical responsibilities of answering constituent inquiries and seeking redress of constituent problems. Personal staff, like other office perks, are provided automatically.[5]

Thus, party leaders have little influence over the attainment of most goals of importance to individual members. Even the goal of exercising power in Congress by attaining a position of formal party leadership can be only sporadically affected by party leaders. In short, automatic rules applying to the allocation of office resources have weakened the ability of leaders to affect the goal attainment of their members and, in the process, strengthened the independence of congressmen.

Electoral Conditions. There are probably a variety of electoral conditions that have bolstered the independence of congressmen, but two of the

FIGURE 1–1 Ticket Splitting in Presidential Elections 1900–1980 [Source: Ornstein et al. (1982, p. 53).]

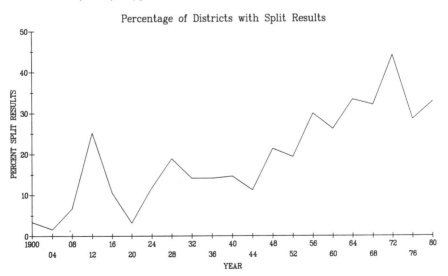

Percentage of Districts with Split Results

the most obvious are the electoral safety of incumbents and the declining influence of party identification on voter loyalties. While party identification remains a potent predictor of vote decisions in presidential and congressional elections, there is little doubt that the influence of party has declined in recent decades (Ferejohn, 1977). Fewer people identify with either of the major parties today than in the past, and more and more voters split their votes between a presidential candidate from one party and a congressional incumbent from the other. For example, in 1920 only 3.2 percent of the congressional districts exhibited split results (i.e., districts carried by a presidential candidate of one party and a House candidate from another), but from 1956 to 1980 more than one of four congressional districts revealed split outcomes (Figure 1-1).

Such "split-ticket" voting reduces the incentives for incumbents to strengthen their ties to their parties. Not only is there little benefit in maintaining a close association with the party, but there is a great deal of potential danger: Few victorious presidential candidates run ahead of the incumbent representative in the district, and more often than not the incumbent's vote total in the district or state exceeds that attained by the president. Some may even accuse presidents of "hurting" candidates from their own party. For example, former President Jimmy Carter ran behind a number of senators who were themselves narrowly defeated in the Reagan landslide in the 1980 election. Close association with the president or the party can produce detrimental effects as voters deliver the same verdict in congressional races that they reach in voting for the president. Close association with a popular president, of course, may pay handsome dividends, and some congressmen and senators, especially newly elected ones, have sought to establish just such close connections. The risks of such a strategy, however, may outweigh the gains, and for most congressmen it is probably all risk. This may explain why congressmen show no reluctance to attack their own political leaders or to criticize their parties: They don't want voters to link their electoral fate to that of their parties.

Most members have good reason to feel that they can pursue their own legislative interests without much interference from constituents or leaders, if we judge their security in terms of the size of their vote margins and the probability of reelection. There is no doubt that incumbents never quite see themselves as electorally safe as their vote margins would indicate, but incumbents have assembled some impressive evidence of electoral safety. For example, over 90 percent of the House incumbents running for reelection have been successful in most elections since the 1940s (Figure 1-2), and over 70 percent of the House incumbents have been reelected with at least 60 percent of the vote in most elections since the late 1960s (Ornstein et al., 1982).

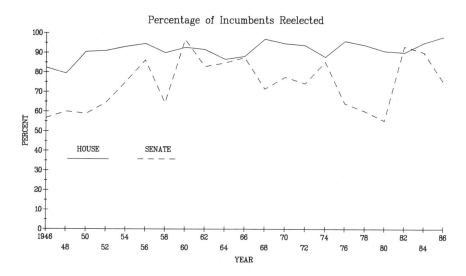

Percentage of Incumbents Reelected

FIGURE 1–2   Reelection Rates of House and Senate Incumbents 1946–1986 (Source: *Congressional Quarterly Almanac,* vols. 2–42.)

Senators cannot boast of the same level of electoral security, but the statistics are nonetheless impressive: At least 70 percent of the senators have been reelected in over 60 percent of the elections since the late 1940s (Figure 1-2), and since the 1950s about 40 percent of the incumbent senators have been reelected with at least 60 percent of the vote. Although the reelection rates and levels of safety achieved by senators cannot rival those attained by representatives, the six-year term of senators may ease electoral anxieties and increase political independence. Elections may be more troublesome for senators than representatives, but senators have more time to adjust to the threat. For instance, the behavior of senators appears to follow an electoral cycle: Voting behavior moderates (Thomas, 1985) and constituency travel intensifies (Taggert and Durant, 1985) as elections approach. During the four years prior to their reelections, however, senators behave more independently. Therefore, even if senators do not enjoy the same level of electoral safety exhibited by most House incumbents, their reelection prospects are still quite encouraging, and the six-year term reduces whatever electoral anxieties might be associated with the greater competitiveness of senate contests. The result is that senators, like representatives, can exercise a great deal of independence in Congress.

Since one of the major functions of political parties is to win elections, the failure of parties to significantly influence the electoral fate of most incumbents weakens party control. With few electoral benefits to offer incumbents, political parties must depend upon nonmaterial incentives, like political symbols and historical traditions, to entice congressional support. Such enticements are generally ineffective in restraining the independence of congressmen.

Home Styles.   Richard Fenno (1978, 1982) first coined the term "home style" to describe the manifold ways in which incumbents relate to their constituents. The home styles of congressmen and senators are the ways in which incumbents cultivate their constituents and nurture images and perceptions that generate voter support. Home styles provide mechanisms for disseminating the type of images that sustain a congressman's independence. They also enable members to gain freedom to pursue their individual legislative goals without interference from constituents. This occurs because home styles are designed to create trust on the part of constituents, which enables members to pursue personal goals without fear of electoral reprisal or of questioning (of their motives) by constituents. More will be said about home styles in the next chapter; let it suffice at this point to note that home styles enhance the independence of congressmen by enabling members to maintain the trust of their constituents and therefore the freedom to pursue personal goals. Freed from critical constituent supervision, incumbents enthusiastically pursue personal legislative interests.

Membership Turnover.   One characteristic of present congresses that has probably strengthened the independence of congressmen is the change in the type of member entering Congress. James Payne (1980) noted a sharp shift in the age and the levels of ambition exhibited by House incumbents: Recent entrants are younger and more likely to harbor aspirations for higher political office. These attributes stimulate the types of behavior that reduce collective action on the part of political parties. Young, ambitious members often seek to establish national reputations and prominence; to attain these goals, members often find it necessary to eclipse party and leadership involvement on legislative measures. The influx of this type of member reduces the ability of leaders to stake out party positions on legislative issues, since their efforts are apt to be overshadowed and perhaps thwarted by these ambitious congressmen. Thus, the entrance of more ambitious members strengthens the extent to which independence is practiced, if not encouraged, within Congress. Perhaps the independence exhibited by senators is due to the ubiquitous nature of ambition within the Senate. As Nelson Polsby (1971) observed, the Senate is a "presidential incubator." In sum, the type of member entering the contemporary House and Senate exhibit many of the characteristics that seem to enhance the motivations for political independence.

POLICY CONSEQUENCES

As independent congressmen and senators pursue personal goals, they shape policy outcomes and decision-making processes. Policy entrepreneurship, which was cited as evidence of the independence of congressmen, poses severe problems in mobilizing coherent policy majorities. A basic reason for this state of affairs is that there is no centralized influence for coordinating policy initiatives, and most members benefit from having it that way, though all bemoan the weaknesses of their parties. Incumbents are primarily concerned with pursuing their own policy interests and in exercising leadership rather than "followership." The lack of a partisan imperative further reduces the incentives to follow the lead of the party. Instead of comprehensive party programs, then, most legislation involves the unconnected legislative efforts of members pursuing individual policy goals.[6]

Congress is infamous for its slow response to national problems. The legislative process is often identified as the culprit in preventing policy majorities from quickly materializing. Just as important is the independence of congressmen, which forces extensive bargaining at many decision points in the legislative process. True, Congress may be partially responsible for this state of affairs since it has decentralized authority (for example, by strengthening subcommittees), but if members were responsive to the will of their leaders, they would fall easily into line behind them. Decentralization might make the process more difficult since legislative majorities are necessary at each decision point, but the majority party's program should survive intact if party discipline prevailed. Party members may require some involvement in a decision, but they are not likely to exact the price that members bent on exercising independence will demand. Instead, decentralization strengthens further the hand of an independent membership. Decentralized decision making provides independent members with opportunities to inject their own preferences into party programs; this necessitates bargaining among members at each decision point to achieve a successful legislative majority. While these majorities may overlap some, there is no assurance that majorities at one stage of the process (for example, the floor of the House) might not contradict the decisions supported by a majority at an earlier phase of the process (for example, in congressional committee or subcommittee). Therefore, party leaders are constantly involved in bargaining for support at multiple decision points in the legislative process, and majorities at each point do not necessarily coincide in policy outlook. Such extensive negotiations produce some of the lack of alacrity associated with the legislative process.

In sum, comprehensive party programs may fail for a variety of reasons, but the independence of congressmen and senators makes such policy decisions improbable. Independent members force leaders to abandon hope of passing comprehensive party programs; party programs are replaced by the aggregate effort of members pursuing individual policy interests. Congressmen may bemoan the lack of party leadership, but if you query them about their willingness to subordinate their own policy interests to that of the party, their enthusiasm for strong parties diminishes rapidly. Party leaders do what they can to mobilize partisan sympathies and support among their members, but most of the time they must resort to bargaining and persuasion, which slows the advance of most policies, fostering legislative stalemate and delay.

SUMMARY

A major characteristic of congressmen, then, is their independence: They exercise considerable latitude in their pursuit of personal goals within Congress. Norms that restrained legislative independence in earlier eras have all but disappeared, and congressional tolerance for individualistic behavior remains strong. The independence of congressmen is evident in their approach to policy making. Incumbents operate as individual policy entrepreneurs promoting policy issues on a unilateral basis. While such behavior may not be conducive to the efforts of the parties to mobilize coalitions, party leaders tolerate such entrepreneurial activity. This approach to policy making is carried over into voting decisions, which often reveal the influence of personal ideology along with the effects of partisan attitudes and constituency interests. The independence of congressmen is also evident in their capacity to construct personal electoral followings that free members from exclusive reliance upon their parties for electoral support. Fidelity to the party is only a secondary consideration for independent congressmen, and they try to implant the same priorities in the minds of their supporters. Another expression of the independence of congressmen is their pursuit of personal goals vis-a-vis committee assignments. Simply put, legislators seek committee assignments that further personal goals and not necessarily electoral ones.

This independence thrives for a number of reasons. First, the seniority system and the automatic allocation of office resources restrict the ability of party leaders to intervene in the affairs of their members. The seniority system offers members protection against the discretionary behavior of their party leaders by restricting the opportunities to replace recalcitrant members on committees; once assigned, only unusual political circumstances or shifts in the composition of Congress can justify removing a member from a committee. Further, the automatic allocation of office resources means that incumbents will have adequate resources to support their personal electoral organizations without having to curry the favor of party leaders. Second, incumbents enjoy unusual electoral safety: There is an unusually high probability of reelection, and electoral safety is quite common, at least in terms of objective indicators. Such safety reduces many of the benefits that can be derived from supporting the party and its leaders. Third, members have adopted attentive home styles that generate trust on the part of constituents, providing members with freedom to maneuver on Capitol Hill and to pursue personal goals in Congress. Finally, membership turnover has resulted in the entrance of a younger and more ambitious legislator—two attributes that often complicate the efforts of party leaders to construct coherent policy majorities. As a consequence, it is difficult if not impossible to organize coherent policy programs since such effort frequently runs counter to the policy entrepreneurial activities of individual members. In addition, the independence of congressmen necessitates extensive bargaining by party leaders, which often disrupts attempts to fashion coherent legislative programs and always slows the legislative process.

Notes

1. In the early 1960s, congressional scholars debated the extent to which senators followed institutional norms—"cultural 'oughts' upon which there is a high degree of consensus" (Huitt, 1961a, p. 566). Ralph Huitt argued in his now famous article on former Senator William Proxmire that the Senate maverick or "outsider" is an institutionally recognized role. The maverick is described by Huitt as one who speaks "out whenever he pleases on whatever subject he chooses without regard to whether he can get any vote but his own" and who looks for support from his constituents and ideological allies across the nation rather than his colleagues in the Senate (p. 571). Huitt claims that the role of maverick has been accepted and esteemed by specialized publics outside of the Senate and recognized as legitimate within the Senate itself. The evidence for Huitt's proposition is indeed fragile. To support his claim, Huitt notes that "men noted for their independence [rank] at or close to the top of lists of outstanding senators" compiled by specialized groups, like political scientists (p. 572), and they "advance without hindrance to the perquisites of seniority, and some of the most powerful committees have had rather odd chairmen" (p. 573).

   Donald Matthews challenges Huitt's interpretation, arguing that the behavior of such "outsiders" may be tolerated by other senators but in no way is it considered a legitimate role: "In my interviews almost all the Senators were *morally indignant* at the behavior of Outsiders. They expressed exasperated tolerance, yes; but I uncovered no evidence that they granted Outsiders legitimacy" (Matthews, 1961, p. 882). According to Matthews, toleration of the idiosyncrasies of Senate mavericks only testifies to the importance of other folkways (or norms) such as courtesy and seniority. In short, Matthews contends that Huitt ignores the difference between legitimacy and tolerance. Matthews' point is a valid one, but changes in the Senate may make Huitt's argument that the Senate Outsider is a legitimate role more compelling today than in the past.

2. Congressman Adam Clayton Powell (D-N.Y.) was accused of willfully and wrongfully appropriating public funds for his own use by allowing salaries to be drawn by people who were not performing their stipulated office duties. For instance, Powell allowed his housekeeper in the Bahama Islands to draw salary as a member of the staff of the House Education and Labor Committee and hired his wife although she performed no official duties in Washington or New York. For an account of the circumstances surrounding congressional attempts to deny Congressman Powell his seat in Congress, see Andy Jacobs' *The Powell Affair* (1973).

3. The existence of ideological voting has been challenged by research conducted by Aage Clausen, and Donald Matthews and James Stimson. Clausen (1973) demonstrates that several policy dimensions—civil liberties, international involvement, agricultural assistance, social welfare, and general management—underlie congressional roll calls, rather than a single (liberal-conservative) continuum. Matthews and Stimson (1975) argue that ideological voting fails to occur with any frequency because: (1) many legislative measures have no easily identifiable ideological content to motivate liberal-conservative voting; (2) the ideological content of bills may be obscured by the complexity of the legislation or legislative strategy; and (3) many bills reflect more than a single ideological view so that the ideological direction of the legislation remains ambiguous. They suggest that the prediction that members with similar views on issues—similar ideological positions—vote together can be explained by members adopting the same voting position as better informed and trusted colleagues—i.e., cue-voting.

4. An alternative explanation for the emergence of the seniority system is suggested by H. D. Price (1975). Price argues that the system represented a rational response to the longevity of congressional careers (lengthening terms of office) resulting from declining electoral competition after 1896. As members began to survive reelection with some degree of frequency, they wanted longevity to count for something; hence, the establishment of longevity, seniority, as a decision rule for allocating legislative power.

5. There is some variation in the size of Senate staffs, based on population size, but these allocations are made on the basis of an established formula; hence, Senate leaders have no greater influence over the size of the staffs of senators than House leaders have over the staffs of representatives.

6. Another policy consequence closely associated with the enhanced independence of congressmen is the increase in the number of decisions that are made on the floors of the House and Senate. For instance, in the House of Representatives, the number of amendments offered to pending legislation more than tripled between the 1950s and the 1980s, and the percentage of legislation subject to floor amendments more than quadrupled during the same period (Smith, 1986). A similar pattern persists in the Senate (Sinclair, 1987).

Chapter Two
ATTENTIVE HOME STYLES

Congressmen spend considerable time cultivating their districts and states and promoting the image that they are personally attentive to the problems and interests of their constituents. The term "home style" refers to how members of Congress go about cultivating their constituencies (Fenno, 1978); attentive home styles drive home the message that the congressman is *personally* involved in looking after the interests of constituents. Incumbents are constantly on the watch for ways to demonstrate such a personal concern, and the opportunities to do so are plentiful. Home styles are an amalgam of three activities: the congressman's allocation of his personal resources and those of his staff, his presentations to constituents, and his explanations of Washington activities (Fenno, 1978).

Allocation of Resources. How a congressman allocates his time between Washington and the district or state tells us a lot about his priorities since time is the scarcest and most valuable resource at his command. If there is one perennial complaint among congressmen, the lack of time is surely it. Incumbents jealously guard their own time, often creating barrier reefs of staff to protect them from claims on it. Members are sensitive to wasting this scarce resource, and activities that squander a member's time are avoided, unless they involve constituents. Protecting their own time has become such a major preoccupation of congressmen and Congress that efforts have been taken to reduce the burdens on a member's time. For instance, Congress has equipped congressional offices with a wide assortment of resources for reducing demands on their time. Personal staff, office space, allowances, expense accounts, and free mailings are just some of the resources provided congressmen, but the personal time of the incumbent is one resource without substitution. While staff perform many constituency-related functions, their efforts only supplement those of their bosses. Moreover, there is no adequate substitution for the personal attention of the congressman in the eyes of most constituents, and some things can only be done personally by the incumbent, like meeting with constituents and addressing large gatherings at home.

The personal time of the congressman is also a resource that is less divisible, unlike personal staff. Staff can be distributed between the Washington and home offices without disrupting either the lawmaking or constituency service responsibilities of congressional offices. Not so with the time of congressmen. The allocation of time to constituent affairs poses a dilemma for most members of Congress, since the time spent in the constituency (or with constituents) could also be spent in legislative activities that might enhance the realization of personal goals. This potential "zero-sum" relationship (time spent with constituents cannot be spent on other things) creates a strain between the desire to attend to legislative business and the need to spend time on district and state matters. Most congressmen would rather devote their time to legislative business, and many see constituency matters as actually interfering with the performance of these responsibilities (U.S. Congress, House, 1977). Yet, members willingly allocate large proportions of their personal time to constituent affairs—one of the clearest manifestations of an attentive home style.

In some cases, attention to the district or state "costs" the congressman very little in terms of the demands on his time. For example, sending newsletters to constituents can be delegated to staff, thereby reducing the impact of such constituency activity on the personal time of the congressman. Staff can address constituent problems and expedite their resolution without the involvement of the congressman in most instances; on less routine matters that might necessitate the congressman's intervention, staff may take action literally in the name of the boss! Members do get personally involved in many of these activities from to time to time, although the costs to them rise precipitously when they do so. Congressmen may complain about getting involved in constituent affairs, but few avoid doing so when the necessity arises because the cost of not being personally involved in constituency affairs significantly outweighs the cost of such involvement. "If these House members failed to see ten people in Maple Grove or cancelled the open meetings or relinquished caucus leadership or left immediately after the clambake, they believe it would cost them dearly in electoral support" (Fenno, 1978, p. 191).

Presentations. The "centerpiece" of an incumbent's home style is the way in which he relates to his constituents: presentation of self (Fenno, 1978). Incumbents believe that support at home is won by the kind of individual self they portray, and they are not the least reluctant to manipulate these presentations. "So members of Congress go home," according to Fenno (p. 55), "to present themselves as a person and to win the accolade: 'he's a good man,' 'she's a good woman.'" Incumbents emphasize three personal characteristics in these presentations: qualification, identification, and empathy. Every congressman creates the impression that he is qualified to hold office; that he can identify with the attitudes and beliefs of his constituents; and that he can empathize with the problems of his constituents. These personal characteristics are transmitted at each and every opportunity that a member has to communicate with constituents: newsletters, constituent mailings, meetings in the constituency, personal visits. The more personal and pervasive the contact, the greater the probability that the message will be retained. Attentive incumbents make considerable use of these presentations to convey the image that they care about constituents, their problems, and their frustrations.

Explanations. The final feature of home styles is the way in which congressmen rationalize their Washington activities to constituents. Fenno (1978) refers to this element of the constellation of activities that form home styles as "explanations of Washington activities." Explanations are the mechanisms through which incumbents describe, interpret, and justify legislative pursuits, especially the two major preoccupations of congressmen—power (Dodd, 1985) and policy (Fenno, 1973). The pursuit of power, for example, can be justified by claiming that such influence is used to further district or state interests within Congress.

Even though they probably have little to fear from electoral reprisals for one or two unpopular votes, incumbent congressmen make a point of explaining their votes and policy positions to their constituents when they are called upon to do so. Since most constituents are unaware of the specific votes of their congressman and perceive their representative as voting in line with constituent sentiment (Parker, 1981a), explaining roll-call votes creates few problems for incumbents. A string of "wrong" votes could pose problems (Kingdon, 1973), but most members avoid creating such patterns in their votes by developing a good sense of the policy stands that are likely to produce adverse constituent reaction. Because there is always some uncertainty as to what votes a member may be called upon to explain (Fenno, 1978), members tend to "stockpile" more explanations than they probably need.

Explanations can be used by members to gain some leeway in their pursuits in Washington. Since it is impossible for constituents to keep tabs on their legislators, especially when they are in Washington, voters are largely uninformed about the behavior of their representatives and senators. This "invisibility" can be exploited by incumbents to pursue personal goals without worrying about constituent reaction. Some members seek independence from the policy preferences of their constituents in order to exercise their own judgment and to promote ideologically satisfying causes. The reservoir of trust built through diligent constituent attention enables members to exercise independence in their pursuit of personal goals. If constituents trust their representatives and senators, they are likely to grant them freedom from surveillance. This is not to say that constituents approve of their congressman's goal pursuits or would approve if they had knowledge of them. It seems more likely that constituents assume that their legislator is fulfilling constituency obligations and congressional responsibilities unless they hear otherwise.

While the actions of incumbents may be invisible to their constituents, the incumbents themselves are not. Constituents normally find their legislators willing and prepared to explain their Washington activities, and their frequent appearances within their constituencies provide ample opportunities to question them about these activities. The fact that members frequently make themselves available to constituents reinforces constituent trust:

> Qualification, identification, and empathy are all helpful in the building of constituent trust. To a large degree these three impressions are conveyed by the very fact of regular contact. That is, "I prove to you that I am qualified," or "I prove to you that I am one of you," or "I prove to you that I understand," by coming around frequently to let you see me, to see you and to meet with you. If, on the other hand, I failed to come home to see and be seen, to talk and be talked to, then you would have some reason to worry about trusting me. (Fenno, 1978, p. 60.)

The major difference between the home styles of senators and representatives has little to do with the activities that they pursue with respect to their constituencies since they generally both do the same sorts of things (Fenno, 1978, 1982). They differ only in the emphasis that they place on certain types of activities: Senators do not feel that they can effectively reach a large number of their constituents through personal contact, while representatives feel that such contact is worthwhile and effective. Thus, senators do not normally spend as much time in their states as House incumbents spend in their districts. Further, the media attention that senators receive ensures that their elections contain a much greater policy component than House races. This may occur because "Senate candidates talk about public policy questions more than House candidates do" (Fenno, 1982, p. 170). As a consequence, there is more evidence of ideological and policy voting in Senate elections than House contests (see, for instance, Kuklinski and West, 1981; Wright and Berkman, 1986). A basic cause of these differences in the home styles of representatives and senators is the size of the constituencies that they represent. The smaller the size differential between a state and a congressional district, the greater the similarity between the styles of the House and Senate incumbents representing these areas. The larger the gap between the size of congressional and senate constituencies, the less the home styles of representatives and senators will come to resemble one another (Fenno, 1982).

In sum, the home-style activities of legislators (allocation of resources, presentation of self, and explanation of Washington activity) are designed to generate constituent trust, thereby enabling incumbents to pursue personal goals in Washington without experiencing a loss of support at home. Constituents willingly invest their trust in their congressman once they are convinced that he is attentive to district or state interests and is likely to sustain that level of attention in the future.

Advertising, Credit Claiming, and Position Taking. These home-style images are transmitted in meetings with constituents at home, in Washington (Fenno, 1978), and through mass mailings. John Saloma (1969) analyzed printed matter sent to constituents by representatives and senators (newsletters, news releases, form letters, and policy statements) during the first session of the 89th Congress. Saloma found that more than one-half of the representatives (55 percent) and senators (63 percent) used their written communications to enhance their own personal image and to advance their own interests (reelection). Three activities associated with such self-promotion are advertising, credit claiming, and position taking (Mayhew, 1974a).

Advertising activities are designed to disseminate the incumbents' name widely among constituents and to associate it with a positive image. They represent attempts to create the belief that the incumbent is personally responsible for the particularized benefits that his constituents are receiving such as federal support for state or district projects. While the notion of constituency benefits generally conjures images of the legislative pork barrel, a large proportion of the particularized benefits that members funnel to their constituents do not even involve legislative action; rather, casework forms the bulk of the particularized benefits distributed to voters (Mayhew, 1974a). Credit-claiming activities involve the efforts of incumbents to create the belief that constituency benefits are solely attributable to their unique efforts. Finally, position taking characterizes the efforts of incumbents to take policy stands that are pleasing to their constituents. There is no better way for a legislator to endear himself to his constituents than by publicly voicing policy positions that are strongly supported in the district or state.

The home-style activities of congressmen are not entirely self-serving since they meet legitimate representational responsibilities. Constituents expect to be kept informed about issues that are relevant to their concerns, and incumbents can oblige their constituents by providing such information, while also taking the opportunity to further their own interests through these communications. Diana Yiannakis' (1982) study of the newsletters and press releases produced by a sample of congressmen during the first six months of both the 94th and 95th Congresses demonstrates exactly how adept incumbents are at fulfilling these dual objectives. Yiannakis found that 42 percent of the paragraphs in these newsletters and press releases were devoted to explaining the incumbent's stands on national issues, and less than 10 percent were devoted to national or local information—an amount of space smaller than that allocated to claiming credit for particularized district benefits (11.6 percent).

EVIDENCE OF ATTENTIVE HOME STYLES

Each congressman leaves a personal imprint on his home style by adopting different variations in, and mixtures of, allocations, presentations, and explanations—all tailored to fit his goals and the constraints imposed by his own personality and constituency. Some members, for example, may allocate more staff to constituency matters than other members, or some may place a greater emphasis on the cultivation of personal relationships while others weight their styles toward the discussion of political issues. Despite this individuality, attentive home styles share a common theme: They reflect a personal commitment to serving constituents, and there is considerable evidence that congressmen have adopted more attentive home styles in recent decades (Fiorina, 1977; Fenno, 1978; Parker, 1986b). This is not to suggest that constituents suffered in the past because of the lack of attention on the part of former representatives and senators. Congressmen have probably always been attentive to their constituents, but today's incumbents are even more attentive than in recent decades. Congressmen display their attentiveness by processing casework, spending time with constituents, exploiting office resources for contacting constituents, and encouraging constituents to see them as an effective source of assistance.

Casework. Casework involves incumbents in helping constituents deal with the federal bureaucracy. It would be extremely rare for a day to pass in a congressional office without letters, visits, or calls from constituents requesting the assistance of their legislator. The range of items on which constituents seek assistance is indeed broad. Sometimes a government check that is late in arriving, or some ambiguity in a federal regulation applicable to local businesses, stimulates constituents to appeal to their congressman for help. Legislator–constituent contact frequently occurs as incumbents seek to resolve or redress such constituent grievances. At times these problems involve the operations of the federal bureaucracy; in these cases, the incumbent performs the role of legislative ombudsman (Fiorina, 1977). At other times, constituents contact their legislator to receive information or to express opinions.

Members of Congress actually spend little time themselves on casework problems; rather, their staffs bear the brunt of most of the daily casework done within congressional offices. The congressman's personal involvement in casework normally is only triggered when staff efforts are unsuccessful in resolving the problem or because the incumbent has a special interest in the case (for example, a district dam or water project). While congressmen are unlikely to get personally involved in constituent casework, they do not give that impression in their communications with constituents. Since staff usually can handle routine constituent inquiries, most constituent requests do not require the personal attention or involvement of the incumbent. Nevertheless, incumbents respond to constituent inquiries as if they were personally involved in resolving their questions. Newsletters to constituents often point to the personal intercession of the member in resolving relatively minor constituent problems. Responses to constituent inquiries carry the member's name in a smearable ink (to impress the truly skeptical), although few incumbents probably read or sign them. In this way, senators and representatives promote the image that they are personally involved in serving their constituents.

The key word here is *personally*. Without doubt, incumbents help their constituents, but their *personal* involvement in such service is often exaggerated. Congressmen may not like the "disguise," but they have little choice since the maintenance of an attentive home style requires the persistence of images that reflect a personal involvement in constituency affairs, no matter how impractical or unrealistic those images may be. Even if their personal involvement in casework is less than they would like their constituents to believe, congressmen allocate a large proportion of the time of their staffs—only the member's own time is a more valuable resource—to constituent affairs. In addition to designating one or several staffers as "caseworkers," most legislative assistants, press aides, personal secretaries, and others without explicit constituent responsibilities also engage in casework from time to time.

The volume of casework processed in congressional offices is difficult to gauge, but one of the best estimates of the casework load is provided by John Johannes' survey of congressmen and their staffs. Johannes queried congressmen and their staffs about a number of issues regarding the processing of constituent requests; he estimated that each week the average office in the Senate processed about 302 cases, and the average House office about 115 cases (Johannes, 1980). Moreover, the casework

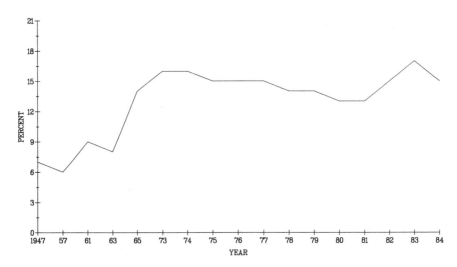

FIGURE 2–1   Percentage of Electorate Writing to Their Congressman 1947–1984 [Sources: AIPO (1947–1965) and Roper (1973–1984) surveys.]

load has apparently increased: 71 percent of the 193 staff surveyed by Johannes perceived an increase in the volume of casework reaching their offices, and more constituents have written to their congressman than in the past. Figure 2-1 displays the trend in the percentage of the electorate who have written to their congressman in the "past year." It is evident that the volume of mail increased significantly during the mid-1960s, about the same time during which incumbents were converting to more attentive home styles (Parker, 1986b).

Congressmen and staff cite two reasons for the growth in casework: (1) growth in government, and (2) the efforts of congressmen to stimulate casework. Not surprisingly, incumbents and their staffs disagree as to who is the culprit. Staff see congressmen as primarily responsible because of their extensive efforts to solicit casework. Congressmen, in contrast, place the blame firmly on the shoulders of government. There is an indisputable logic to the congressman's argument: Congressmen have always engaged in casework, but the expansion of government programs resulting from "Great Society" legislation passed in the 1960s created more laws, regulations, bureaucracies, paperwork, and problems with government. Members found themselves besieged by constituents who were now more dependent than ever upon governmental action.

Despite the logic of their argument, congressmen must bear a significant proportion of the guilt for the rise in casework loads since senators and representatives have exploited their office resources to increase casework. Staffs and offices in the district or state have expanded their operations, and mobile offices—vans equipped with office furniture—have become increasingly popular with incumbents (Light, 1979). Newsletters constantly remind constituents to bring their problems to their congressman; community forums and councils are encouraged to do the same. Johannes (1981) estimates that about 50 percent of the congressmen exploit at least two sources of contact with constituents to solicit casework. The emphasis on soliciting casework is not hard to explain: Such effort helps to validate a congressman's claim of being attentive to constituent affairs.

Personal Time of Congressmen. Unlike other congressional resources, time spent in the district or state reflects a personal investment in constituency affairs. While a portion of the burden of constituency service can be shifted to staff, the jobs of image building and explaining are tasks that each senator and representative must do personally. This is not to deny the fact that staff frequently travel to the district or state at the request of their bosses, but such constituency attention usually supplements the attention given the district or state by the congressman; it rarely compensates for the lack of a member's *personal* attention.

Congressmen do indeed spend considerable time attending personally to constituent business. John Saloma (1969) estimated that more than one-quarter (28 percent) of a representative's average work week is devoted to constituency affairs, and a similar amount of the legislator's staff time is also spent on constituency matters (25 percent). More recent data suggest an even higher percentage of time may be devoted to constituency affairs, since a large proportion of a congressman's time in Washington, as well as in the district or state, is spent on constituency matters. About one-third of the average day of a senator is spent in Washington dealing with constituent mail or talking with constituents or groups (U.S. Congress, Senate, 1976), and congressmen devote a similar proportion of time to district affairs while in their Washington offices (U.S. Congress, House, 1977). In the district or state, almost all of a congressman's time is taken up with presentations to constituents, and incumbents spend considerable time there: Representatives spent about one of every three days in their districts, while senators spent one of every four days in their states in 1980 (Parker, 1986b). An attentive home style necessitates such expressions of personal attention to constituent affairs. What better way is there to demonstrate one's attentiveness than to personally spend time with constituents?

There is evidence that congressmen have altered their existing home styles to emphasize their personal attention to constituency affairs. One indicator of this change in attentiveness is the increased amount of time that congressmen personally spend in their districts and states. Figure 2-2 presents data describing the mean number of days that congressmen and senators have spent in their constituencies between 1959 and 1980. It is

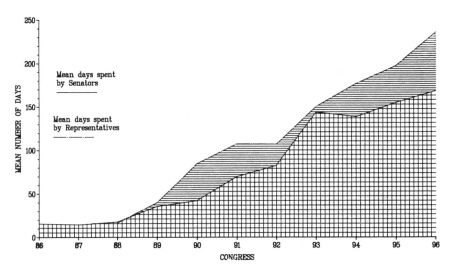

FIGURE 2–2   Time Spent in the Constituency 1959–1984 [Source: Parker (1986b, pp. 74–75, 78–79). House data for the 86th and 87th Congresses are not available.]

obvious from this graph that there have been significant increases in the amount of time that incumbents spend in their districts and states, and that the trends in the time spent by representatives and senators tend to coincide, beginning an upward movement during the middle of the 1960s and then following a largely monotonic course. The major difference between the trends in district and state attentiveness is that representatives spend more time in their constituencies than senators.

What is particularly unusual about these trends is that they occur at the same time that institutional demands on representatives and senators were also expanding (Figure 2-3). Incumbents were being pulled in two directions during these years: Legislative demands were absorbing more of the energies of congressmen and senators at the same time that constituency affairs were consuming more and more of their time (Parker, 1986b). As Figure 2-3 illustrates, congressmen and senators were spending more time in session than in the past; they were also spending more time in their constituencies during the same period of time. While these activities seem to be zero-sum in terms of their demands on the time and energies of incumbents, Congress has developed ways of reducing these conflicts in demands, such as structuring the legislative schedule to facilitate constituency attention.

Exploiting Office Resources.   Congress has equipped its members with a vast arsenal of office resources for serving constituents. Each office receives an allowance for hiring personal staff—who serve at the pleasure of the congressman—to address constituent problems and promote the in-

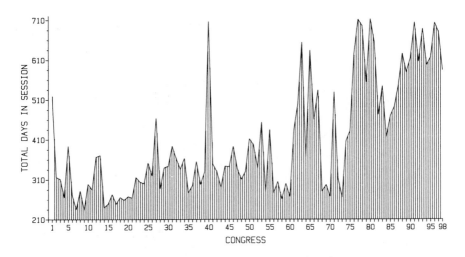

FIGURE 2–3 Time Spent in Session: U.S. Congress 1789–1984 [Source: *Congressional Directory* (1985).]

terests of their boss (Salisbury and Shepsle, 1981). In 1982, the personal staff allowance in the House was $352,536 per year, which could be used to hire up to 18 full-time and 4 temporary staff in Washington and district offices. The personal staff allowance for senators varies with the size of the state; it ranged from $621,154 for states with a population of less than 2 million residents to $1,247,879 for states with over 21 million citizens (Inside Congress, 1983).

A second office resource is the official expense allowance, which is separate from the clerk-hire allowance. The expense allowance covers a variety of costs incurred in maintaining the types of personal contact with constituents that mark an attentive home style: travel, stationary, newsletters, postage, telephone service, and office rental. In addition to the official expense allowance, congressmen receive a variety of government publications free of charge. Particularly invaluable are the allotments of publications frequently requested by constituents; among these items are pamphlets on American history and the legislative process, historic documents, and attractive calendars. Perhaps the most important office resource is the franking privilege that permits members free mailings to constituents. Despite restrictions, a wide range of material qualifies for use of the congressional frank, such as newsletters, questionnaires, biographical material, federal laws and regulations, and nonpartisan election information (for example, registration dates and places). These resources are exploited to serve constituents, and to promote the image that the incumbent is attentive to district or state interests. It is almost impossible to separate the two.

TABLE 2–1 Voter Likes and Dislikes of Their Representative: 1978–1984

CONTENT OF LIKES AND DISLIKES	DEMOCRATIC INCUMBENT				REPUBLICAN INCUMBENT			
	1978	1980	1982	1984	1978	1980	1982	1984
Experience	21.0%	14.6%	14.3%	15.7%	22.1%	18.3%	15.3%	17.6%
Trust	14.2	13.1	11.2	12.3	12.9	11.0	12.6	12.9
Leadership Qualities	3.1	2.4	3.6	3.4	2.3	2.0	3.3	3.7
Constituency Attention	23.9	25.5	22.3	19.4	18.3	21.9	17.9	19.9
Personal Qualities	16.0	16.4	17.6	21.2	16.7	17.3	18.4	15.2
Party Connections	3.4	4.4	5.6	3.7	4.1	6.9	10.0	6.6
Ideology	3.5	4.7	4.1	3.7	7.4	5.7	4.0	6.0
Domestic Policy	4.7	7.3	8.1	5.4	5.7	5.2	5.8	5.7
Foreign Policy	1.0	1.4	0.7	1.6	0.7	1.2	1.5	1.8
Group Connections	5.3	6.2	8.7	8.5	5.2	6.2	7.5	4.4
Miscellaneous	3.9	3.8	3.7	5.2	4.6	4.3	3.7	6.2
Total Responses	1088	834	749	1203	754	562	602	564

Source: University of Michigan, American National Election Studies, 1978–1984.

Perceptions of Congressmen. Since congressmen work exceedingly hard to promote the image that they care about their districts and states, it should not be too surprising to find that constituents see their congressmen in exactly these terms. The personal qualities of congressmen and their attention to district or state affairs are two reasons frequently cited by constituents as a basis for evaluating incumbents (Parker and Davidson, 1979); other "reasonable" criteria, such as political party identification, ideology, or issues, are rarely mentioned. Table 2-1 describes what voters liked and disliked about their own representatives; the data are from national opinion surveys conducted between 1978 and 1984. It is clear from this table that the constituency attentiveness of congressmen, their experience, and personal qualities dominate constituent evaluations. Other home-style presentations also emerge in the evaluations, though they are less pervasive: constituent trust and leadership qualities. Few constituents, however, see their legislators in terms of policies or ideology, which probably adds to an incumbent's popularity since such factors are more likely to tarnish than to polish a congressman's image among constituents.

How can we explain the mirror image of congressmen held by constituents and promoted by incumbents? There is no real way to tell whether the criteria used by constituents to evaluate their representative's performance is the result of the importance that constituents attach to attentive home styles or because incumbents emphasize these characteristics in their constituent contacts and communications. I suspect that it is a combination of both factors that conspire to make attentiveness salient in constituent perceptions of their congressman. In any event, the attentiveness of an incumbent is not lost on his constituents.

As might be expected, popular images of senators are not as colored by their constituency attention. The differing responsibilities and representational arrangements of representatives and senators, such as length of term and constituency size, may make constituency attention less relevant for evaluating the performance of senators. Clearly, the smaller size of the Senate, and the broader set of interests normally represented by senators, suggest that the performance of senators is judged differently from the performance of representatives. Robert Swansborough's (1982) analysis of the constituent images of representatives and senators in four southern states illustrates the different emphasis that constituency behavior receives in voter images of representatives and senators. Swansborough found that 34 percent of the constituents in these states cited the constituency behavior of their representative as "something they liked," but less than one-fifth of these respondents cited the constituency behavior of their senators as something liked. This should not be construed to suggest that the constituency service provided by senators cannot rival the level or quality of district attention, since few constituents have anything negative to say about the constituency behavior of senators (Swansborough, 1982). I suspect that constituency attention is less central to the images of senators because they gain the public's eye in so many other (less controllable) ways. Nevertheless, constituency attention provides a positive component to the images of senators in the same way that such attention generates positive evaluations of representatives.

At the encouragement of their representatives and senators, constituents view their legislators as successful manipulators and movers of governmental action. These images, and the reported success of incumbents in dealing with constituent problems, have created constituent expectations of service and successful bureaucratic interventions: More than 8 of every 10 constituents feel that their congressman could help them in some way (Parker, 1986b). What is most remarkable about this expectation is that few constituents have actually contacted their representative (over 80 percent of those interviewed in national surveys have *never* contacted their representative or senator). Therefore, constituents perceive their representative to be helpful even though they have never had the type of personal experience upon which to base such a judgment. Since there is no evidence that the constituency service provided by senators is any less effective in promoting similar images, I suspect that senators are also viewed as helpful and successful in attending to constituent problems. These perceptions mirror the types of messages that attentive incumbents disseminate.

WHY CONGRESSMEN ADOPT ATTENTIVE HOME STYLES

Members adopt attentive styles for different reasons, and the exact mixture of objectives probably varies from member to member. The electorally insecure view an attentive home style as a mechanism for enhancing their safety. Members representing constituencies that are heavily dependent upon governmental programs and services view the adoption of an attentive style as the best way to respond to constituent needs. For the politically ambitious, an attentive style provides the measure of leeway necessary to further career, policy, or personal goals. Even if members do not rank these goals in the same order, the satisfaction of one goal could occur simultaneously with the satisfaction of other goals without incurring additional costs. Hence, there are strong incentives for most congressmen to adopt attentive home styles. As the personal costs associated with constituency attention were reduced, the attraction of an attentive home style rose still further.

Some of this cost reduction was accomplished by increasing the subsidies for various constituency activities and expanding the perquisites available for maintaining contact with constituents. Other costs were made more transferrable. I have already noted the ability of a member's personal staff to shoulder much of the routine work associated with constituent casework; hence, members could expand their constituency services without feeling the full brunt of the increased contact with constituents.

There have also been efforts to reduce the competition for a member's time created by legislative (Washington) and constituency demands. For instance, the legislative schedule has been structured to facilitate constituent contact by confining legislative business to certain days (Tuesday to Thursday). Thus, the office perquisites and the legislative schedule have been altered to promote attentive home styles on the part of representatives and senators. By manipulating the legislative schedule and reducing the costs associated with constituency attention, Congress altered the opportunity structure and facilitated the conversion of members to more attentive home styles.[1]

Satisfying Multiple Goals. Stylistic changes in constituency attention have occurred because they satisfy major needs of members: the needs to maintain electoral safety, to alleviate constituent problems, and to gain a degree of freedom from their constituents to pursue policy interests or positions of power within Congress. These needs provided the motivation for the adoption of more attentive home styles (Parker, 1986b). Constituency service, political leeway, and electoral safety are member needs that could be satisfied through diligent constituency attention. While specific needs may vary in importance from member to member, the adoption of an attentive home style could simultaneously satisfy all of them. This feature of an attentive home style made it attractive to House and Senate incumbents at every level of seniority.[2] The attraction of an attentive home style increased further as the personal costs (to the member) of an attentive style were minimized by cost-cutting measures such as increased office perquisites and adjustments in the legislative schedule to minimize conflicts between Washington and home responsibilities.

Cost Subsidization and Shifting. The most direct way in which institutional incentives for constituency attention are provided is through direct subsidies for these activities. Many services are subsidized through legislatively authorized allowances. Prior to recent reforms in Congress, separate allowances were maintained for such expenses as telephones and telegrams, postage and special delivery, and staff and travel.[3] Since unused portions of these allowances were returned to the Treasury, there were strong incentives for members to take full advantage of them.

The franking privilege is just one example of a subsidy that can serve as a direct incentive for increasing levels of constituency contact.[4] American households are bombarded at regular intervals with an assortment of mail that bears the signature of a member of Congress in lieu of postage. The ease with which such mail can be addressed, the number of constituents that can be reached by these mailings, and the absence of direct costs to members for exercising this privilege make mass mailings useful mechanisms for maintaining contact with constituents. Further, there is an economy-of-scale incentive for expanding this type of service if subsidies are increased: Once established, the direct marginal cost to the member of expanding such a service is small. Mass mailings, for instance, can be distributed to a broader group without the member incurring any additional *personal* costs.

The restrictions placed on the use of the congressional frank are quite narrow and specific: Members are prohibited from using the frank for mailings that are designed to solicit political support. However, even mailings falling into this prohibited category are subsidized through a postage allowance. Another example of direct subsidization is the provision of al-

TABLE 2-2   Increases In House Perquisites: 1945-1975[a]

SPECIFIC ALLOWANCE	1945–1960	1961–1975
Clerk Hire (number of staff)	5 (1945) 6 (1949) 7 (1954) 8 (1955)	9 (1961) 10 (1964) 11 (1966) 12 (1969) 15 (1971) 16 (1972) 18 (1975)
Postage (dollars per session for airmail and special delivery)	$90 (1945) 125 (1952) 200 (1954) 300 (1957) 400 (1959)	$500 (1963) 700 (1968) 910 (1971) 1140 (1974)
Telephone and Telegraph (units)	40000 (1959)	45000 (1962) 50000 (1963) 70000 (1967) 80000 (1970) 100000 (1973) 125000 (1975)
Travel Allowance (round trips per session)		2 (1963) 4 (1965) 12 (1967) 18 (1973) 26 (1975)

[a]These separate allowances were consolidated into the Official Expense Allowance in 1978.
Source: Committee on House Administration.

lowances to defray the monetary costs of traveling to the district or state. The establishment of this allowance in the Senate in 1958 and in the House in 1963 meant that this expense no longer had to be covered out-of-pocket or by friendly lobbies. The expansion of subsidies for mailings, travel, and staff were critical factors in facilitating stylistic changes in the way in which members relate to their constituencies (Parker, 1986b).

In Table 2-2, the postwar increases in four categories of House office expenses are enumerated. It is clear that most of the increases in these expense categories occur after 1960. All of the increases in the travel allotment occur in the 1960s and 1970s, and the clerk-hire allowance doubled between 1961 and 1975. This pattern of post-1960 increases in office perks also can be found in the growth of Senate allowances. For example, the Senate postage allowance rose $150 between 1956 and 1960, but the allowance increased by about $500 between 1961 and 1966; between 1966 and the consolidation of the postage allotment with other expenses in 1973, the postage allotment was increased by about 50 percent. The increases in these allowances provided the resources necessary for maintaining an attentive home style and expanding constituent–legislator contact. Further increases in these allowances reduced the costs associated with constituency attention and increased the incentives to exploit these opportunities. The comments of one House incumbent interviewed by Fenno (1978) suggest the importance of subsidies in generating attention to district affairs:

> In the early years, I didn't make many trips home. It was simply a matter of money.... I come home more now. I get a bigger travel allowance and I get asked to speak more. I never pay any of my own money to come home. I can't. (pp. 52–53)

Increases in the subsidies for staff provide an example of a more indirect method of reducing the costs attached to constituency attention—cost shifting. As noted earlier, one of the inherent limitations on the member's ability to engage in constituency attention is that a member's time is finite. If there were some way of shifting the personal costs of constituency service to someone else, a member could increase the number of constituents served. The use of staff for constituency service activities helps members to shift the burden of such activities and expand the range of services without reducing the level of service to their constituents or increasing demands on themselves.

Personal staff are at the center of the "small business" operations that characterize House and Senate offices. These offices have been termed "member enterprises" (Salisbury and Shepsle, 1981) because of the multiplicity of activities performed by legislative offices to further member interests, especially district interests. Senators and representatives have long recognized the value of staff in serving as their surrogates. This recognition is evident in the efforts of members to increase the level of constituency travel permitted by their staffs. Senator Mark Hatfield (R-Oreg.) echoed the sentiment of most senators when he urged the passage of legislation that would reimburse staff for travel within the home state:

> What staff members are able to do in all states when they assist constituents in this manner is to help cut red tape facing everyone dealing with the government. In addition, better communication is achieved. Eyeball-to-eyeball contact is what should be encouraged. This bill will assist in enabling our staffs to better serve our constituents. (U.S. Congress, Senate, Committee on Rules and Administration, 1972, p. 7)

Legislative Scheduling. Another method to reduce the costs attached to constituency attention is to structure the legislative schedule to allow members to spend time in their districts and states without detracting from their Washington responsibilities. As a general rule, time spent in the district or state is time well spent for incumbents because it contributes to their visibility and provides valuable opportunities to focus attention on activities that create favorable images in the minds of constituents. By structuring the legislative schedule so that members can spend time with their constituents without jeopardizing legislative interests or responsibilities, Congress has helped to reduce the costs of constituency attention. In the process, home-style changes in constituency attention (increased attention to constituency affairs) on the part of representatives and senators have been encouraged.

There are several ways in which the legislative schedules in the House and the Senate have been structured to facilitate the adoption of attentive home styles. Congress, especially the House, is infamous for its Tuesday-to-Thursday schedule of legislative business. This truncated schedule enables House members to spend weekends in their districts (a good time for maximizing contact with constituents) without missing any legislative business. The House has also institutionalized periods for constituency travel by setting aside blocks of time in the legislative schedule each year for incumbents to travel within their districts. Thus, there is generally little relationship between voting participation in Washington and time spent in the district or state, since most legislative business is scheduled to minimize conflicts with constituency travel. Few members need to worry about their absenteeism becoming a campaign issue because incumbents rarely miss a vote unless they really want to avoid taking a position on an issue.

In the Senate, the scheduling of most business is, by definition, acceptable to all since it is conducted under unanimous consent agreements. These agreements are negotiated between the minority and majority party leaders and must receive the unanimous approval of the Senate; once approved, they serve as the schedule for Senate business.[5] It is interesting to note that the use of unanimous consent agreements in the Senate increased at the same time that institutional changes encouraging increased attention were occurring among senators: Use of unanimous consent agreements (per the number of days in session) increased from 14 percent in 1959 to 37 percent in 1975 (Oleszek, 1978). Such accommodations helped to facilitate changes in the attentiveness of senators by reducing the conflicts between legislative business in Washington and time spent at home.

Perhaps the most obvious way in which Congress structures the legislative schedule to reduce the costs of constituency attention is through the proliferation of recess periods. Congress normally conducts no legislative business during recess periods, so members need not worry about forsaking their legislative responsibilities while spending time with their constituents. Some recess and holiday periods are even dictated by legislative statute. For example, the Legislative Reorganization Act of 1970 specified that Congress was to adjourn from the thirtieth day before, to the second day following, Labor Day during the first session of each Congress. In essence, the legislation set aside the entire month of August for a congressional recess period. Although the establishment of the August recess had a significant effect on the overall number of recess days allocated, the rise in recess days began even before the declaration of this special recess period. As Figure 2-4 reveals, the number of days that the House and Senate were in recess began to rise in the mid-1960s (after the 89th Congress); this increase coincides with the growth in other office perks that facilitated constituent–legislator contact.[6]

FIGURE 2–4 Days in Recess: U.S. Congress 1943–1984 [Source: Congressional Directory(1985).]

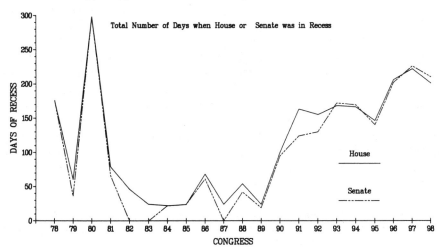

POLICY CONSEQUENCES

One of most obvious consequences resulting from the widespread conversion of congressmen to attentive home styles is pork barreling. Pork barreling describes the processes through which congressmen divert federal funds to their districts and states. Members have always been involved in some sort of pork-barreling activity, so it wasn't too difficult for incumbents to make this activity an integral aspect of their home styles. What better way to demonstrate concern for the district or state than to bring home the bacon! And the opportunities to do so have never been greater. There is a variety of pork to be found in the federal budget, some of it the product of efforts by congressmen, bureaucrats, or both (Fiorina, 1977; Arnold, 1979). Grants to local governments and universities, federal aid for specific constituent groups (for example, subsidies for certain agricultural products), federal buildings and installations (for example, military bases), or plain old federal dollars in the form of contracts to local businesses for government work are just a few of the "standard" items available at the pork barrel.

> The creative pork barreler need not limit himself to dams and post offices—rather old-fashioned interests. Today, creative congressmen can cadge LEAA [law enforcement assistance] money for the local police, urban renewal and housing money for local politicians, educational program grants for the local education bureaucracy. And there are sewage treatment plants, worker training and retraining programs, health services, and programs for the elderly. The pork barrel is full to overflowing. (Fiorina, 1977, p. 48)

A second policy consequence is the emphasis on serving constituents. Congressmen devote a large proportion of their resources to addressing constituent problems, which diminishes their capacity to engage in lawmaking activities by absorbing their time as well as that of their staffs. Even though Congress has attempted to ease the burden of constituent service by reducing the direct costs to incumbents of maintaining an attentive home style, some costs are nontransferable. Congressmen must incur some costs just to sustain the image of an attentive representative or senator, and one basic cost cannot be shifted to someone else: personal attention to constituent affairs. The personal attention allocated to constituency affairs diminishes the amount of time that can be devoted to strictly lawmaking functions (e.g., committee business). Representatives seem quite aware of the trade-offs necessary to maintain an attentive home style. As one representative observed:

> I spend every Saturday in the mobile office, listening to people complain.... I would like to shift time from that to the legislative side. I spend too much time on things like finding a high school band a place to stay. (Cavanagh, 1981, p. 68)

Yet, the priorities for members are all too clear:

> Legislation takes a back seat. It can be neglected without any immediate adverse impact on a congressman. He can miss a committee hearing, not be on the floor, neglect material necessary for an informal discussion, and who's ever gonna know? But he cannot avoid, except at the risk of the peril of constituent hostility, responding to constituent requests. So constituent requests take a priority over legislation. (p. 68)

Congressional oversight of executive agencies is another by-product of the widespread adoption of attentive home styles. Casework can sometimes lead directly to formal oversight of an agency or the introduction of remedial legislation. At the very least, casework sounds a "fire alarm" that gets the attention of Congress and may be even more effective than subcommittee investigations in rooting out bureaucratic misfeasance (McCubbins and Schwartz, 1984). In many instances, attention to constituent problems provides congressmen with feedback regarding the weaknesses in programs or the inefficiencies of federal offices operating within the constituency. There are three major ways in which constituency service can generate oversight:

> First, it could lead directly to formal oversight techniques (hearings, investigations, audits).... Second, when successful in resolving a case, correcting an error, or catching an abuse of power, casework in and of itself achieves some of the goals of oversight.... Third, as a result of incoming congressional complaints and requests, departments and agencies might change regulations or procedures, conduct their own internal oversight, or at least be more careful the next time similar cases arise.... (Johannes, 1979, p. 328)

In short, an attentive home style strengthens a congressional strength—oversight (Huntington, 1965). Of course, there are any number of causes for congressional oversight (Aberbach, 1979), and constituency casework is only one of them. Nonetheless, it is a quite effective means for conducting oversight, at least in the eyes of caseworkers and agency liaison personnel (Johannes, 1979).

SUMMARY

Home style describes the ways in which legislators cultivate their districts and states—how they allocate their resources, present themselves to constituents, and explain their actions to voters. Attentive home styles are designed to promote the image that the incumbent is personally looking after the interests of his constituents. By advertising their activities and claiming credit for benefits received by district residents, incumbents endear themselves to their constituents. Congressmen demonstrate their attentiveness by processing casework, spending time with constituents, exploiting office resources in contacting constituents, and encouraging their constituents to view them as effective sources of assistance.

While members actually spend little of their own time on casework, they behave as if they were personally involved in resolving constituent complaints. And even if members are not as personally involved in constituency services as they would like the voters to believe, they allocate a large proportion of their staff's time to constituent affairs; only the legislator's own time is a more valuable resource. Personal time spent with constituents is another indicator of an attentive home style: Incumbents actually have increased the time they spend in their districts and states in recent decades, reversing the persisting decline in the time spent with constituents that began in the twentieth century with the lengthening of legislative sessions. The diligence with which legislators exploit their resources, such as office and staff allowances, is another indicator of the widespread adoption and conversion to attentive home styles by House and Senate incumbents. These efforts seem to have the desired effects since constituents tend to see their congressmen in terms of the presentations they make: Incumbents are perceived as qualified, attentive, trustworthy, personally attractive, and effective "shakers and movers" of bureaucratic action.

What factors underlie the persistence of attentive home styles among congressmen? First, the adoption of an attentive home style persists because it enables members to satisfy a variety of goals (reelection, political leeway, and constituency service) *simultaneously*. Second, the attractiveness of attentive home styles is also a result of institutional changes that have minimized the personal costs to the incumbent of maintaining an attentive style. Cost-cutting measures such as increased office perquisites and adjustments to the legislative schedule (to reduce conflicts between Washington and home responsibilities) created incentives for members to adopt and maintain attentive home styles. Simply put, by manipulating the legislative schedule to reduce the competition for a member's time, increasing the subsidies for constituency activities, expanding perquisites for constituency contact, and allowing incumbents to transfer the costs associated with maintaining an attentive home style, Congress created an incentive structure conducive to the persistence of attentive home styles.

There are three policy consequences that can be linked to the maintenance of attentive home styles. One result is pork barreling—the diversion of federal funds to districts and states—which is an effective way for incumbents to demonstrate their attentiveness to their constituencies. Another policy effect is the emphasis on serving constituents and addressing their problems. Finally, attentive home styles may enhance legislative oversight by bringing bureaucratic problems to the attention of incumbents: Encouraging constituents to seek assistance from their legislative offices alerts congressmen to bureaucratic omissions and commissions that may result in formal congressional, or internal agency, oversight.

Notes

1. Richard Fenno (1978) suggests that changes in home styles can occur as a result of three kinds of changes in the personal circumstances confronting incumbents:

   The most common contextual causes would be a redrawing of district boundaries and a marked population shift within old boundaries. The most common strategic cause would be a substantial decline in support among primary or reelection constituencies. The most common personal cause would be a shift in personal circumstances or goals. Singly or in combination, these factors probably produce home style change. (p. 195)

   There is no evidence, however, that contextual, strategic, or personal causes of home-style change have influenced changes in the time congressmen spend in the districts or states (Parker, 1986b).

2. While there is evidence of a generational change in home styles—representatives elected since 1958 are more attentive to their districts than those they replaced—this alone cannot explain the changes in the time spent by representatives described in Figure 2-2; older House incumbents have also converted to more attentive home styles. In the Senate, all of the change in the time spent in the state can be attributed to the conversion of senators to higher levels of attention. For an analysis of the question of home-style change, see Parker (1986b).

3. Presently, members have two allowances: one for hiring personal staff (clerk-hire) and the other for all expenses previously covered by separate allowances (telephone and telegraph, postage, travel newsletter, stationery, and general office expense). The size of a House member's official expense allowance is determined by combining expenses from several fixed categories and expenses from three variable allowances: travel, telephone, and district office rental. The amount of these expenses depends upon the location of a member's district and its distance from Washington; the amount of a senator's allowance is based upon the size of the state represented and its distance from Washington.

4. This privilege was first enacted into law by the Continental Congress in 1775 to enable members to keep their constituents fully informed of constitutional developments; one of the earliest acts of Congress was to continue this practice. The franking privilege has remained virtually intact, though the law was revised in 1973 to regulate and police the usage of the congressional frank.

5. Major legislation, as well as noncontroversial measures, reaches the Senate floor by unanimous consent. This occurs because a strict observance of the Senate rules would mire the chamber in parliamentary procedures and delay. As a result, the Senate expedites its business by setting aside the rules with the unanimous consent of its members (on the floor):

   ...the Senate has evolved a highly flexible legislative scheduling system that responds to individual, as well as institutional needs. The system bears little resemblance to what the formal rules specify and rests largely on usage and informal practice. Unlike House members, all senators have an opportunity to participate in scheduling legislation for floor action. Minor or noncontroversial bills are expedited to save time for major and controversial measures. Insofar as possible, consideration of important bills is scheduled to suit the convenience of members.... (Oleszek, 1978, p. 135)

6. The question naturally arises as to whether the increase in the number of days of congressional recess can be attributed to the increased length of legislative sessions (see Figure 2-3). Since the number of days in legislative session declines after the 88th Congress but the number of recess days continues to increase after this period, it seems unlikely that the rise in recess days is merely a function of the lengthening of legislative sessions.

Chapter Three
POPULAR CONGRESSMEN AND AN UNPOPULAR CONGRESS

Americans generally hold their politicians in low esteem. Every vocation has its presumed seamy side with an appropriate set of terms to describe the practice and the practitioners; unscrupulous lawyers are "shysters" and incompetent physicians are "quacks." In government, the seamy side is "politics" and the infamous practitioners are "politicians." Americans steadfastly hope for the best from their politicians, but most expect far less, perhaps the worst, from their elected officials. Few vocations are held in such contempt; parents even caution their children against entering politics (Mitchell, 1959).

In sharp contrast to this sordid image of politicians, congressmen are seen in far more positive terms. While politicians are generally viewed as dishonest and guided by pure self-interest, congressmen are perceived as maintaining high ethical standards (U.S. Congress, House, 1977). Most surveys find that individual congressmen are popular with their constituents and that they are rarely seen in a negative light by them. Congress, however, consistently serves as a focal point for public ridicule and attack. Disapprobation of Congress may be something of an American pastime for many citizens, groups, newspaper reporters, journalists, and even congressmen themselves. It seems that we poke fun of Congress at every opportunity: in newspaper articles, editorial opinions, cartoons and comic strips, jokes, and in all forms of graffiti.[1] Criticism of Congress is so common that one must wonder if the institution will ever be popular with Americans! This contradiction—popular congressmen serving in an unpopular Congress—creates something of an anomaly:

> If our congressmen are so good, how can our Congress be so bad? If it is the individuals that make up the institution, why should there be such a disparity in our judgments? (Fenno, 1975, p. 278)

In this chapter we examine public attitudes toward Congress and congressmen and why we seem to love our congressmen so much more than our Congress.

EVIDENCE OF THE POPULARITY OF CONGRESSMEN
AND THE UNPOPULARITY OF CONGRESS

As we noted, the popularity of congressmen and the unpopularity of Congress is a finding that occurs regularly in public opinion research. How unpopular is Congress? Popular dissatisfaction with Congress is evident in its low levels of public confidence, poor performance ratings, and perceived lack of responsiveness. The contrast between the images of Congress and congressmen is indeed stark: Congressmen are viewed as trustworthy, responsive to the needs of their constituents, and performing their responsibilities.

Confidence. It is a rare reading of public opinion that shows Americans to have even a modest amount of confidence in Congress. The ability of Congress to deal with specific problems in a competent manner, whether they be reforms of Congress or economic malaise, is always questioned. For example in 1977, 78 percent of those surveyed in a national opinion survey supported the efforts of party leaders to make ethical reform a major legislative priority but 49 percent doubted that anything would come of it (U.S. Congress, House, 1977). Like most negative impressions of Congress, the lack of confidence seems to be a persisting characteristic.

Figure 3-1 presents data drawn from national surveys conducted by Louis Harris between 1973 and 1981 on public confidence in three branches of the national government. Respondents were queried in these surveys about their confidence in 10 institutions: "As far as the people running (name of institution) are concerned, would you say you have a great deal of confidence, only some confidence, or hardly any confidence at all in them?" Restricting attention to the institutions of the national government, Congress is the institution least able to command consistently the

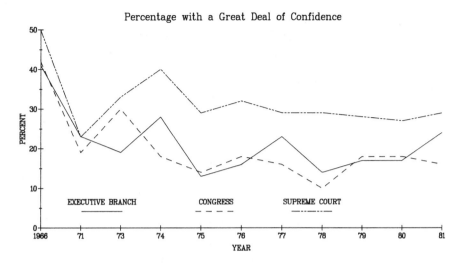

Percentage with a Great Deal of Confidence

FIGURE 3–1   Confidence in Leaders of National Institutions 1966–1981 [Source: Lipset and Schneider (1983, pp. 48–49); Louis Harris surveys only.]

confidence of Americans. Only once during the nine-year span of the surveys did more than 18 percent of the respondents express a "great deal" of confidence in the "people running Congress." Congress falls far behind the Supreme Court, with about 30 percent of the respondents consistently expressing confidence in the Court, and fares only slightly better when its public confidence is compared with that of the executive branch. The percentage of respondents with a great deal of confidence in Congress is almost identical to the proportion having a similar level of trust in the executive branch in five years (1975, 1976, 1978, 1979, and 1980), but in three of the other four surveys (1974, 1977, and 1981) a greater percentage of the respondents expressed confidence in the executive branch. Whether judged in absolute terms, or relative to the other branches of the national government, Congress seems unable to induce much public confidence.

A different approach to the question of institutional confidence has been followed by the Gallup Poll organization. They sought to measure confidence in the "institutions" themselves, rather than the "people running them" as Louis Harris had done; in addition, the Gallup Poll offered respondents four rather than three options to describe their level of trust in each institution—"a great deal," "quite a lot," "some," or "very little." By offering respondents two positive expressions of confidence ("a great deal" and "quite a lot"), Gallup generally has found higher levels of institutional trust than reported by other survey organizations: between 1973 and 1981, 34 to 42 percent of the public indicated that they had either a "great deal" or "quite a lot" of confidence in Congress. While this magnitude represents a higher level of confidence than that reported by Louis Harris during the same time span (Figure 3-1), Congress still lagged behind organized religion, public schools, and the Supreme Court, and only ranked slightly ahead of organized labor in terms of public confidence (Lipset and Schneider, 1983). In fact, in 1981 only 12 percent of the respondents surveyed could be categorized as having high levels of confidence in Congress—only the stock market failed to instill more trust (Lipset and Schneider, 1983).

To the best of my knowledge, there are no survey data directly measuring confidence in individual congressmen that parallel queries about trust in Congress; hence, it is virtually impossible to contrast confidence in Congress with confidence in congressman. There is some evidence, however, to suggest that constituents have a great deal of confidence in their own congressmen. For example, a large number of constituents perceive their representative as voting in Washington in agreement with constituency opinion[2] without any awareness of a single vote cast by their representative (Parker, 1986b).

One indication of the level of trust among constituents is the extent to which trust is mentioned in a positive or negative fashion by constituents in evaluating their congressman. These evaluation questions have been asked in national surveys conducted by the University of Michigan between 1978 and 1984. Indications of constituent trust can be found in questions that ask respondents to describe the things they like and dislike about their representative.[3] (The responses categorized as reflecting constituent trust are listed in the Appendix.) Generally, distrusting responses refer to the incumbent's pursuit of self-interest, lack of integrity (principles), stupidity, untrustworthiness, dishonesty, or lack of independence (controlled by political bosses or parties), and constituent trust is reflected in responses that are the opposite of these (e.g., honesty, trustworthiness, integrity).

While the categorization of such open-ended responses is always somewhat subjective, the effort to identify trusting and distrusting comments is guided by the nature of the standard trust in government questions.[4] The useful properties of this scale, such as its predictive validity and reliability, provide the rationale for using these items as a guide to classifying trusting and distrusting responses. It provides some assurance that the responses used as indicators of constituent trust reflect the same underlying concept—trust. For example, the responses categorized as reflecting constituent distrust capture the content of the items included as measurements of distrust in the standard "trust in government" scale: Government officials are stupid, crooked, run by interests looking out for themselves, cannot be trusted to do what is right, and are undeniably self-interested.

The constituent trust measure is operationalized by subtracting the number of distrusting responses from the number of trusting responses:

Number of trusting responses — Number of distrusting responses

This calculation results in an index of constituent trust that ranges from a high of +3 to a low of -3. The frequency of high trust responses on this measure suggests that constituents maintain fairly high levels of confidence in their congressman: More than 75 percent of the respondents expressing a trusting *or* distrusting response gave more trusting evaluations of their congressman than distrusting ones (Figure 3-2). This finding is consistent with Richard Fenno's observation that congressmen are persistently concerned about levels of constituent trust and make concerted efforts to maintain and boost that trust (Fenno, 1978). Such high levels of constituent trust suggest that the effort is quite successful.

Evaluations of Performance. The performance of Congress and congressmen also produce divergent evaluations: Congressmen are viewed as performing at the highest levels, while Congress' performance is normally judged as below par. Simply put, congressmen are popular with their constituents but Congress is not.[5] The survey query normally used to elicit citizens' evaluations of Congress asks respondents to rate the performance of the institution during the past year; the same general survey item elicits constituent evaluations of their own congressman.[6] The differential in the affective responses to these two items is quite impressive: In 1978 for example, over 60 percent of a national sample evaluated their own representative as doing a "good" or "very good" job, but only 20 percent of the

FIGURE 3–2 Constituent Trust 1978–1984 [Source: University of Michigan. Percentages based upon the total number of respondents who mentioned trust or distrust in evaluations.]

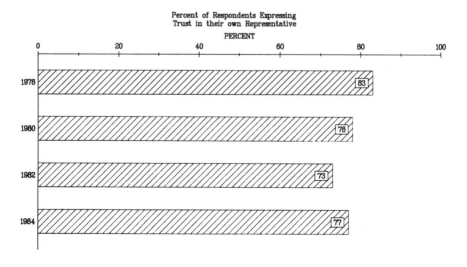

respondents expressed a similar evaluation of Congress. In 1980, 61 percent of a national sample *approved* of their representative's performance, while 51 percent *disapproved* of Congress (Davidson and Oleszek, 1981).

The performance of Congress, like confidence in the institution, has historically received low grades from the public. Figure 3-3 describes the trend in the performance ratings—unpopularity—of Congress between 1939 and 1984: The percentage of the public who expressed either a "fair" or "poor" evaluation of the performance of Congress in a particular year. During most of this period, more than one-half of those interviewed were unwilling to rate the performance of Congress as above average. Some may argue that a "fair" rating is not so bad since it indicates satisfactory performance! When one examines the content of these "fair" evaluations of congressional performance, however, it is clear that this type of evaluation implies dissatisfaction, not satisfaction, with Congress.[7] The persistence of this negative image of Congress is also evident in the fact that the institution has received more negative than positive evaluations of its performance in over 80 percent of the survey measurements of congressional popularity (Parker, 1981b).

This is not to ignore the fact that, from time to time, Congress has received favorable evaluations of its performance; however, these are aberrations to the normal pattern. For instance, the extremely low level of dissatisfaction with Congress recorded in 1953 (Figure 3-3) probably is influenced by the fact that a truce in the Korean War was initiated while the survey was underway. This coincidence may have increased positive feelings toward Congress, especially since events of this nature—those

FIGURE 3-3   Congressional Unpopularity 1939–1984 [Sources: AIPO, Louis Harris, CBS-New York Times Poll (1980), University of Michigan (1982, 1984).]

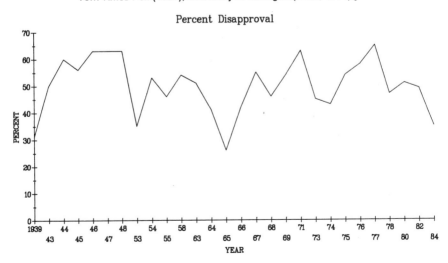

Percent Disapproval

that "rally" public feeling behind institutions and officials (Mueller, 1973)—reduce congressional unpopularity (Parker, 1977). Another major deviation in the normal pattern of congressional unpopularity occurred during the 89th Congress. This was an unusual period of cooperative legislative-executive relations: Approximately 70 percent of the over 450 presidential measures submitted to Congress were approved during the first session (1965). Thus, the remarkable productivity of the 89th Congress, and its cooperative relationship with the president in the aftermath of his landslide election, probably contrived to promote citizen satisfaction with the general performance of Congress during this period. Such conditions are indeed rare, especially in the contemporary Congress.

Perceptions of Responsiveness. The same theme that we observed in public assessments of confidence and performance is also apparent in voter perceptions of the responsiveness of Congress and congressmen: Congressmen are viewed as responsive to their constituents, but Congress, the institution, is perceived as unresponsive. The positive image of the responsiveness of congressmen is apparent in survey reports of citizen satisfaction with the services their legislators provide. For instance, over 65 percent of those interviewed in national opinion surveys in 1977 and 1978 (U.S. Congress, House, 1977; University of Michigan, 1978) indicated that they were "mostly" or "very" satisfied with the assistance that they received from their congressman; 65 percent of those interviewed in 1977 believed that neither the congressman nor his staff could have been any more helpful (U.S. Congress, House, 1977). Although the number of constituents who seek assistance from their congressman is relatively small—about 15 percent—perceptions of responsiveness extend beyond this small group. Most constituents perceive their representative to be effective in handling their problems if the need to seek his assistance should ever arise.

Just as important as the effectiveness of congressmen in helping people is the perception that congressmen can render that assistance over a whole range of problems. Some of the problems that constituents bring to their congressman could conceivably fall within a category of assistance that congressmen might be able to provide for constituents. For instance, a national survey found that respondent requests for (specific) assistance from their representative dealt with such matters as military discharges (10 percent), public policies (13 percent), social security (11 percent), and government employment (9 percent) (U.S. Congress, House, 1977). Congressmen might be expected to be successful in dealing with constituent problems in these areas, especially given the effectiveness of their dealings with federal agencies (Arnold, 1979). These problems, however, only scratch the surface of what people think their congressman can do for them.

A 1973 national survey (U.S. Congress, Senate, 1973) asked respondents a series of questions dealing with *personal* problems that they might encounter and who they would turn to for help with these problems. The list of people or organizations that the respondent might turn to included: president, governor, U.S. senator, U.S. representative, state legislator, top local official, influential friend, clergy, lawyer, local groups; respondents could cite more than one source of help. These data are presented in Table 3-1; I have truncated the original table by eliminating several sources of assistance, but this will not affect the conclusions drawn from it—i.e., that congressmen (representatives more than senators) are frequently viewed as sources of assistance for resolving personal or local problems.

Not unexpectedly, most people see their local officials as likely sources of assistance for most local problems, like dirty streets or the building of gas stations. People seem more willing, however, to turn to their representative than to their state officials (governor and state legislator) on some local issues, like airline routes. It is fairly reasonable to expect people to bring certain types of local or personal problems to the notice of their federal officials. For instance, personal problems relating to military service and federal investigations could conceivably be areas that warrant assistance from the congressman, but issues of aircraft noise and a local government's control over information seem rather odd problems to bring to the representative or senator. Yet, a substantial number of citizens would do just that (Table 3-1). In sum, citizens tend to see their congressmen as responsive to, and effective in resolving, a whole range of constituent problems.

Congress, in contrast, is generally perceived to be ineffective, primarily because it seems incapable of dealing with national problems or pressing societal issues, and therefore takes the blame for most unresolved problems. The large federal deficits are Congress' work because it has failed to make needed cuts in federal programs; the cost overruns in federal contracts are evidence of inadequate legislative oversight; and the mounting national debt reflects the unwillingness of Congress to raise taxes. Certainly Congress cannot be absolved from guilt for these problems, but it seems to bear a disproportionate share of the blame in most instances.

The unresponsiveness of Congress seems to be a persisting perception. Figure 3-4 describes the trend in the proportion of respondents in national surveys who perceived "most" congressmen as "paying a good deal of attention" to their constituents when "deciding what to do in Congress." In 1964, the first year for measuring the trend in the perceived responsiveness of Congress, over 40 percent of the respondents in the survey felt that most congressmen paid a "good deal" of attention to their constituents, but this proportion declines over time, reaching a low of 16 percent in 1980. In sum, congressmen are perceived as responsive and effective in dealing with

TABLE 3–1 Whom People Would Turn to for Help if Faced with Specific Personal Problems[a]

PERSONAL PROBLEMS	PRESIDENT	GOVERNOR	U.S. SENATOR	U.S. REPRESEN-TATIVE	STATE LEGISLATOR	TOP LOCAL OFFICIALS
Income tax refund unfairly turned down.		3%	11%	22%	3%	13%
You or family member suspected by police of a crime not involved in.		2	1	3	1	17
Federal investigation asked about personal political beliefs.	1%	3	16	26	4	15
Plans to put up a gas station nearby.		1	1	5	3	49
Son in army treated unfairly.	6	6	27	46	4	5
Street too dirty.		1		2	2	75
Airplanes taking new route making noise over your house.		6	8	18	13	30
Local government holding back information affecting your taxes.	1	10	7	15	15	20

[a]Answers do not equal 100% because some respondents named more than one source of help and because the table has been truncated, eliminating some categories of assistance (for example, clergy).

Source: U.S. Congress, Senate, 1973, p. 326.

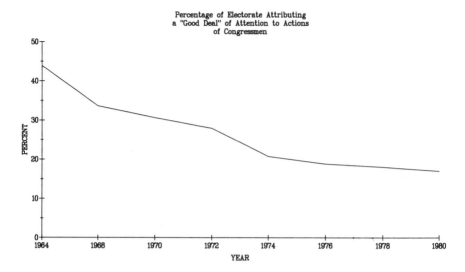

FIGURE 3-4   Perceived Responsiveness of Congressmen 1964–1980 [Source: University of Michigan.]

constituent problems, no matter how personal those problems might be, but Congress is viewed as neither responsive nor effective.

WHY WE LOVE OUR CONGRESSMEN BUT NOT THE CONGRESS

The contrasting levels of public esteem for congressmen and Congress persist for three major reasons: citizen expectations, the behavior of congressmen, and media treatment of congressional politics. Differences in the expectations that people hold for Congress and its individual members account for some of the differences in affect. Constituent expectations almost guarantee that congressmen, especially attentive ones, will be popular with voters since they are assigned tasks that they can readily accomplish, like constituency service. Congress, in contrast, is expected to effectively tackle major problems and policies with speed and efficiency— two attributes historically uncharacteristic of the legislative process. With such expectations, Congress is doomed to failure. The popular esteem of Congress is not helped by the actions of congressmen, who tend to "polish" their own reputations at the expense of Congress. Congressmen frequently attack Congress and encourage their constituents to think ill of the institution. In this way, incumbents disassociate themselves from the institution and the negative feelings that most constituents harbor toward Congress. This strategy, however, also reduces the popular standing of

Congress. Finally, the local and national media tend to treat Congress and individual congressmen quite differently. The national media is more critical in its treatment of Congress than is the local media, which tends to picture individual congressmen in a far more favorable light.

Expectations. Americans assign different responsibilities to their congressmen and the larger entity, the Congress, and the expectations that constituents hold for the performance of their representative are more easily satisfied than those they hold for Congress. Congressmen are expected to serve, and to communicate with, constituents. For Congress as an institution, however, citizens expect the resolution of pressing national issues and problems (Parker and Davidson, 1979). Congress faces the far more hazardous assignment since many problems are virtually unsolvable on a national scale, or the resolution of them is many decades away; even if these problems were solved, would that fact be evident and who would receive the credit—the president, political parties, individual congressmen?

This contrast in expectations can be observed in the criteria that constituents use in evaluating the performance of Congress and their own congressman. Four categories of responses account for the vast majority of the reasons given by respondents in national surveys for evaluating Congress: political issues, the conduct of legislative-executive relations, the congressional environment (style and pace of the legislative process, congressional ethics, and self-interest), and the treatment of specific groups (Figure 3-5). The most prominent reasons given for evaluating Congress

FIGURE 3–5 Criteria Used in Evaluating Congress [Sources: AIPO (1939, 1954) and Louis Harris (1968, 1977).]

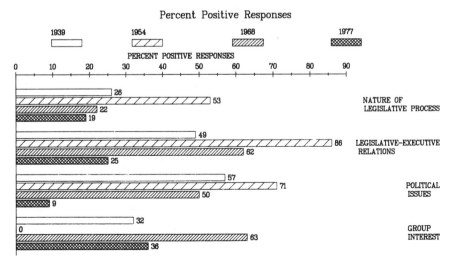

were political issues and the congressional environment—two criteria that frequently place Congress in an unfavorable light. While Congress may take policy actions that please some citizens, the same actions alienate still others; even if Congress is successful in resolving one set of problems, its failure to solve other problems normally catches the attention of citizens and the media. As for the legislative process, when have citizens praised Congress for delaying legislative action or for being a deliberative assembly?

In light of the saliency of these criteria, it is not too surprising that attitudes toward Congress are frequently negative. The range and volume of policies for which Congress is held responsible create numerous opportunities for dissatisfaction to accumulate; the cumbersome legislative process is also a feature with little popular appeal. The data in Figure 3-5 demonstrate the extent to which certain criteria are laden with negative affect. As these data demonstrate, rarely is mention of the congressional environment associated with anything positive to say about Congress' performance. Political issues can boost congressional popularity on occasion (1939 and 1954), but of late they fail to enhance its public esteem. In short, some of the most salient concerns of Americans appear to be those that cast Congress in an unfavorable light.

The criteria for evaluating Congress and those used in evaluating individual congressmen exhibit few parallels. The personal attributes of incumbents (experience, personal qualities, and honesty) and their attention to their constituents are the most frequently cited reasons for evaluating one's own representative (see Table 2-1), and these criteria tend to place representatives in a favorable light. Personal qualities usually reflect well on incumbents, and the adoption of attentive home styles by most congressmen ensures them a revered place in the minds of their constituents. Senators are more frequently evaluated in terms of political issues than representatives, perhaps because they emphasize issues more in their constituency presentations than representatives (Fenno, 1982) or because citizens tend to see their senators as more involved in national issues than their representative, who is viewed as more attentive to local problems. Nonetheless, the attention of senators to their states meets with the emphatic approval of their constituents (Swansborough, 1982).

Thus, evaluations of representatives are more likely to rest on service to the district than on matters of public policy, and such criteria place the performance of congressmen in a favorable light. Congress, on the other hand, is assessed more in terms of institutional features like the style and pace of the legislative process and its policy actions (or inactions), which tend to produce negative or mixed evaluations of its performance. The different criteria used in evaluating Congress and its members go a long way in explaining divergent attitudes toward the institution and individual congressmen.

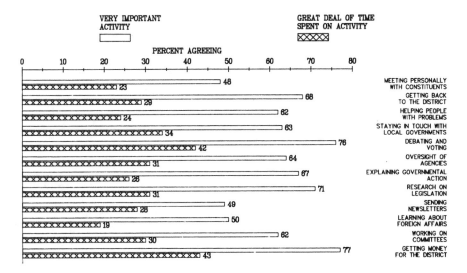

FIGURE 3–6   Perceived Importance and Time Spent on Congressional Activities [Source: U.S. Congress (1977, pp. 826–29).]

One reason why constituency service may be so important to constituents is because they don't perceive congressmen, in general, as devoting a great deal of time to district or state affairs. Figure 3-6 presents data drawn from a national survey that asked respondents to rate the importance of various legislative activities and to estimate the amount of time that their own representative spent on these activities (U.S. Congress, House, 1977). The categories of importance were: "very important," "fairly important," "only slightly important," or "not important," the categories describing the amount of time their representative devoted to each activity were: "a great deal," "some," "only a little," or "hardly any." Figure 3-6 presents the percentage of respondents who agreed that an activity was "very important" and the percentage who perceived their representative as spending a "great deal" of time on each activity (shaded areas).

There is a consensus among constituents about the importance of constituency and legislative activities. Over 60 percent of the respondents felt that getting back to the district, helping people with problems, maintaining contact with local governments, explaining governmental action to constituents, and bringing federal dollars to the district were very important constituency tasks (see Figure 3-6). Similar levels of support are accorded activities with a more legislative bent to them: debating, voting, overseeing federal agencies, researching legislation, and working in committees. The interesting point about Figure 3-6 is that several constituent activities are viewed by many respondents as consuming less of the time of their representative than other legislative tasks, even though both types of activities are viewed as equally important. For example, a larger percentage of respondents felt that congressmen devoted a "great deal" of time to debating political issues and public policies than to either getting back to the district or helping people with problems; a higher percentage of respondents also saw their representative as spending more time on overseeing agencies, researching legislation, and working in committees than in helping constituents or explaining governmental actions to them.

It seems clear that congressmen can create a sacred place for themselves in the minds of their constituents by being attentive to district matters. It's a good way to distinguish yourself from others in Congress who are perceived to spend more of their time on legislative business than on constituency affairs. This may explain why over one-third of the reasons given by respondents in a national survey (U.S. Congress, House, 1977) for believing their representative to be better than most other incumbents made mention of some aspect of his or her service to the district (communicates with constituents, cares about constituents, tries to solve constituent problems, obtains federal funds for the district). It is easy to understand why attentive congressmen are so popular with their constituents: They are spending time on activities important to constituents that are perceived to receive too little attention.

Congressmen are judged differently from Congress because of the divergent expectations constituents harbor, and congressmen are more popular with their constituents than Congress because less is expected of them. Surely, serving constituents is more easily accomplished than balancing the budget or reversing economic trends. What constituents expect of their congressman is nonetheless important, and the fulfillment of these tasks boosts the esteem of the congressman in the eyes of his constituents. Congress, on the other hand, is characterized by processes and policy actions that tax the patience of most citizens. The result is that Congress is rarely able to sustain high levels of public approval, while congressmen have no such trouble with their own levels of popularity.

Behavior of Congressmen. There is little doubt that the constituency service of incumbents is salient to constituents: It is mentioned frequently in evaluations and is one accomplishment that constituents seem to remember.[8] One reason why such constituency activity is so salient to voters is because they feel it is an important activity that most incumbents neglect too often. For instance, 37 percent of a national sample indicated that they thought that the most important thing for a "good" congressman to do would be to "work to solve problems in his district" and to "help the people"—the most frequently mentioned responsibility. Keeping in touch with constituents (17 percent) and soliciting constituent opinion (12 percent) were the third and fourth most frequently cited functions for "good" congressmen to accomplish (U.S. Congress, House, 1977, p. 822). Another reason for the saliency of the constituency service function in the images of individual congressmen is the emphasis that such service receives in the home presentations and explanations of incumbents.

The images of congressmen held by constituents mirror the messages that congressmen disseminate through their communications and presentations. Congressmen are constantly on the prowl for opportunities to deliver these messages because they realize that such repetition reinforces their positive image and makes it less susceptible to change. A radio spot here and there, an article in the local newspaper, or a meeting with constituency groups provide the types of ubiquitous contact that give members the opportunity to promote home-style messages. Thus, the emphasis of attentive congressmen on serving district and state interests finds a receptive audience and also guarantees that constituents see their congressman in the most favorable light. This may explain why congressmen are so popular with constituents, but how does the behavior of congressmen enhance negative attitudes toward Congress?

As congressmen polish their own images among constituents, they also denigrate Congress. Incumbents are not the least bit apprehensive about joining the chorus of attacks on Congress. For instance, all of the 18 House members that Richard Fenno (1978) observed in their districts took advantage of opportunities to picture themselves as better than others serving in Congress. It is also fairly easy to find someone in Congress to blame for an ineffective policy or the lack of action on a pressing national problem:

> The performance of Congress is collective; but the responsibility for congressional performance is not. Responsibility is assessed member by member, district by district. It is easy for each congressman to explain to his own supporters why he cannot be blamed for the performance of the collectivity. It is doubly easy to do because the internal diversity and decentralization of the institution provide such a variety of collegial villains to flay before one's supporters at home. There are the "old chairmen," "the inexperienced newcomers," "the tools of organized labor," "the tools of big business," . . . . (Fenno, 1978, p. 167)

In sum, incumbents run for Congress by running against it; in the process, they lower citizen opinion of Congress. This strategy costs incumbents very little, since constituents find blaming Congress a very convincing explanation for all kinds of malaise. In fact, members may actually endear themselves to their constituents when they shift the blame to Congress because most constituents are already very critical of the institution: By telling constituents what they already suspect, congressmen are able to increase constituent identification and trust (Fenno, 1978, p. 167). Unfortunately, one of the latent consequences of this "addictive, cost-free, and fool proof" strategy is that the institution suffers, bleeding from "435 separate cuts" (Fenno, 1978, p. 169). Is it any wonder that we love our congressmen but not the Congress? Our congressmen wouldn't have it any other way!

I should note that congressmen are not ignorant of the adverse results of their efforts to separate themselves from the institution. For example, when a sample of House incumbents were asked in 1977 what "individual members could do by *themselves* to increase public esteem for the House," a large number of representatives offered the suggestion that members be encouraged to limit their attacks on Congress (U.S. Congress, House, 1977). It is doubtful that incumbents will see this as sufficient rationale for altering their constituent presentations, especially since such changes may have dire consequences for their own popularity with constituents.

Media Treatment. Congress generally receives hostile treatment at the hands of the national press, which tends to emphasize the negative aspects of the legislative process. Congressmen, in contrast, are normally pictured in far more positive terms (when they receive media attention). This differential in media treatment accounts for some of the difference in popular attitudes toward Congress and individual congressmen. The contrasts in media treatment stem from the different media that cover Congress and individual members: The national media tend to cover the institution while the local media cover individual members. Further, the national media tends to be "tougher" in dealing with items on its "beat"—national politics—than the local media, which tends to be "soft" on individual members when reporting news about them. As Michael Robinson (1981) observed, "the nationals look hard at the institution. The locals exchange glances with their representatives" (p. 88). Thus, local press treatment promotes favorable images of individual congressmen, whereas the national media reaches everyone with critical coverage and images of Congress. In this way, positive images of congressmen and negative images of Congress are reinforced.

Another reason why the media treatment of congressmen by the local media is so positive is that incumbents exercise a virtual monopoly over the dissemination of information about themselves. Congressional news found in the local press usually has its genesis in the office of individual members, and the information that incumbents provide the local media tends to draw constituent attention to actions or characteristics that create positive images of them. Anthony Downs (1957) noted this dilemma in discussing some of the problems inherent in attempting to rationally reduce the costs of becoming informed: "Whenever information is provided to consumers at a low cost either because of mass production or subsidies or both, each consumer gains financially only by sacrificing control over the selection principles behind the information" (p. 230).

While the information provided to constituents is not apocryphal, it can be constructed in such a manner as to lead to the conclusion that the incumbent is performing well. Incumbents can be viewed as behaving much like the propagandists that Downs (1957 p. 84) refers to as "persuaders": "they present correct information organized so as to lead to a specific conclusion." The conclusion that legislators want their constituents to reach is obvious: The incumbent has served the district or state well during his term of office. This may explain why most citizens see their representative as doing a "good" or "very good" job in Washington.

POLICY CONSEQUENCES

Members of Congress try to protect and increase their popularity among their constituents. To accomplish this objective, congressmen promote policy outcomes that will contribute to their standing among constituents, and they avoid association with policies that could damage their popularity. This leads them to engage in activities that ensure that they will win favor with their constituents. Since federal projects and money for the district impress constituents, one policy-related activity that congressmen can exploit to enhance their popularity is pork-barreling. The opportunities to engage in pork-barreling, as noted earlier, are indeed great. So congressmen constantly raid the federal budget for projects that might benefit constituents or their districts and states. The capacity of such "pork" to enhance a congressman's popularity guarantees that it will be a priority on the legislative agenda of most incumbents.

Congressmen can also protect their esteem among constituents by avoiding association with unpopular policies. There are two major ways in which congressmen can escape responsibility for policies or problems that create constituent dissatisfaction. First, they can place the blame for the problems or policies (or lack of policies) on Congress. Congress is a handy whipping boy, and constituents are accustomed to thinking ill of the institution; hence, congressmen can escape the adverse effects that unpopular policies and societal conditions (e.g., unemployment) can have on the attitudes of their constituents. This enables congressmen to maintain high levels of approval among their constituents. Thus, another policy consequence of the divergent set of attitudes toward Congress and congressmen is that incumbents seek to affix the blame for problems on Congress.

Finally, congressmen can protect their public image by avoiding taking stands on controversial issues.[9] Controversial votes may endear some members to their constituents, but they can also induce widespread defections from a member's supportive electoral coalition. In most cases, incumbents have little to gain by promoting controversial causes or issues, though some members may occasionally endure the risks that go along with espousing controversial causes because it satisfies personal legislative goals. Controversial issues cannot always be prevented from emerging upon the legislative agenda, but most members have strong incentives to avoid taking stands on them. To do otherwise risks irreparable damage to one's popularity among constituents. The strategic use of absenteeism by congressmen to avoid controversial votes is one example of how members can avoid taking stands on these matters. As noted earlier, the scheduling of legislative business is designed to avoid conflicts with home activities; when members miss votes, they often do it intentionally.[10]

At times, the legislative agenda is set so that members cannot avoid dealing with controversial matters. For instance, congressmen must vote on the size of the federal deficit. When forced to take a stand on a controversial issue, congressmen try to obfuscate the issue or principle involved or structure constituent perceptions in such a way that a stand on a controversial issue can be interpreted in a manner that is bound to please constituents. Congressmen are very adept at executing both of these strategies. In any event, the concern for their own esteem among constituents leads incumbents to try to distance themselves from controversial actions, policies, or problems. Above all, they try to maintain a distance between themselves and the institution in which they serve.

SUMMARY

As a collectivity, Congress lacks public esteem; individual congressmen, however, are far more popular with constituents. Congress is viewed as unresponsive, and its actions fail to instill confidence or provoke positive evaluations. This unflattering view of Congress can be contrasted with the glowing image of the congressman. There appears to be a broad consensus that one's congressman can be trusted and that he will be responsive to the interests of his constituents; the popularity of Congress pales in comparison to the popularity levels attained by individual congressmen. Some of this differential in affect can be explained by the less demanding expectations that constituents harbor for their congressman, such as service to the district. Congress, on the other hand, is expected to solve national problems with speed and effectiveness. The penchant of the national media for focusing public attention on the least attractive aspects of Congress and the efforts of congressmen to polish their own reputations at the expense of Congress also contribute to public disapprobation of Congress but not the congressman. The concern for their own popularity leads congressmen to espouse popular policies and avoid unpopular ones, and to engage in pork-barreling—a popularity-generating activity.

NOTES

1. One of my favorite graffiti regarding Congress was etched into a bathroom door: Congress is the opposite of progress.

2. When respondents were asked in 1978 the extent to which they agreed or disagreed with their representative's voting record, fewer than 15 percent disagreed with his voting record. This persists even when controlling for the party loyalties of the respondent and their representative (Miller and Katosh, 1981).

3. The following questions are used in creating the trust in government scale:

   1) Do you think that people in government waste a lot of the money we pay in taxes, waste some of it, or don't waste very much of it?

   2) How much of the time do you think you can trust the government in Washington to do what is right—just about always, most of the time, or only some of the time?

   3) Would you say the government is pretty much run by a few big interests looking out for themselves or that it is run for the benefit of all the people?

   4) Do you feel that *almost* all of the people running the government are smart people who usually know what they are doing, or do you think that quite a few of them don't seem to know what they are doing?

   5) Do you think that quite a few of the people running the government are a little crooked, not very many are, or do you think hardly any of them are crooked at all?

4. How valid is this measure of constituent trust? One way of evaluating the validity of this measurement of constituent trust is to examine its relationship to other variables that are hypothetically and logically linked to trust. In the following table are shown the correlations between constituent trust and the perceived helpfulness of the respondent's congressman as well as between trust and the extent to which the respondent agrees with the votes cast by his or her congressman in each survey between 1978 and 1984. I expect that respondents with high levels of trust will more frequently perceive their congressman as being helpful (if called upon) and as voting as they would like him to. As the table indicates, trusting respondents are indeed more likely to perceive their congressman as helpful and as casting votes in tune with constituent opinion: There are substantial positive correlations between constituent trust and perceptions of helpfulness and voting agreement. These predicted relationships support the contention that this measurement of constituent trust is a valid one.

Correlations Between Constituent Trust and Perceptions of Helpfulness and Voting Agreement (Pearson product-moment correlations)

Variable	1978	1980	1982	1984
Perceived[a] Helpfulness	.46	.44	.52	.45
Perceived[b] Voting Agreement	.33		.44	

[a] Question wording: If you had a problem that Representative (name of incumbent) could do something about, do you think (he/she) would be very helpful, somewhat helpful, or not very helpful to you?

[b] Question wording: Now we would like to know how much you generally agree or disagree with the way (name of House incumbent) has voted on bills that have come up in the U.S. House of Representatives in Washington. Looking at this list, would you say you agree, agree somewhat, neither agree nor disagree, disagree somewhat, or disagree with the way (he/she) has voted on bills, or haven't you thought much about this? (This question was not asked in the 1980 and 1984 studies.)

5. It might seem tautological to associate popularity with congressmen: Congressmen are naturally "popular" with their constituents, or else they would no longer be incumbents! On the other hand, popularity can be viewed theoretically and conceptually as an intervening mechanism (construct) that translates the behavior of incumbents into increments of electoral support. That is, congressmen and senators can be viewed as acting in ways that promote their popularity among their constituents and therefore their electoral safety.

6. The exact wording is normally some variant of the following:

   In general, how would you rate the job that your U.S. Representative has been doing—very good, good, fair, or poor?

   In general, how would you rate the job that the U.S. Congress has been doing during the past year—very good, good, fair, or poor?

7. Some of the responses to "fair" assessments of Congress include mention of such things as too much politics, failure to pass needed legislation, lack of cooperation with the president, passing foolish legislation, lack of effort to resolve problems, and insensitivity to public opinion (American Institute for Public Opinion, August, 1939, no. 166A).

8. When asked to recall anything their representative has done in office, 14 percent of the respondents recalled their representative's contacts with constituents — the second largest category of recall-responses (U.S. Congress, House, 1977).

9. The Gramm-Rudman-Hollings balanced-budget measure is a good example of the "devious" ways in which congressmen avoid the unpleasant task of cutting budgetary support and thereby antagonizing constituent interests. The law initially provided for an automatic, across-the-board cut in all programs if Congress cannot agree upon a way of reducing the federal deficit. In this way, congressmen could avoid the blame of the adverse effects on constituents that stem from reductions in federal programs.

10. Political journalists Rowland Evans and Robert Novak reported that the failure of gas deregulation to pass the House in 1976 could be attributed to "planned" absenteeism: 14 of the 15 representatives who favored deregulation but missed the vote had no valid excuse for their absenteeism. Some were back in their districts, while others were in Washington but not on the floor of the House (Evans and Novak, 1976).

Chapter Four
STABILITY IN THE MEMBERSHIP OF CONGRESS

An important characteristic of the present Congress is the relative stability of its membership: Few new members enter Congress because few old ones leave. This stability represents a large-scale change in the turnover of representatives and senators—a change that may be responsible for the development of the seniority system, the persistence of professional norms, and the increased power of Congress vis-a-vis the executive branch (Polsby et al., 1969). While members in the contemporary Congress rarely leave office either voluntarily or involuntarily, this was certainly not the case in earlier congresses. H. Douglas Price (1975, p.5) suggests that senators in the 1st Congress set the tone for that chamber in the early years of the Republic: "They fled the Capitol—not yet located in Washington—almost as fast as was humanly possible." It is not surprising, then, that most career patterns in the senate during these early years ended rather abruptly. "Prior to the Civil War one just did not make a long run 'career' out of continuous Senate service," Price concludes, "except perhaps as a fluke" (p. 7).

Service in the House during this period, like the Senate, was not characterized by longevity: Careers in the House amounted to little more than one or two terms for many representatives throughout most of the nineteenth century. The proportion of first-term representatives entering

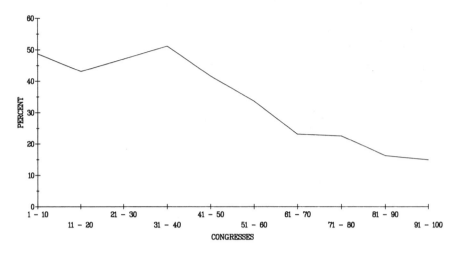

FIGURE 4–1 Percentage of First-Term Members in House of Representatives 1789–1986 [Sources: Polsby (1968) for data from 1st to 89th Congresses. Data for 90th to 100th Congresses are calculated from the Congressional Directory (1967–1987)].

Congress during this period ranged from one-third in the 9th Congress to three-quarters in the 28th Congress (Fiorina et al., 1975); the House elected in 1900 was the first in history in which new members comprised less than 30 percent of the membership. In short, membership in earlier congresses was characterized by high levels of turnover of senators and representatives.

Turnover in the present Congress is another story: very little membership change and increased terms of service. Prior to the 1900s, the average amount of service in the House of Representatives amounted to less than three years, but after 1955 the average increased to more than five years. During the 92nd Congress, the mean terms of service in the House reached an all-time high of six years (Ornstein et al., 1982). Thus, the lack of membership turnover reflects the continuation of a trend that predates the emergence of the contemporary House and Senate. While some of the same forces that added longevity to the careers of congressmen at the turn of the century may still influence turnover today, other influences, not readily apparent before the 1960s, seem equally potent in reducing turnover.[1] Before discussing these influences and how they have diminished turnover in the twentieth century, historical trends in congressional turnover are described.

HISTORICAL TRENDS IN TURNOVER

There are two general trends in turnover in the House of Representatives: Turnover increased until the 1850s and has declined since that time

(Fiorina et al., 1975). Figure 4-1 presents data regarding turnover in the House between 1789 and 1986. This gross change in the membership of the House masks some interesting variation in the turnover rate. There is considerable fluctuation in the turnover rate in the early Congresses, but a distinct upward trend in turnover is visible until the 17th or 18th Congress. House turnover rates stabilize around the middle of the 1850s before beginning an erratic decline. The turnover rate reaches another high point in the 54th Congress (1895–1896) but declines again after this period. Turnover rises a little during the Woodrow Wilson presidency then drops to another low point in the 70th Congress (election of 1926) before increasing with the approach of the Great Depression and the 1932 landslide election of Franklin D. Roosevelt. During the 1970s, turnover in the House appears to increase slightly, though the level of turnover still remains below the levels reached before 1950. These changes in the turnover rate tend to coincide with different periods in political history that parallel changes in the party system.

Political historians define five periods in the development of the present-day party system in the United States on the basis of differences in the degree and nature of party competition. The first party system encompasses the years between 1788 and 1824 and features the dominance of the Republican Party after the Federalist Party began to disappear as an effective opposition party (after 1808); during this period of dominance, Republicans won from 61 to 85 percent of the House seats. The second party system, 1824–1854, crumbled with the rise of the Republican Party in the elections of 1854 and 1856.

The Civil War system, 1860–1892, reflects Republican control until 1874, after which control of the presidency and Congress alternates between the parties. The Civil War weakened the Democratic Party outside of the South, as Democratic candidates suffered from the party's association with the southern cause. This weakness in the Democratic Party helped Republicans maintain control of the presidency until 1885, of the Senate until 1897, and of the House until 1875. The polarization of the country along sectional lines in the 1890s marks the end of the Civil War party system.

During the fourth party era, 1896–1932, Republicans maintained domination until 1912, when Theodore Roosevelt's Bull Moose Progressive Movement split Republican loyalties and provided presidential victories for Woodrow Wilson and the Democratic Party. Republican domination returned, however, in 1920 and lasted until FDR's election in 1932, the start of the fifth party system. There is no consensus among political historians as to the end of the fifth party system and the start of the sixth, but some suggest that a major realignment in the parties brought to a close the fifth party system in 1968. Regardless of whether we are in the fifth or sixth party system, it seems clear that changes in these systems coincide with changes in electoral competition between the political parties.

The instability and decay of party systems appear to have promoted high levels of turnover in Congress.

The turnover trend among senators is very similar to that exhibited by House members: The percentage of new senators experienced a sharp decline after the 1880s, though the decline is not as steep as that among new House members. Increasing tenure also appears somewhat later in the Senate than in the House of Representatives:

> The Civil War period marks the end of a declining trend in mean terms of service, and the beginning of a gradual increase. This increase apparently signals the beginning of professionalization in the House. The professionalization of the Senate seems to have begun somewhat later. A corresponding period of increase is not seen in the Senate until the 48th Congress. Once begun, though, the speed of the process is remarkable. With the Tilden-Hayes election, and the end of Reconstruction, the number of Congresses served by senators begins a dramatic increase. By the 54th Congress, the average number of Congresses served has increased from three to nearly five. (Brookshire and Duncan, 1983, p. 4)

In addition to the nature of the party systems and the levels of electoral competition associated with them, historical patterns of membership turnover are related to the attractiveness of Congress as a decision-making body and the existence of local norms that required incumbents to retire after short periods of service. It is customary to think of the Senate as one of the nation's most powerful political institutions—certainly more powerful than the House—because of its constitutional role in foreign affairs and executive branch appointments. However, H.D. Price (1974) reminds us that in its initial decades the Senate was little more than an "honorific nothing" (p. 6). After the Civil War and Reconstruction, the attractiveness of the Senate increased as the institution reached a pinnacle of influence:

> The executive branch was in a long eclipse, and senators extended their sway into effective control of state party machines (or vice versa). The national government was by then of vital importance in regard to tariff policy, monetary policy, and—for the South—race policy. Senators controlled the allocation of federal patronage, and increasingly lorded it over the House. Thus by the 49th Congress (1885) resignations were only one-third the number for 1845, though the Senate was twenty members larger. The ratio of members seeking re-election to those not doing so is no longer half and half, but stands at 55 to 13. By this time most states were predominantly either Democratic or Republican, so that electoral hazards were reduced. By this time also, Senate committee chairmanships were being quite rigorously handled in terms of continuous committee service. The Senate was a good place for a politician to be. (Price, 1974, pp. 8–9.)

The attractiveness of the House of Representatives also increased for some of the same reasons, especially the enhanced role of the House in the formation of public policy. One example of the enhanced role of the House in the making of major policy decisions was the tariff barriers created to protect domestic industries. Not only did the tariff question give each congressman a constituency stake in the issue and influence over national policies, but the tariff produced substantial surpluses for congressmen to spend (Kernell, 1977). Thus, the job of the representative became more important and more prestigious. Increased congressional tenure is indicative of the desire of incumbents to serve in Congress, and the improved status of the House and the Senate were indeed handsome incentives to return to Washington. In fact, Samuel Kernell (1977) estimates that about one-half of the decline in turnover in each decade between the 1850s and the 1900s can be attributed to the interest of incumbents in serving additional terms of office.

Another factor that appears responsible for some of the decline in congressional turnover is the norm of rotation: The rotation of the nomination for a congressional seat among party faithful for specific periods of time. These rotation practices declined during the last half of the nineteenth century and disappeared by the twentieth century, but in the interim they increased congressional turnover (Kernell, 1977). Two forces that hastened the demise of the rotation norm were the challenges on the part of enterprising incumbents, and the substitution of the direct primary on a national scale for the party caucus in the selection of nominees for office (Kernell, 1977). By loading the district convention with supportive delegates or by exploiting access to patronage appointments, incumbents occasionally succeeded in overturning the traditional two-term limit on their careers. Direct primaries virtually liberated incumbents from dependence upon unpredictable caucuses for their nominations, allowing them to exploit their proven campaign skills and the resources of their offices to maximum electoral and political advantage.

Structural changes in the electoral system also affected turnover. H. D. Price (1975) argues, for example, that the election of 1896 was particularly critical in altering levels of congressional turnover:

> This decade was marked by the emergence of the really solid Democratic South, by the rapid spread of ballot reform and registration systems, but above all by the collapse of the Democrats in the 1896 Bryan campaign. Democratic gains in the silver states and some farming states proved temporary, but massive Democratic losses in the Northeast and Mid-west were to last until Al Smith and the Great Depression. As a result, re-election became more probable and more incumbents came to seek re-election. Successive new all-time records for amount of prior service in the House were set in 1900, then a higher record in 1904, then a yet higher record in 1906, and that one was broken in 1908. Successive new all-time low records for proportion of new members were set in 1898, again in 1900, again in 1904, and yet again in 1908. (p.9)

In addition to these forces, reapportionments, economic panics, and electoral reforms, like the direct election of senators (Brookshire and Duncan, 1983b), have influenced levels of congressional turnover (Fiorina et al., 1975; Kernell, 1977).

TURNOVER IN THE CONTEMPORARY CONGRESS

The decline in congressional turnover that marks early periods of political history in the House and Senate continues to persist, though the form it takes differs from that exhibited in the past.[2] Declining turnover in contemporary congresses is revealed in the survival rate of incumbents, the weakness of presidential coattails in inducing party turnover in congressional elections, and the decline of "marginally" elected congressmen—those most susceptible to replacement. These influences give declining turnover in the contemporary Congress a quite distinct flavor since some of these influences seem to be post-1960s phenomena.

Survivability. Perhaps the clearest evidence of the lack of turnover in Congress is the survivorship rate of representatives: Legislators elected in recent congresses appear to be surviving at a higher rate than in the past. T. Richard Witmer (1964) created a "political actuarial table" that estimated the rates of survival among House incumbents by computing the percentage of representatives elected during five successive congresses who continued to serve in the House in later congresses. Witmer's analysis extended from the 53rd Congress (1893) to the 88th Congress (1965); in Table 4-1, I have updated Witmer's study through the 97th Congress (1982).

Witmer contended that the survivability of House members had increased, and the data in Table 4-1 support that conclusion: The percentage of first-term representatives who go on to serve additional terms in subsequent congresses has increased over time. For instance, the percentage of first-term members serving two additional terms increased from 41.3 percent between the 53rd–57th Congresses to 74.6 percent between the 83rd–87th Congresses and reaches 82.4 percent in the 95th Congress; freshmen re-election rates rise from 84.5 percent between the 83rd–87th Congresses to 91.4 percent in the 96th Congress. Thus, extending Witmer's study reveals that the survivability of representatives has actually increased beyond the levels attained in his study; beyond the third term, however, survivorship rates seem to fluctuate less from the levels attained in the final years of Witmer's study (83rd–87th Congresses).

Witmer also predicted that there would be an emerging stability in the proportion of senior members (10 or more terms) because of the small size of the entering classes of freshmen from which (later) senior members would be drawn (Witmer, 1964 p.537). "If this is correct," he concluded, "there will be a corresponding increase in the availability of seats for first-term members. We may, in other words, expect to see a reversal of the trend toward fewer and fewer freshmen members in the not far distant future." I suspect that Witmer was too optimistic about the extent to which there would be an infusion of new members into the House of Representatives since the survival rates of representatives appear to increase in many congresses.

In Table 4-2, data on the membership of classes in the House of Representatives and the entering classes from which they are principally derived is shown. If Witmer is correct, there should be a decrease in the percentage of members with 10 or more years of congressional service after the 83rd–87th Congresses. As Table 4-2 indicates, however, there has been no falling off in the survival of these senior members since the conclusion of Witmer's study: tenth-, twelfth-, and thirteenth-termers have actually survived at higher rates than Witmer anticipated. For instance, the percentage of tenth- and eleventh-termers increased by about 6 percent after the 83rd–87th Congresses, and the percentage of thirteenth-termers nearly doubles between the 83rd–87th Congresses and the 93rd–97th Congresses. While other congressional classes exhibit less of an increase in the rate of survival, there is no instance in which the survivor rate in later Congresses falls more than one or two percent below the rate attained between the 83rd–87th Congresses. Moreover, the survivorship rates during the 93rd–97th Congresses are in every instance higher than the rates existing during the 83rd–87th Congresses. Thus, despite Witmer's prediction of a decline in the survival rate of incumbents, survivorship rates have actually increased in the House of Representatives.

It should not be too surprising, in light of the increased survivability of congressmen, to find voluntary retirements in the 1970s replacing electoral defeat as the prime source of turnover in the House of Representatives. Retirements peaked in the late 1970s; but since 1980 there has been a reversal of this trend, especially in the House of Representatives (Figure 4-2). Joseph Cooper and William West (1981) found that the number of voluntary retirements increased in both the House and the Senate: Between 1957 and 1969, an average of 32 representatives and 5 senators resigned each Congress, but between 1969 and 1979, House retirements averaged 46 members and Senate retirements averaged 7. Cooper and West argued that the increase in voluntary retirements in the House was due to a growing dissatisfaction with service in the House of Representatives. Simply put, some of the attraction of congressional service that enticed members in earlier Congresses to stay around for additional terms had disappeared:

> ...the job of a member of Congress is far more onerous and unpleasant than a few decades ago. Members now lead very hectic and frenetic lives. The combination of their Washington and district duties results in long office

TABLE 4–1 Percentages of First-Term Members in Specified Congresses to Members Serving Additional Terms in Subsequent Congresses[a]

	53rd–57th	58th–62nd	63rd–67th	68th–72nd	73rd–77th	78th–82nd	83rd–87th	88th	89th	90th	91st	92nd	93rd	94th	95th	96th
First-termers at:																
Beginning of	623	481	536	368	499	403	302	65	83	60	36	48	66	87	63	75
End of	668	526	603	409	562	465	335	77	92	66	49	58	71	95	68	81
2nd-termers one																
Congress later	66.9	76.0	73.6	78.5	77.9	74.8	84.5	87.0	65.2	97.0	89.9	84.5	88.7	96.8	88.2	91.4
3rd-termers two																
Congresses later	41.3	54.8	58.0	65.8	60.3	60.9	74.6	75.3	59.8	83.3	85.7	65.5	78.9	80.0	82.4	
4th-termers three																
Congresses later	32.9	39.5	47.6	53.3	48.4	52.5	65.7	71.4	51.1	72.7	65.3	50.0	62.0	64.2		
5th-termers four																
Congresses later	27.2	29.1	37.6	40.3	39.3	43.4	57.9	62.3	43.5	45.5	59.2	46.6	50.7			
6th-termers five																
Congresses later	22.6	21.1	30.7	31.3	30.1	37.4	49.3	55.8	39.1	34.8	44.9	32.8				
7th-termers six																
Congresses later	16.2	16.2	25.2	24.0	24.9	33.1	41.2	48.1	32.6	25.8	38.8					
8th-termers seven																
Congresses later	11.1	11.6	19.9	19.1	19.2	25.8	35.5	39.0	28.3	22.7						
9th-termers eight																
Congresses later	8.5	8.6	11.4	15.3	21.1	29.0	32.5	19.6								
10th-termers nine																
Congresses later	6.4	7.4	10.6	11.2	13.2	18.7	22.7	20.8								
11th-termers ten																
Congresses later	4.2	4.8	7.3	7.8	10.7	15.1	17.0									

TABLE 4–1 (con't.)

	53rd–57th	58th–62nd	63rd–67th	68th–72nd	73rd–77th	78th–82nd	83rd–87th	88th	89th	90th	91st	92nd	93rd	94th	95th	96th
12th-termers eleven Congresses later	2.5	3.0	5.5	7.3	8.9	11.2	12.0[b]									
13th-termers twelve Congresses later	1.3	2.3	4.0	6.6	7.1	9.9	10.6[c]									
14th-termers thirteen Congresses later	0.9	1.1	3.3	5.1	5.7	7.5										
15th-termers fourteen Congresses later	0.8	1.0	2.5	4.2	3.7	5.6										

aThe figures for first-termers are absolute numbers as of the beginning and end of the Congresses specified; all other figures are percentages of the numbers of first-termers at the end of the Congresses.
bBased on the 83rd–86th Congresses.
cBased on the 83rd–85th Congresses.

Sources: Witmer (1964) for data from 53rd to 87th Congresses. Data for 88th to 96th Congresses are calculated from *Congressional Directory* (1963–1981).

TABLE 4-2 Membership of Classes in the House and the Entering Classes from Which They Principally Derive

	2nd-Termers			3rd-Termers			4th-Termers			5th-Termers		
	(I)	(II)	(III)	(I)	(II)	(III)	(I)	(II)	(III)	(I)	(II)	(III)
58th–62nd	365	493	74.0	278	518	53.7	233	566	41.2	190	652	29.1
63rd–67th	472	616	76.6	337	588	57.3	241	600	40.0	153	562	27.2
68th–72nd	333	444	75.0	306	482	63.3	278	507	54.8	244	56	43.5
73rd–77th	440	572	76.9	303	523	57.9	214	480	44.6	153	450	34.0
78th–82nd	346	472	73.3	296	493	60.0	247	486	50.8	223	511	43.6
83rd–87th	290	339	85.6	258	359	71.9	254	417	60.9	204	440	46.4
88th–92nd	291	350	83.1	272	388	70.1	221	372	59.4	184	333	55.3
93rd–97th	339	373	90.9	272	341	79.8	223	339	65.8	171	336	50.9

	6th-Termers			7th-Termers			8th-Termers			9th-Termers		
	(I)	(II)	(III)	(I)	(II)	(III)	(I)	(II)	(III)	(I)	(II)	(III)
58th–62nd	151	668	22.6	93[a]	570[a]	16.3	53[b]	459[b]	11.5		X	
63rd–67th	111	526	21.1	85	493	17.2	62	518	12.0	58	566	10.2
68th–72nd	185	603	30.7	148	616	24.0	106	588	18.0	77	600	12.8
73rd–77th	129	409	31.5	101	444	22.7	87	482	18.0	69	507	13.6
78th–82nd	169	562	30.0	134	572	23.4	82	523	15.7	55	480	11.5
83rd–87th	174	465	37.4	146	472	30.9	133	493	26.6	100	486	20.8
88th–92nd	164	342	48.0	140	345	40.6	113	362	31.2	111	421	26.4
93rd–97th	144	342	42.1	134	350	38.3	124	388	32.0	95	372	25.5

	10th-Termers			11th-Termers			12th-Termers			13th-Termers		
	(I)	(II)	(III)	(I)	(II)	(III)	(I)	(II)	(III)	(I)	(II)	(III)
63rd–67th	46	652	7.1	28	668	4.2	15[a]	570[a]	2.6	7[b]	459[b]	1.5
68th–72nd	48	562	8.5	25	526	4.8	17	493	3.4	11	518	2.1

TABLE 4–2 (con't.)

	10th-Termers			11th-Termers			12th-Termers			13th-Termers		
	(I)	(II)	(III)	(I)	(II)	(III)	(I)	(II)	(III)	(I)	(II)	(III)
73rd–77th	58	561	10.3	44	603	7.3	30	616	4.9	17	588	2.9
78th–82nd	46	450	10.0	32	409	7.8	31	444	7.0	32	482	6.6
83rd–87th	85	511	14.7	60	562	10.7	46	572	8.0	28	523	5.4
88th–92nd	93	448	20.8	76	474	16.0	58	482	12.0	47	503	9.3
93rd–97th	70	333	21.0	57	342	16.7	37	345	10.7	37	362	10.2

	14th-Termers			15th-Termers		
	(I)	(II)	(III)	(I)	(II)	(III)
68th–72nd	6	566	1.1	5	652	0.7
73rd–77th	11	600	1.8	8	562	1.4
78th–82nd	24	507	4.7	15	561	2.7
83rd–87th	22	480	4.6	16	450	3.6
88th–92nd	37	497	7.4	24	520	4.6
93rd–97th	30	421	7.1	26	448	5.8

aThree Congresses only
bFour Congresses only
Column (I) = Number of members at the beginnings of the Congresses indicated.
Column (II) = Number of members of entering classes from which the membership shown in Column (I) is principally derived.
Column (III) = Column (I) as percentage of Column (II).

Sources: Witmer (1964) for data from 53rd to 87th Congresses. Data for 88th to 97th Congresses are calculated from *Congressional Directory* (1963–1981).

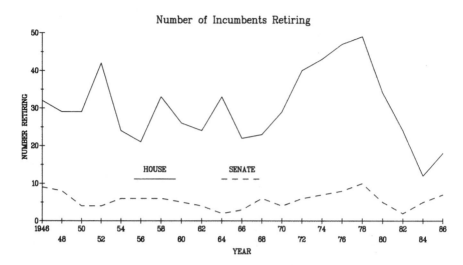

FIGURE 4-2   House and Senate Retirements 1948–1986 [Sources: Ornstein et al. (1982, pp. 46–48) and *Congressional Quarterly Almanac*, vols. 38–42.]

hours and frequent travel. They have little time left to spend with their families. When in Washington, members are confronted by the need to vote on hosts of issues they know little about, frustrated by scheduling conflicts in committee meetings and overlaps in jurisdictions, and debilitated by the need to race continually back and forth from office to committee to floor. Practicing the basic politician's art of compromise is far more difficult. (Cooper and West, 1981, p. 87)

At the same time that legislative pressures and demands on incumbents have increased, the ability of Congress to handle its workload in a coherent and deliberate manner, and the capacity of members to master the volume of complex and interrelated issues they confront, have declined considerably; the growing burden of servicing and cultivating constituents has also contributed to dissatisfaction among incumbents. Legislative service has become more "costly" to incumbents, and the rewards derived from that service have not kept pace.

...the satisfactions members receive from realizing policy goals have declined as the difficulties of building majorities behind coherent and meaningful programs have increased. More and more members today doubt that they can have an impact on the course of our nation, that they can play a vital and significant role in shaping national policy. (Cooper and West, 1981, p. 89)

Furthermore, John Hibbing (1982) contends that the demise of the seniority rule for selecting committee and subcommittee leaders also increased voluntary retirements from the House of Representatives during the 1970s:

Representatives are motivated by the desire to acquire committee power. When the seniority rule was an iron law, the way to maximize power was to stay in the House for an extended career. When the application of the seniority rule became a question mark, the value of an extended congressional career declined. As a result, the voluntary retirement rate shot up and the typical congressional career was shortened. (p. 482).

Despite the increased retirements from Congress during the 1970s, the survival rates of representatives suggests that the vast majority of congressmen continue to find legislative service sufficiently rewarding to seek additional terms.

Retirements in the Senate reveal the same trend as in the House (Figure 4-2). Voluntary retirements in the House amounted to 11 percent per Congress during the 1970s, in contrast to 7 percent in the late 1950s and 1960s; in the Senate, retirements accounted for 22 percent of the turnover among senators during the 1970s and 15 percent in the late 1950s and 1960s (Hibbing, 1982). These similarities notwithstanding, retirements among senators seem to be based upon a different set of factors: Age, electoral marginality, and ambition account for the vast majority of retirements among senators during the 1970s and 1980s. Dissatisfaction with service in the Senate might be expected to register at lower levels since individual senators possess more power than their counterparts in the House. Nonetheless, we cannot completely dismiss the discord that results from time pressures, electoral demands, and policy frustration, since these undesirable features of legislative service affect House and Senate incumbents alike. As former Senator James Abourezk (D-S.D.) described the wear and tear on a senator: "Each time you run, you have to peel off a principle here, a principle there" (Hibbing, 1982, p. 100). Few senators can escape these problems, though they do not seem to drive many senators from office.

Decline of Marginal Districts and States. David Mayhew (1974b) was one of the first scholars to call attention to the decline in electorally marginal districts. Mayhew constructed histograms of the percentage of the vote obtained by Democratic representatives in every election between 1956 and 1972. He was interested in the percentage of congressional districts in which the vote outcome indicated that the district was electorally marginal (i.e., successful incumbent elected by less than 55 percent of the vote).[3] Mayhew's examination of the shapes of these vote distributions over time revealed that fewer and fewer districts had election results that fell into the marginal range. Mayhew observed that the vote distributions in the 1950s and early 1960s had a majority of congressional election outcomes located in the middle of the distribution—the competitive range of election results. In the late 1960s, however, the vote distributions shifted so that

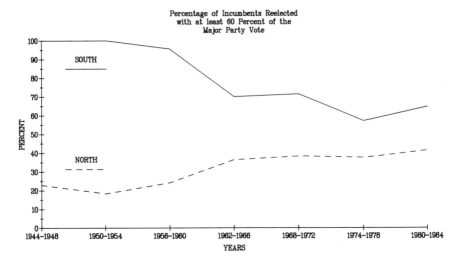

FIGURE 4-3   Senate Elections Won by 60 Percent of the Vote 1944–1984 [Sources: Ornstein, et al. (1982, p. 51) and *Congressional Quarterly Almanac*, vols. 36–40.]

considerably fewer election victories fell into this marginal range. Mayhew concluded that turnover in Congress had declined because the kind of congressional district that produced electoral turnover in the past was becoming an endangered species—marginal districts.

If the disappearance of the marginal district can account for declines in House turnover, then the decline of marginal Senate seats can account for some of the lack of turnover of senators during the 1960s and 1970s. As Figure 4-3 reveals, the percentage of incumbent senators reelected with at least 60 percent of the two-party vote has declined in the South and risen among northern senators; the vast majority of the safe Senate seats remain in the South, however. During the 1944–1948 period of elections, all southern incumbents were reelected with at least 60 percent of the vote, while only 22.9 percent of the incumbent northern senators exhibited a similar level of safety. This stands as true testimony to how electorally safe the South was in earlier decades.

After 1960, however, the electoral safety of southern senators begins to decline with the improved electoral position of the Republican Party in the South. The percentage of "safe" southern senators drops from 70 percent during the 1960s to 57 percent during the 1974–1978 period; during the 1980–1984 period, the electoral safety of southern senators rises though it remains below the levels of safety observed prior to the 1974–1978 period. At the same time that southern senators were becoming less safe as a group, northern senators were actually increasing their electoral safety. Before the 1960s, less than one-quarter of the northern incumbent senators could claim safe election margins, but after this time period

TABLE 4–3   Safe Democratic and Republican Senate Seats in Northern States: 1946–1980

Election Period	Number of Safe[a] Democratic Senators	Percentage of Winning Incumbents	Number of Safe[a] Republican Senators	Percentage of Winning Incumbents
1946–1950	3	9%	7	22%
1952–1956	2	4	10	20
1958–1962	10	20	5	10
1964–1968	17	30	9	16
1970–1974	16	30	6	11
1976–1980	14	41	6	18

[a]Senators winning by at least 60% of the major party vote.

Source: *Guide to U.S. Elections* (Washington, D.C.: Congressional Quarterly, 1975), pp. 485–509; *Congressional Quarterly Weekly Reports* (1976, 1978, and 1980) provided the data for recent elections.

(1944–1960) more than one-third of these incumbent senators were reelected by safe margins.

It is evident from Table 4-3 that the electoral safety of northern senators differs between the two parties: The shift in the electoral safety of northern senators occurred primarily among the Democrats, since safe Republican seats remain fairly constant throughout the 1946–1980 period. Specifically, between 1946 and 1962, Democrats averaged 5 safe seats while Republicans averaged 7 safe seats over the three election triplets. This pattern is dramatically altered by northern Democratic senators after 1964 when the average number of safe Democratic seats increases to 16, while the average number of safe Republican seats shows no change over the last three election triplets.

In sum, the lack of turnover in contemporary congresses has occurred in part because the types of congressional districts that normally show the greatest vulnerability to short-term electoral forces have declined in number. Even Senate seats, historically highly competitive (especially outside of the South), have become less so since the 1960s. The result has been an increased stability in the membership of Congress.

Weakness of Presidential Coattails. Among the many problems that confront presidents, one of the most perplexing is how to persuade members of Congress that is in their best interests to deliver what the president wants. Presidents are most persuasive when they can convince congressmen that their electoral fortunes are intertwined with those of their president, and that their success at the polls depends upon *his* legislative successes in Congress. The most explicit way in which presidents can demonstrate this relationship is when congressional candidates knowingly owe their electoral success to the popular appeal of a victorious president. When congressional candidates ride to victory on the "coattails" of their party's presidential candidate, the president is certain to be persuasive in eliciting support. It is unlikely that a president can gain much political mileage if his candidacy raises or lowers a congressman's normally substantial election votes by only a few percentage points. If, on the other hand, the president's coattails are efficient—those who favor a presidential candidate also vote for that party's congressional candidate—the change may be far more dramatic, resulting in the election of many new members whose electoral verdicts reflect the popular national appeal of the victorious president. Thus, presidential coattails are a viable mechanism for changing the composition of Congress and inducing turnover.

The most obvious way in which coattail voting could occur is if voters base their decisions for lower offices upon their vote in the presidential race. This could occur if a voter, who is always predisposed toward the congressional candidate of one party, ignores this predisposition and votes for the opposition candidate because of the attractiveness of that party's presidential candidate. Another way in which coattail voting could occur is if previous nonvoters sympathetic to the candidate of one party are mobilized to go to the polls by the presence of an unusually attractive presidential candidate on that party's ticket; in this case, increases in turnout benefit one party over the other. We can expect sizable coattail victories, therefore, when a president induces a substantial number of new voters, and those already inclined to split their presidential and congressional votes between the parties, to vote a straight ticket.

Political mechanisms that could produce a linkage between electoral outcomes at the presidential and congressional levels have steadily atrophied in the last several decades, along with the strength of the connection between presidential and congressional election outcomes. Before the 1900s, party organizations were often strong and salient features of the electoral landscape: Voters used party-supplied ballots, and nominations were under party control. In these years, congressional and presidential votes were strongly correlated (Burnham, 1975; Calvert and Ferejohn, 1984). This relationship is considerably weaker in the contemporary Congress, and it may be declining even further. For instance, Congress and the White House have been controlled by different parties for about one-half of the postwar years, but during the preceding 50 years, divided government persisted for only six years!

In addition, the proportion of congressional districts producing split outcomes (a majority of voters favoring the candidate from one party for the House seat, and the candidates of the other party for president) have increased significantly (see Figure 1-1). Clearly, today's House incumbents should be less fearful of the strong national tides commonly associated with presidential elections since voters show a willingness to split their loyalties between presidential and congressional candidates:

> The evidence presented here suggests that the cross-sectional relationship between the congressional and presidential vote, already quite weak in 1956, has become substantially weaker since 1968 and that a substantial portion of this decline results from a decline in coattail voting. In other words, at the same time that the influence of partisan factors in vote determination have been declining and that the more or less local forces producing incumbency voting have been increasing, citizens have been making less use of their evaluations of the presidential candidates in making their decisions about how (and whether) to vote in the congressional contest. (Calvert and Ferejohn, 1983, p. 417)

Moreover, when voters do split their ballots, incumbents usually benefit.

The lack of coattail voting has reached the point where an incoming president cannot routinely expect to have a majority of his party in control of both branches of Congress or that members of his own party will see their own electoral fates as linked to his success in office. Some scholars are even prepared to relegate presidential coattails to the history books. "Incumbents have become quite effectively insulated from the electoral effects, for example, of adverse presidential landslides. As a result, a once notable phenomenon, the so-called coattails effect, has virtually been eliminated" (Burnham, 1975, p. 412). In sum, presidential coattails, a viable mechanism for membership turnover in past congresses, has become almost extinct as a potent force in congressional elections. Without the periodic disturbance of presidential elections to disrupt the stability of the membership of Congress, congressmen can count on very long careers in the House or Senate.

CONDITIONS PROMOTING STABILITY
IN THE MEMBERSHIP OF CONGRESS

There are several factors that have promoted and sustained the stability in the membership of the House and Senate. First, the decline in partisan predispositions may have loosened the ties of Americans to their political parties, thereby reducing the dependence of voters on party loyalties as a means of choosing between congressional candidates. In the absence of strong partisan predilections, many voters have substituted incumbency for party identification as the principle on which to base their votes. Second, the resources available to incumbents may provide them with a campaign edge over their normally unknown, underfinanced, and inexperienced challengers. Thus, the resources of incumbents enhance their electoral position and reduce the probability of electoral defeat. In contrast to the electoral positions of most incumbents, congressional challengers are impoverished: They have difficulty raising money and gaining the attention of the electorate and, in many cases, recruiting someone to challenge an incumbent results in inferior candidates. Finally, the adoption of attentive home styles may enhance the survival of incumbents because being attentive to constituency affairs enables them to win the trust and support of constituents. Moreover, attentive home styles provide a ubiquitous means for promoting popular images among constituents and for disseminating them widely and repeatedly within the district or state.

Decline of Partisanship. I have already noted the importance of the weak attachments of Americans to their political parties in promoting the individuality of congressmen and in sustaining their electoral independence. Declining partisanship among voters may also enhance the stability of the membership of Congress by weakening the pull of presidential coattails and reducing the influence of short-term partisan forces on congressional elections. There are at least two ways in which declining partisanship could reduce turnover in Congress. First, the absence of strong attachments to the parties has eased the incumbent's task of assembling personal electoral followings. Second, the decreasing value of party identification as a rule of thumb in voting choices may have led voters to seek a different basis for their voting decisions, and "reelect the incumbent" appears to have become just such a principle.

Party identification reflects an individual's psychological attachment to one of the major parties. In the 1950s, these loyalties seemed quite stable. Party loyalties remained intact, even when voters supported candidates from the opposition party, and party identification was the single best predictor of voting decisions in presidential and midterm elections. By the mid-1960s, however, the influence of party was beginning to wane. More individuals deserted their party attachments in making their vote decisions in presidential and congressional elections, and fewer voters expressed loyalties to either of the parties. Since party loyalties were abandoned increasingly in congressional vote decisions, congressmen sought other bases for constructing their voter coalitions. Party might remain an incentive for support, and party identifiers might comprise a significant segment of a congressman's voter coalition, but it was an unreliable basis of support. At the very least, voter coalitions composed entirely of strong partisans were too minimal to consistently ensure reelection. In sum, incumbents needed to expand the partisan basis of their voter coalitions to avoid dependence upon an increasingly unreliable basis of support and to ensure a safe and dependable margin of victory.

In the process, congressmen developed personal electoral followings that vowed loyalty to the incumbent rather than his party. These personal followings helped members to withstand the types of partisan electoral pressures that often spelled electoral defeat in earlier decades. National forces that produce landslide elections, election mandates, coattail victories, or other types of abnormal rates of turnover were rendered impotent.

The intense and unstable national politics of the 1960s also led some voters to abandon party as a guide to voting in congressional elections. When parties are clearly defined by contrasting stands on issues and policies, adherence to party as a cue for voting made some sense, especially given the relative obscurity of most congressional contests. By the late 1960s, however, many political issues crosscut party alignments; the voter had good reason to look elsewhere for a guiding principle on which to base his congressional vote. Incumbency provided just such a simple cue for a number of voters: If voters haven't heard anything too disgusting or outrageous about their congressman, they might rationally assume that he is performing his duties in Washington. Why change? After all, an incumbent's successor might be a good deal less admirable—a likely occurrence in the minds of most constituents. Thus, incumbency provided voters with a simple cue for voting in congressional elections where information about the candidates is normally difficult to obtain. As incumbency replaced party as a cue in congressional voting, partisan electoral forces lost their potency. With the subjugation of partisan considerations in the minds of voters, incumbency assumed greater significance in determining the outcomes of congressional elections, and partisan turnover dissipated.

The declining influence of party in congressional elections is evident in Figure 4-4. This figure reports the percentage of voters who defected

FIGURE 4–4   Partisan Defections to House and Senate Incumbents 1956–1982 [Source: Bullock and Scicchitano (1985, p. 37).]

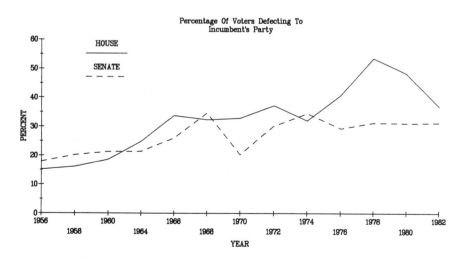

Percentage Of Voters Defecting To Incumbent's Party

from the ranks of party supporters to support the incumbent. This figure makes clear the potency of incumbency in congressional elections during recent decades: Voters defecting from their party's candidate has more than doubled in House elections. The percentage of defections was less than 20 percent in House elections before 1964 but rose over 30 percent since that time. While partisan defections in Senate elections are considerably less, such defections have also grown. Until the mid-1960s, the percentage of partisan defections in Senate races never rose above 26 percent, but for most senate elections in the 1970s and 1980s, the percentage of defections was about 30 percent.

Office Resources. Office resources, or "perks" as they are commonly called, help to minimize turnover by enhancing the reelection chances of incumbents.[4] I have already noted the vast array of resources available to incumbents for maintaining contact with their constituents when discussing the independence of congressmen and their attentive home styles. I need only add that these resources have an undeniable electoral function, or, at the very least, the use of these resources satisfies electoral as well as representational needs. Many of the services that members provide to their constituents, such as mass mailings, fulfill representational obligations. A newsletter is one means through which constituents can learn about the activities of their congressman and the impact of national policies on the district or state. On the other hand, fulfilling such a representational obligation may simultaneously satisfy electoral needs: The same newsletter that keeps constituents informed about government can be packaged to convey images that have electoral appeal.

Claiming "credit" for a federal project or "advertising" one's record of constituency service can be easily integrated with less political information. Government-subsidized travel to the state or district helps congressmen maintain contact with their constituents, but meetings with constituents also provide congressmen with a ubiquitous channel for disseminating the types of messages that elicit voter support. The similarity between the congressman's messages between (Fenno, 1978) and during congressional campaigns (Jones, 1966) testifies to the dual objectives that these office resources serve. The intertwining of electoral and representational purposes in the use of these resources makes it difficult to effectively regulate usage without impairing representational responsibilities.[5] Because of these electoral benefits, office "perks" have helped incumbents stave off electoral defeat, thereby minimizing congressional turnover. The constituent contact that results from the use of most of these resources provides opportunities for incumbents to engage in electioneering. Incumbents use these contacts to enhance their visibility among constituents, to project electorally rewarding home-style images, and to mobilize supporters for an approaching election.

Senators can also exploit their contacts with their constituents for electoral advantage, but their efforts face more obstacles. The feelings of trust that bind constituents to their representative are nurtured through personal contacts (Fenno, 1978), and although senators have increased the time they spend with their constituents, the size of most states precludes the development of such personal ties between senators and their constituents. Senators also exercise less control over the dissemination of information about themselves, unlike representatives. This is not to say that senators gain less from the exploitation of office resources; rather, the nature of the office—greater prestige, power, competitiveness, and campaign costs—makes senators more vulnerable to forces beyond their control. For example, the higher levels of "free" information in Senate elections make challengers far more visible to voters than in House elections (Parker, 1981a).

Newsletters, trips to the state or district, and the use of other office resources do more than increase constituent contact and therefore voter support. These resources also discourage competitive challenges by influencing perceptions of vulnerability. If an incumbent can convince potential opponents, and those who would financially support their candidacies, that he is unbeatable, few formidable challenges will be made by the opposition party. For one thing, it is difficult to recruit a candidate to run against a popular incumbent; often the activity degenerates into recruiting "losers" rather than high quality candidates. Thus, by maintaining extensive contact with voters, incumbents are able to enhance their support among their constituents and thereby weaken the opposition they face at the next election.

We should not underestimate the financial edge that incumbents gain as a result of these office perks. Incumbents not only start their campaigns earlier than their challengers—the day after they are sworn in signals the start of the next campaign for many incumbents—but they begin with a sizable advantage in campaign resources. This occurs because office perks can be converted easily into campaign resources. For example, staff responsibilities can be reassigned from the office to the campaign with few problems; hence, the difficulties associated with organizing a campaign staff are minimized for most incumbents. Furthermore, the names of constituents writing to request assistance from their congressman can be added to the long lists of potential supporters and contributors. Thus, incumbents maintain a clear financial edge over their opposition as a result of their ability to exploit the resources of the office and to make it difficult for challengers to attain the financial support they need to wage a competitive campaign. Resources do not guarantee victory; it depends on what the incumbent does with those resources and how he works to build trust and support among his constituents. Nonetheless, incumbents have an extensive array of office resources that can be converted into electoral advantage.

Weak Challengers. Another reason there is so little turnover of incumbent congressmen is because they often face nominal competition in their reelections—underfinanced and weak opponents. The electoral strength of most incumbents scares off the type of candidates who would wage the most competitive elections: Voters are more familiar with them, and like them better, than their challengers; the public also has many more contacts with incumbents than those who challenge them. Opportunities to exploit incumbency are limited only by an underdeveloped imagination. Recruiting challengers under such circumstances is akin to asking someone not only to join a losing cause, but also to lead it! As a consequence, it is extremely difficult to find able politicians who are willing to challenge entrenched incumbents.[6] Gary Jacobson and Samuel Kernell (1981) argue that the weakness of these candidacies produces lopsided electoral victories for incumbents.

Challengers to senate incumbents, in contrast to House challengers, are better equipped to make a contest of it. They are normally more experienced, visible, and frequently have access to substantial sources of financial support. The prestige of the office and the greater vulnerability of senate incumbents ensures that Senate elections attract better qualified challengers than are found in House contests. Moreover, politicians rarely contest a Senate seat unless they feel that they have a good chance to succeed—the costs of such campaigns are far too high for frivolous candidacies. Thus, Senate contests normally attract serious challenges by able and well-financed candidates at a higher rate than we observe in House races; this may account for some of the greater electoral vulnerability of Senate incumbents.

One thing that guarantees an ineffective challenge is the absence of adequate funding to wage a campaign. Regardless of ideological or policy differences, most interest groups channel their contributions to incumbents; with these funds, incumbents purchase television and radio time for their campaign messages, staff their campaign organizations, and design and circulate campaign paraphenalia. Because the resources at the disposal of incumbents are extensive and electorally potent, congressmen appear to spend only in response to electoral threat: "Incumbents, then, acquire and spend funds in proportion to the perceived necessity to do so. And they can usually get all they feel they need, although they may not enjoy doing it" (Jacobson, 1980, p. 139).

Congressmen do not usually find it necessary to spend lavish sums of money on their campaigns because the electoral threat posed by most challenges is not severe enough to warrant huge expenditures. If an incumbent is forced to compete with a challenger in terms of campaign expenditures, he is in real trouble and probably faces electoral defeat. In most cases, however, campaign spending is of marginal value to incumbents because of the vast array of campaign resources subsidized by the government and the weak financial position of most challengers. Challengers, on the other hand, benefit from campaign spending, perhaps because it generates the visibility and campaign resources necessary to wage a competitive race. Incumbents also deter serious challenges by pre-emptive spending: The accumulation of large "campaign war chests" through continuous fund-raising activities and the expenditure of these funds well in advance of the general election. If successful, incumbents may have little need to worry about trying to match the campaign expenditures of their challengers because "potential strong opponents have dropped out...in the face of large sums of money stockpiled by an apparently invincible incumbent" (Goldenberg and Traugott, 1984, p. 94).

Finally, there is some evidence that the quality of challenges, especially in House elections, is affected by national tides that favor one party over the other (Jacobson and Kernell, 1981), and by local partisan forces (Bond, Covington, and Fleisher, 1985). Gary Jacobson and Samuel Kernell argue that when the outlook for electoral victory is dim, able and qualified candidates eschew the opportunity to contest the election of an incumbent. However, when the electoral tides turn against the incumbent's political party, more and better candidates are attracted to the race; hence, incumbents face competitive challenges. In sum, when national conditions (tides) appear to favor one party over the other, the favored party is able to field an unusual group of formidable and well-financed challengers.[7] Jon Bond and his colleagues found that local partisan forces, in addition to national forces, were also important influences on the quality of challenges to House incumbents. Close elections and the general partisan nature of their districts affected the vulnerability of incumbents to electoral challenges: "The most important reasons why most House incumbents do not face formidable opponents are because most incumbents did not have a close race in the preceding election and because most have been selected from the dominant party in the district" (Bond, Covington, and Fleisher, 1985, p. 526).

Attentive Home Styles. Attentive home styles make members popular with their constituents, and popularity within the district or state often translates into electoral success (Parker, 1981a). "All else being equal, a very favorable image as a good constituency representative is more important to the candidate in determining the vote than having the same party affiliation as the voter" (Cain, Ferejohn, and Fiorina, 1984, p. 119). Constituency attention can be viewed as an electoral advantage that largely falls to incumbents since they are the only ones in a position to take advantage of it. Simply put, actions speak louder than words, and incumbents can boast about their attention to their constituents, while challengers can only promise what they would do if elected. Further, since most incumbents are fairly diligent in looking after their constituents, the challenger's promises of maintaining a comparable level of attention, or of increasing it, may not sound very convincing to constituents already satisfied with their representative's performance.

Attentive home styles also serve as a mechanism for expanding voter coalitions, and the over-time change in home styles accounts for some of the decline in marginal elections. That is, electorally marginal congressmen and senators have increased their electoral safety by adopting more attentive homes styles; as these marginal congressmen and senators became safe, they reduced membership turnover in Congress (Parker, 1986b).

Fenno (1978) views the processes of building and maintaining electoral support as involving two stages of constituency careers: the expansionist and protectionist stages. In the expansionist stage, members "solidify a primary constituency, a core of strongest supporters who will carry a primary campaign, if necessary, and who will, in any case, provide the backbone for a general election campaign" (p. 172). This stage of the constituency career gives way to the protectionist stage in which incumbents seek to maintain and stabilize their support. Although Fenno describes these stages as sequential, he notes that some members may find it necessary to lapse into the earlier expansionist stage in response to events. Therefore, incumbents elected from areas with strong opposition party traditions, or who are ideologically divergent from their constituencies, may find it necessary to cultivate state or district voters on a more or less continuous basis. Such members may need to engage in expansionist-stage activities for most of the duration of their terms in office!

This should not be construed as suggesting that the quantity, or even the quality, of constituency attention differs as members progress through the stages of their constituency careers; rather, the focus, diversity, and breadth of that attention may differ depending on whether the aim of the incumbent is to build or to maintain his electoral coalition. Incumbents in the expansionist stage of their careers need to broaden their bases of support by cultivating a wider assortment of groups within the district or state than incumbents in the protectionist stage, who have the luxury of concentrating their attention on a more limited subset of constituency groups. Northern Democratic senators from Republican areas, for example, have an obvious incentive to expand their electoral coalitions: They must direct their constituency activities toward more diverse groups in order to weave majority and minority party voters into successful coalitions. Republican senators from these same areas, on the other hand, can move more rapidly into the protectionist stage and limit their attention to those groups that consistently provide sufficient partisan support to ensure victory.

In short, congressmen and senators who are politically atypical of their constituencies are most inclined to expand their voter coalitions. Members can be atypical of their constituencies in a number of ways, but the most dramatic seem to relate to partisan loyalties and ideological orientations. Liberals representing conservative constituencies or Democrats elected from Republican areas are two examples of the types of political conditions that can make incumbents atypical. These representatives and senators have the greatest incentive to expand their voter coalitions because their electoral survival depends upon their ability to create coalitions composed of constituents with partisan loyalties to the opposition party or ideological beliefs that would impel loyalty to their opponents. The more politically atypical the area represented, the greater the incumbent's need to expand his voter coalition.

I have demonstrated elsewhere (Parker, 1986b) that incumbents from politically atypical areas who adopted attentive home styles expanded their voter coalitions. In the aggregate, these changes produced an increase in electoral safety during the 1960s and 1970s in House and Senate elections. Thus, incumbents elected from areas with strong opposition party traditions and loyalties found a way to increase their electoral safety during the 1960s and 1970s without switching parties or subjugating their political positions to constituent opinion. The method was quite simple: Demonstrate a thorough concern for the district by emphasizing how attentive you are to the needs, demands, and problems of your constituents. Bolstered by the expansion of office perks during the 1960s and 1970s, the adoption of, and conversion to, attentive home styles made these messages a permanent feature of legislator-constituent interactions. Therefore, changes in attentiveness enabled these atypical members to hold on to their congressional seats despite their deviance from the bulk of their constituents. The consequence was a decline in the electoral insecurity of congressmen during the 1960s and 1970s who would be *a priori* the most marginal. This accounts for some of the aggregate shift in the electoral safety of representatives and senators since the 1960s and the continuing stability in the membership of Congress.

POLICY CONSEQUENCES

Turnover in the membership of Congress is critical to the formation of public policy: New members help alter the liberal-conservative balance within Congress, and the "natural" drift of senior members to greater conservatism (Clem, 1977), and they introduce different perspectives and values into Congress. For example, the large Senate class of 1958 was responsible for a number of major changes in the Senate, and in national policies, during the 1970s:

> It was the massive influx of liberals in the late 1950s and early 1960s, however, that embodied the changes in public opinion and precipitated so many of the changes that occurred inside the Senate. In terms of the general

> life-style of the Senate, it is generally agreed that the liberals introduced "a greater informality of general demeanor and relaxed the stuffiness of the chamber." In the process, the liberals made the Senate a less cocooned and cloistral institution, they reduced the mystique of its introverted and private operations, and they undermined the whole notion of a structural hierarchy of personal status and privilege. Distinctions between juniors and seniors became blurred as the atmosphere within the institution became one of individual assertion. The liberals' disparate ideas and high expectations enlivened the Senate, made it more heterogeneous in composition, and brought it more into the mainstream of national political pressures and trends. (Foley, 1980, p. 253)

When large numbers of new members are elected to Congress as a result of a pronounced shift in the attitudes and opinions of voters, their entrance signals significant policy changes—changes in the legislative agenda and in voting coalitions. In short, membership turnover seems essential for policy change to occur within Congress, and the stability of Congress precludes large-scale changes from occurring.

The high rate of electoral success on the part of incumbents tends to promote stability in the policy agenda and the solutions to political questions. Not only are very few new members entering Congress every two years, but there is little evidence that existing members change their attitudes once they have developed a "voting history" on an issue—a standing decision on an issue produced by background characteristics such as party, ideology, and constituency, and the incumbent's experiences with votes on similar issues (Asher and Weisberg, 1978). These voting histories promote stability in the voting records of congressmen:

> ...the forces of continuity predominate in congressional voting. Stability in individual voting was much more common than change even when the partisan control of the White House was altered and even in issue areas—such as foreign aid and the debt ceiling—where presidential impact was considered substantial. On the school construction votes, where membership replacement best accounted for the ultimate passage of the bill, it nevertheless was the case that the most frequent vote pattern on the issue was one of constancy. And while the dimensional structure of civil rights did change over time, there remained a substantial correlation between the old and new dimensions. (Asher and Weisberg, 1978, p. 423)

This stability means that most policy decisions will be conservative, favoring the status quo position on issues:

> ...there is scant reason to expect it [Congress] to come forth with legislative proposals that depart sharply from previous settlements. Old policies have a tendency to look strictly modern to those who originally made them. Moreover, newcomers to the system, who might be more inclined to abandon past policies and practices, ordinarily lack the political resources to make their preferences count. Finally, what sometimes impresses outsiders as

curious or irresolute legislative response to new demands or nagging problems may appear to legislators themselves as both appropriate and necessary. The stakes are rarely quite the same for non-members as for members. Left mainly to their own devices, legislators stay in office by viewing large questions in parochial light and by making self-preservation one of their chief priorities. (Keefe and Ogul, 1985, p. 108)

Second, the lack of competition for most seats in the House and a substantial number of Senate seats reduces most of the potential for legislative policy innovations. Safe members have little incentive to offend constituents with controversial stands or policies. This helps to "freeze" the legislative agenda to include politically acceptable solutions, not necessarily innovative ones.

Finally, for significant policy changes to occur, a change in the partisan composition of Congress is probably necessary, but such changes are relatively rare. The disappearance of presidential coattails and marginal districts as major sources of party turnover have reduced the susceptibility of congressional elections to national tides and short-term forces. While these national forces may grant a presidential candidate a handsome election victory, he is apt to assume office without a sufficient number of congressmen committed to his programs to ensure passage. Insulated from national waves of opinion, congressmen feel no compulsion to follow the mandate provided a popular president. Incumbents may follow the lead of a victorious president, but they normally do so under their own volition; ideological compatibility may be more important in inducing presidential support in Congress (Parker and Parker, 1985) than a huge election margin run up by a victorious president.

On occasion, party turnover has been quite significant, and the policy changes that resulted have indeed altered the course of government. Political scientists frequently refer to such periods of party government as realignments in the party system. Critical elections that lead to these partisan realignments reflect the altered electoral bases of the parties themselves and create a more cohesive majority party capable of enacting major policies:

In both the 1896 and 1932 realignments, it was the newly created, cohesive majority party that voted through the shifts in policy. The cohesiveness of the new majority party was the result of the turnover in membership (switched-seat districts) which reduced cross pressuring and disrupted committee continuity. The new members had high party-support scores and provided the votes that enacted the policy changes. Thus, on this reasoning, any election that generates a substantial turnover in membership can create the conditions necessary for major shifts in policy. (Brady, 1978, p. 95)

Such critical elections are rare, however, and in the absence of these periodic disturbances, policy changes are more incremental and less comprehensive.

One final point: The lack of turnover may actually enhance the execution of a major congressional responsibility—legislative oversight of the executive branch. The stability in the membership of Congress assures that those who oversee governmental agencies have familiarity and understanding of the operations of these agencies. Agencies are mazes of organization, and layers of personnel and structure—factors that inhibit effective legislative oversight. Certainly, the congressional neophyte lacks the experience of senior members in dealing with agencies and their programs. The senior committee member who has analyzed agency programs and budgets over a number of terms is better able to ask the "right" questions because of greater familiarity with an agency resulting from years of congressional and committee service; knowing the "right" question to ask agency officials may be the only way to unlock areas of agency misfeasance and incompetence to public exposure. Thus, more effective levels of oversight might be accomplished as a consequence of the stability of the membership of Congress since that stability generates expertise that is useful in overseeing federal agencies.

On the other hand, long years of congressional service may also lead congressmen to adopt a more friendly and protective attitude toward certain agencies with which they have dealt during their tenure on a committee. Rather than being a critical audience, then, congressmen would be apprehensive about interfering in the operations of those agencies that have strong ties with individual members. And there are plenty of reasons for members to protect, rather than to oversee, such agencies. For instance, some agencies may provide benefits to a congressman's district that might be reduced if an oversight investigation proved embarrassing or critical. In short, senior congressmen may be in the best position to conduct effective oversight of federal agencies, but their motivations to do so are suspect.

SUMMARY

Congress can be characterized as a relatively stable institution—there is little turnover in membership. This stability is evident in the increased survivability of congressmen, the decline of marginal districts and states during the 1960s and 1970s, and the declining potency of presidential coattails in congressional elections. Legislators elected in recent congresses appear to be surviving at higher rates than past representatives, and congressional districts susceptible to national trends and short-term forces are disappearing. Membership turnover resulting from the electoral success of a president's coattails is also an historical curiosity.

The lack of membership turnover appears related to several factors. First, the decline in partisan loyalties among voters has weakened the "pull" of presidential coattails and has reduced the impact of short-term partisan forces on congressional elections. In addition, the reduced importance of party as a voting cue has led voters to seek other bases for their votes, and incumbency provides many voters with just such a rule of thumb. Second, incumbent congressmen are able to remain in office for long periods because they frequently face weak competition in their reelections. Inexperienced and underfinanced challengers unseat very few incumbents. Since entrenched incumbents only have to face nominal competition, they are able to win frequently and by safe margins of victory. Finally, the adoption and conversion to attentive home styles has made incumbents popular with their constituents, reducing the incentives to challenge them and helping to insulate their congressional contests from the vagaries of national forces. Attentive home styles have also helped "protect" those who are politically atypical of the partisan loyalties and identifications of the vast majority of their constituents and therefore extremely susceptible to defeat.

This stability in the membership of Congress reduces the likelihood of widespread policy changes since such policy innovations are normally associated with a large influx of new members or the existence of electorally marginal ones. As a result, most policy decisions favor the status quo, and solutions to political questions remain unaltered. While such job stability provides legislators with the type of experiences that equips them to ask searching questions of the agencies they oversee, longevity in office may reduce the willingness of senior members to engage in critical oversight of "pet" agencies.

NOTES

1. James Garand and Donald Gross (1984) have examined the electoral safety of congressional candidates between 1824 and 1980. They note that there has been a long-term trend toward electoral safety since 1932, and perhaps since 1894. They argue that since the decline of competition has occurred prior to the 1960s, the explanation for the decline of competition after 1966 cannot be explained by post-1965 developments. They assume that the same forces that produced earlier declines in electoral competition continue to operate, and that *no* new influences might arise to weaken competition further by bolstering, complementing, or replacing these historical forces. This, of course, discounts the well-documented declining influence of presidential coattails—a post-1966 phenomenon—on congressional turnover. I do not deny that some historical forces, such as the weakening of partisan influences on voter decision making, continue to reduce congressional turnover; I would add, however, that other forces have arisen during the 1960s to reduce competition further in congressional elections.

2. Declines in turnover in the contemporary Congress do not match, however, the magnitude of the declines in electoral competition exhibited in earlier periods of change. For instance, the decline in competition that occurs after the 1890s is far greater than the decline in competition that occurs after 1965.

3. We must be cautious about equating marginality solely in terms of reelection margins. Gary Jacobson (1987) demonstrates that while vote margins have increased, the electoral security of incumbents remains the same:

> An incumbent elected in the 1970s with between 60 and 65 percent of the vote was just as likely to lose in the next election as was an incumbent in the 1950s who had been elected with 55 to 60 percent of the vote; incumbents in the 1970s with previous margins in the 65–70 percent range were more vulnerable than those in the 1950s with margins in the 60–65 percent range. (p. 130.)

Clearly, marginality implies more than just an incumbent's previous election margin. Measures of the heterogeneity of the district (Fiorina, 1974) and the partisan tradition in the state in subnational elections (Parker, 1986b) are just two additional factors that need to be considered in defining truly marginal districts. I feel that the essential criterion for defining a marginal district is whether or not the district has been susceptible *historically* to partisan change in control of the seat. There may have been a closer correspondence between this latter definition of marginality and reelection margins in the 1950s than in the 1970s.

4. Establishing an electoral connection between perquisite usage and election results has met with mixed results. Richard Born (1982) has found no relationship between several measures of perquisite usage and reelection, while Cover and Brumberg (1982) have demonstrated a linkage between the mailing of baby books to their constituents and vote support.

5. There have been some notable attempts to restrict the exploitation of office perquisites for electoral objectives. For example, there are limits on the timing of mass mailings to prevent their distribution at or near an election. The Senate has also restricted the number of references that a senator can make to himself in newsletters mailed to constituents.

6. Lyn Ragsdale and Timothy Cook (1987) present evidence that the weakness of challenges is unrelated to the adroit use of campaign and office resources by incumbents:

> ...to the limited degree that incumbents affect challenges, it is not what incumbents do right that fends off successful opponents; it is what incumbents do *wrong* that somewhat increases the viability of challengers' campaigns. Members with policy views divergent from those of their districts and those confronted by ethical allegations faced challengers able to secure greater financial backing. (pp. 56–57)

In short, they contend that incumbent victories are less the result of the skillful use of office resources to minimize the campaign efforts of challengers and more the result of the weakness of the challengers themselves. A similar point is made by Bond, Covington, and Fleisher (1985).

7. Empirical studies of this thesis, however, have cast some doubt on its validity. See, for instance, Uslaner and Conway (1985) and Born (1986).

Chapter Five
CAREER PATHS IN CONGRESS

Congressional service was rarely viewed as a legitimate vocation by members in the early Congresses, most of whom maintained commitments to their primary occupations. Congressmen were farmers and merchants first, and legislators last. Serving in the Capitol during their early years was not only a hardship because of the dismal surroundings of Washington, but also because of the need to abandon one's primary occupation. The idea of citizen-legislators eventually vanished with the emergence of the congressional career, which was brought about by the gradual professionalization of Congress. "The Senate emerged as a highly stable professional body only after the end of Reconstruction. The House remained fluid, both in membership and in committee structure, up to the massive realignment of 1896" (Price, 1975, p. 3). Thus, the "professional" legislator entered, distinguished from those serving in earlier congresses by his commitment to long-run career goals, subject only to the risks of the electoral process and the practices of congressional leaders.

Congressmen follow well-traveled routes (career paths) in attaining personal goals associated with their career aspirations. The personal goals that commonly occupy the attention of career-oriented congressmen are power, policy influence, and reelection (Fenno, 1973). These goals are pursued within the structure of the political parties or within the organization of the committees; each arena provides numerous opportunities for members to attain these goals. This chapter examines patterns in the careers of members as they seek these goals.

PATTERNS IN CONGRESSIONAL CAREERS

While positions of party leadership may help incumbents realize their reelection goals, such positions are normally sought for the power and influence attached to them. Party leaders exercise influence over legislation and their political parties; hence, leadership positions provide opportunities to realize goals of power and policy influence. There are a variety of offices within the political parties that elevate their occupants to positions of legislative influence. Each party has a number of special committees that perform basic party functions such as assisting in reelection (campaign committees), assigning members to committees (steering committees or committees on committees), or formulating policy (policy committees). And, of course, each committee has a chair to direct its operations. These chairmanships are highly prized, but the most desired positions are the Speaker, majority (or minority) leader, and the chief whips. These offices confer a status upon their occupants that entails considerable congressional influence.

In the House, the major elements of the leadership structure consist of the Speaker, who serves as both the presiding officer of the assembly and the majority party's titular leader; the majority and minority floor leaders; and the assistant floor leaders or whips, who also have cadres of assistants. In the U.S. Senate there is no institutional or party official comparable in power and prestige to the Speaker. The vice president of the United States is designated by the Constitution as the presiding officer (president) of the Senate, and the Senate president *pro tempore* presides in his absence, but neither office has very much power or authority. Aside from the position of Speaker, the Senate leadership apparatus tends to parallel the functions performed by their House counterparts.

Congressional committees are also good places for realizing reelection, power, and policy-influence goals. "Each member of each committee wants his committee service to bring him some benefit in terms of goals he holds as an individual congressman" (Fenno, 1973, p. 1). Congressional committees provide forums for members to assume leadership on matters of policy within a committee's jurisdiction, and the expertise that results from committee work can enhance a member's reputation and visibility. Further, committees provide members with positions of legislative power—chairs of committees or subcommittees—which have increased in number during recent decades. "The House's major career incentive is the opportunity accorded a tenth to a fifth of its members to possess the substance of power in the form of a committee or subcommittee chairmanship or membership on a key committee" (Polsby, 1971, p. 6).

The opportunities to achieve specific goals (reelection, power, and policy influence) vary from committee to committee; hence, members "match their individual patterns of aspiration to the diverse patterns of opportunity presented by House [and Senate] committees" (Fenno, 1973, p. 1). For example, according to Fenno (1973), the Appropriations and Ways and Means Committees are populated by influence-oriented members, Interior and Post Office Committees are dominated by reelection-oriented members, and Education and Labor and Foreign Affairs committee members tend to be policy-oriented. Given the ability of the committee system to help members realize diverse legislative goals, it should not be too surprising to find patterns in how members gravitate to certain committees.

Opportunities for Party Leadership in the House and Senate. In the early decades, the Speaker of the House was largely a figurehead, but by the eve of the War of 1812, he had become the predominant elected official of the legislative branch. Although the power of the Speaker fluctuated during most of the nineteenth century, the office commanded unparalleled influence over the House from the 1880s to the early 1900s. The power of the Speaker reached its historical zenith under Joseph G. Cannon (R-Ill.), who embellished upon the powers exercised by autocratic Speakers of the past. Cannon developed a hierarchical system of authority relations based on the manipulation of the House's formal organizational structure and reinforced by strong party discipline. In 1910, Republicans joined Democrats in a revolt against Cannon's arbitrary rule. The Speaker was stripped of most of his powers, including his authority to appoint all House members to committees, his control over recognition of members wishing to speak or offer motions, and his seat on the powerful Rules Committee. Never again would the speakership be given such influence over the House; subsequent Speakers have achieved influence primarily as a result of their personal prestige, persuasion, and bargaining.

The powers of the Speaker presently include presiding over the House and deciding points of order (with advice from the parliamentarian); referring bills and resolutions to the appropriate House committees; appointing members to select, ad hoc, special, and conference committees; and designating members to preside over the Committee of the Whole during his absence from the chair. While these are usually routine tasks that grant Speakers little power, most twentieth century Speakers have used these powers creatively to aid their own parties whenever possible. "Tradition and unwritten law require that the Speaker apply the rules of the House consistently," writes former Senate Parliamentarian Floyd M. Riddick

(1949, p. 67), "yet in the twilight zone a large area exits where he may exercise great discretion and where he has many opportunities to apply the rules to his party's advantage." Nevertheless, the effectiveness and success of Speakers rest "less on formal rules than on personal prestige, sensitivity to member needs, ability to persuade and skill at mediating disputes" (Davidson and Oleszek, 1981, p. 170).

The Speaker's principal assistant is the majority leader (floor leader) who, like the Speaker, is nominated at the beginning of each Congress by a secret ballot in the majority party's caucus, and then formally elected by the entire House. The majority leader was an appointment at the discretion of the Speaker until the revolt against Speaker Cannon, when House incumbents took it upon themselves to make this appointment through the party caucus, or conference, as Republicans call their party caucus. The majority leader's job has revolved around several tasks: formulating the party's legislative program in consultation with other party leaders; steering the party's legislative program through the House; persuading committee leaders to take action on legislative measures before their committees that is favorable to the aims of party leaders; and arranging the legislative schedule with the cooperation of key party members. The daily duties of the minority leader correspond to those of his majority counterpart, except that the minority leader has no authority over the scheduling of legislation. The minority leader's principal duty has been to organize the forces of his own party to counter the legislative program of the majority; it is also his duty to consult ranking minority members of House committees and to encourage them to adopt party positions, or to follow the lead of the president if the party controls the White House.

Whips of both parties assist floor leaders in keeping track of the whereabouts of party members and in pressuring them to vote the party line. They are also responsible for ensuring the attendance of party members on important roll calls and for canvassing their colleagues as to their likely support or opposition to party-formulated legislation. Whips also are involved regularly in the formation of party policy and in the scheduling of legislation. Although the duties of Senate whips are essentially the same as those of their House counterparts, Senate whips are rarely as effective as House whips. "For one thing, the functions and duties of Senate whips are less institutionalized; for another, party leaders have chosen to assume many of the functions under the whip's auspices in the House. Moreover, Senate whips at times have openly defied stands taken by their own party leaders" (*How Congress Works*, 1983, p. 28).

As this brief description of the responsibilities of the Speaker, majority and minority leaders, and party whips indicates, positions of party leadership entail the type of power that would be attractive to congressmen committed to the pursuit of legislative and/or policy influence. The attainment of these positions tends to follow distinct patterns.

Patterns in Leadership Careers. There is a large measure of longevity in most leadership positions. Garrison Nelson (1977) reports that 46 percent of all the leadership changes in the House resulted from career-related factors. Since 1911, personal factors (retirement from the House, death in office, resignation) are more important than political factors (defeated for reelection, elected or appointed to another office, defeated for another office) in inducing leadership change. Clearly, a House leadership career is an end in itself, rather than a springboard to other offices. Leaders now are more likely to stay in office until they die or retire. When leadership changes occur within the political parties, they tend to follow one of five patterns:

> (1) Interpositional mobility when a leader holding one post moves to another within the hierarchy; (2) defeat on the floor for the speakership when disaffected members of the leader's own party join with the opposition to deny a reelection; (3) a defeat in the caucus for any of the party's elective leaders; (4) replacement of an elective leader as a nominee without a formal denial of support; and (5) demotion to the ranks of the ordinary members of an appointed leader by an elected one. (Nelson, 1977, p. 928)

Since 1911, interpositional change in leadership offices has been the largest single category of intraparty leadership change in the House (Nelson, 1977, p. 927, Table 4). The established succession pattern appears to be the movement from either the whip position to the majority leadership office, or from whip to majority leader to Speaker; House Republicans, however, do not exhibit as clear a pattern of succession. In the Senate, Republicans and Democrats frequently resort to election contests in choosing their party leaders, yet both parties have increasingly adopted a two-step succession route: whip to floor leader. "In both parties and in both Houses, party leaders have served an apprenticeship, in terms both of years of experience and, more generally, occupancy of lesser party positions. Hence, the rise in importance of a hierarchy of party offices, which, in turn, has led to emerging or established patterns of leadership succession" (Peabody, 1976, p. 475). These patterns in leadership careers in the party parallel the pursuit of careers within the committee system:

> Although formally elected, the selection of party leaders exhibits remarkable stability over time and shows some indications that apprenticeship posts lead to higher posts. Once in office, party leaders are rarely removed. They enjoy security and the expectation of advancement when a higher post becomes vacant. This pattern is close to that of the seniority system for selecting chairs. Once in office a chair is rarely removed. Committee members move up the committee ladder as vacancies occur. Of course, there are fewer steps in the apprentice stage for party leaders. (Hinckley, 1983, p. 184)

Patterns in Careers Within Committees. The committee system, like the political parties, affords opportunities to realize important personal goals. Party leadership positions in the House that entail substantial authority are limited in number, but committee leadership positions are far more plentiful. In the Senate, it is just a fact of life: There are more committee leadership opportunities than senators! The small number of senators relative to the number of leadership positions guarantees that most members will have a position of committee authority. In the 96th (1979–1980) and 97th (1981–1982) Congresses, over 95 percent of the members of the majority party chaired a Senate committee or subcommittee, and many of these senators controlled more than two committee leadership positions (Ornstein et al., 1982). The larger size of the House membership makes committee leadership positions scarcer than in the Senate, but about one-half of the members of the Democratic majority chair either a House committee or subcommittee. In sum, there are numerous opportunities for members to realize the legislative goal of attaining a position of committee leadership.

One factor that accounts for these opportunities to exercise committee power is the change in House and Senate rules (reforms) that restricted the number of leadership positions that a single member could hold. In the House, this limitation immediately expanded the opportunities for members to attain a position of committee leadership. "In the 91st Congress, the House had 110 legislative subcommittees with 93 different chairmen; in the 92nd Congress [after the change in rules] there were 108 legislative subcommittees and 108 different chairmen. Altogether there were 29 new subcommittee chairmen in 1971; sixteen got their positions solely because of the reform" (Ornstein, 1975, p. 102). Some years later, the Senate instituted similar rules, which spread power precisely and evenly across the majority party:

> The Senate also prohibited a senator from serving as chairman of more than one committee at the same time; prohibited a senator from serving as chairman of more than one subcommittee on each committee of which he was a member; prohibited the chairman of a major committee from serving as chairman of more than one subcommittee on his major committees and as the chairman of more than one subcommittee on his minor committee ... ; prohibited the chairman of a minor committee from chairing a subcommittee on that committee and prohibited him from chairing more than one of each of his major committees' subcommittees. ... (*How Congress Works*, 1983, p. 99)

Movement to positions of committee leadership is governed largely by the seniority system. The seniority system refers to the practice of ranking committee members in each party according to years of consecutive service on the committee. This system automatically designates the chair of each committee as that member of the majority party with the longest record of consecutive service on the committee. If the present chairman leaves the committee, his place is taken by the majority party's next ranking member. The same rule applies to the ranking of the minority party's members on the committee: The committee member with the greatest seniority on the committee becomes the ranking minority member of the committee. New members to the committee, initially added to the bottom of the seniority list of their respective parties, climb the seniority ladder by remaining on the committee and accruing years of consecutive service. Members who stay in Congress but switch ("hop") committees are also placed at the bottom of the "new" committee's list. Clearly, the seniority system discourages members from making committee assignments anything less than a career.

The seniority system has been adhered to quite faithfully, even though it is mentioned nowhere in the formal rules of Congress and despite the adoption of procedures for selecting committee leaders by a vote of the majority party's caucus. It is a tradition—a customary practice—that has the force of law due to its observance over the years. In the twentieth century, the seniority rule has rarely been violated, and then only in exceptional circumstances. For instance, two southern Democrats, John Bell Williams and Albert Watson, were stripped of their committee seniority in the House in 1965 because they had supported the Republican presidential candidate, Barry Goldwater, in 1964; Williams later left the House to become governor of Mississippi and Watson joined the Republican Party. Such odd exceptions aside, the informal custom that longevity counts provides a good description of how and why members gain committee leadership positions. Even requiring the election of committee leaders has done little to disrupt the seniority ladder to committee power: Senate and House members of the majority party have generally reaffirmed the selections of committee leaders that would result from adherence to the seniority rule. Rule changes in the House that made subcommittee leaders subject to a vote by the majority party members of the committee also have failed to alter the effects of the seniority system on the selection of subcommittee chairmen.

Before 1973, House subcommittee chairs were appointed by the chair of the full committee, but the selection of these leaders is now determined by a vote of the Democratic (majority party) members of the committee. Thomas Wolanin (1974) analyzed the use of seniority under the *appointment system* and concluded that committee seniority was generally followed in selecting subcommittee leaders. Exceptions to the seniority rule were rare and occurred infrequently after 1950. Simply put, senior members who ranked high enough in terms of committee seniority to merit a subcommittee chair usually received one: "Application of the rule of committee seniority predicts which committee members will chair subcommittees in about 90 percent of the cases" (Wolanin, 1974, p. 701). In some instances, committees emphasized subcommittee seniority in appointing their subcommittee chairs (Appropriations, District of Columbia, and House Administration), but most followed full committee seniority in making these selections (Goldstone, 1975).

Adherence to the seniority norm did not dissipate after 1973 when subcommittee chairmen were elected by the majority party members on the committee. Under the new system, most senior members who ranked high enough in seniority to warrant a subcommittee chairmanship still received one. In fact, the number of violations of the seniority rule in selecting subcommittee leaders appears to have declined further (Hinckley, 1983). There are, of course, instances when seniority failed to guide the selection of subcommittee chairs, like Henry Waxman's election as chair of the Health Subcommittee in 1979, but "for every Henry Waxman challenging a more senior member for a key subcommittee chair ten junior Representatives moved routinely into their bits of committee turf" (Loomis, 1984, p. 199). In short, despite the change in the method of selection, seniority continues as a dominant criterion for choosing committee and subcommittee leaders in Congress.

In 1975, three House committee chairmen were denied reappointment by a vote of the Democratic Caucus—W. R. Poage (Agriculture), Edward Hébert (Armed Services), and Wright Patman (Banking, Currency, and Housing). Barbara Hinckley (1983) has interpreted these defeats as signaling challenges to the seniority system:

> In contrast to the earlier twentieth-century exceptions [to seniority appointments], none had switched party, blatantly broke congressional norms, jumped into tidal basins, or in any way called institutional attention to themselves. ... They were the only committee leaders *both* old *and* southern whose committee had a senior northerner as a rallying point for a challenge. (p. 126)

Hinckley suggests that the seniority and the unrepresentativeness of these three leaders led to their forced exits from the ranks of committee leaders. This was truly a brief episode, since seniority has been followed for the most part in subsequent selections of committee leaders. But even the defeat of Hébert, Poage, and Patman cannot be construed as an attack on the seniority system. The unfairness of these three leaders in running their committees is perhaps more important. These disposed leaders were, as Hinckley suggests, out of touch with the majority of members in their party, but so were others who were reelected to their committee leadership positions. The difference is that the defeated chairmen not only took stands against party policies, but also twisted the rules to alter or to prevent these policies from becoming law (Parker, 1979). Violations of their positions of authority, rather than their policy differences with the party, explain the defeats of these three committee leaders. "Simply put, the greater the abuse of power and the greater the violation of procedural and personal fairness, the lower the level of membership support" (Parker, 1979, p. 80). The seniority system withstood such an assault because the tradition was not really under attack. The autocracy of a past chairman would no longer be tolerated, but succession to leadership positions by right of seniority remained the dominate path.

One final pattern to careers within the committee system is the inclination of some members to transfer among committees. While most members now receive their preferred committee assignment early in their legislative careers (Gertzog, 1976), this was certainly not the case in the past when freshmen were notoriously assigned to the least desirable committees. It is not hard to understand why junior members would want to sacrifice their accumulated seniority on one committee to transfer to another: New members generally received the committee assignments that their more senior colleagues avoided. With so little to lose, freshmen were often willing to sacrifice their seniority on an undesirable committee for the opportunity to gain assignment to a better committee. And the successful reform of the rule of seniority in designating committee leaders reduced the disincentives associated with changing committee assignments still further. "One can abandon accumulated seniority and still hope to move quickly into a leadership position. Conversely, members are no longer guaranteed that they will receive a committee or subcommittee chairmanship simply because they remain on a committee longer than anyone else" (Copeland, 1987, p. 555). Although freshmen have gained better treatment in terms of committee assignments (Asher, 1975), and most members receive respectable assignments relatively early in their congressional careers, some incumbents still seem willing to sacrifice their accumulated tenure on one committee to move to another one.[1] What, then, are the features of a committee that make it so attractive that incumbents are willing to sacrifice their accumulated seniority on one committee to transfer as a novice to another?

Relatively few members change committees after their freshman year, but those who do tend to gravitate to a small number of prestigious committees (Ways and Means, Appropriations, and Rules). "Members become even more selective as their seniority on their present committee increases" (Jewell and Chi-hung, 1974, p. 441). The rankings of the attractiveness of committees appear to reflect a committee's potential to shape public policy, gain recognition from the press and colleagues, and influence other congressmen by passing their pet bills (Bullock, 1973). Generally, congressmen with less prestigious initial assignments are more likely to vacate those positions for better ones. That is, when incumbents transfer they seek to improve their lot; otherwise, the loss of committee seniority and all that it entails is not worth the sacrifice.

Table 5-1 presents rankings of House committees in terms of the total transfer activity involving that committee (arrivals and departures) relative to the number of transfers to the committee. Clearly, the exclusive committees (Ways and Means, Appropriations, Rules) are the most desired

TABLE 5-1 Index of House Committee Prestige and Corresponding Rank: 80th-96th Congresses

| | 80th-91st Congress | | | | | | 92d-96th Congresses | | | | | |
| | Index of Prestige[a] | | | Committee Rank | | | Index of Prestige[a] | | | Committee Rank | | |
Committee	Rep.	S. Dem.	N. Dem.	Rep.	S. Dem.	N. Dem.	Rep.	S. Dem.	N. Dem.	Rep.	S. Dem.	N. Dem.
Ways and Means	1.00	1.00	1.00	1	2	1.5	1.00	1.00	1.00	1.5	2	2
Appropriations	.98	1.00	.98	2	2	3	.97	1.00	1.00	3	2	2
Rules	.95	1.00	1.00	3	2	1.5	1.00	1.00	1.00	1.5	2	2
Armed Services	.91	.80	.74	4	4	6	.45	.50	.60	7	6.5	6
Foreign Affairs	.84	.67	.94	5	6	4	.88	.40	.44	4	9	11.5
Education and Labor	.70	.43	.14	6	13	17	.21	.00	.11	18	18.5	20
Judiciary	.58	.68	.68	7	5	7	.57	.00	.31	6	18.5	17
Interstate and Foreign Commerce	.57	.64	.84	8	7	7	.73	.00	.50	5	18.5	10
Internal Security[b]	.50	.25	.00	9	16	20						
Banking, Finance, and Urban Affairs	.44	.45	.22	10	11.5	14	.06	.13	.57	21	14	7
Agriculture	.42	.47	.54	11	10	8	.44	.50	.44	8.5	6.5	11.5
Public Works and Transportation	.31	.50	.41	12	8.5	9.5	.29	.33	.43	13	11	13.5
District of Columbia	.25	.42	.17	13.5	14	15.5	.25	.00	.17	15.5	18.5	19
Science and Technology	.25	.45	.36	13.5	11.5	11	.33	.33	.23	11.5	11	18
House Administration	.24	.12	.30	15	17	12	.08	.50	.40	20	6.5	15
Interior and Insular Affairs	.16	.50	.17	16	8.5	15.5	.22	1.00	.53	17	15	9
Veterans Affairs	.14	.08	.10	17	19	18.5	.38	.00	.38	10	18.5	16
Post Office and Civil Service	.11	.05	.10	18	20	18.5	.25	.00	.00	15.5	18.5	21
Merchant Marine and Fisheries	.10	.11	.26	19	18	13	.33	.33	.43	11.5	11	13.5
Government Operations	.08	.33	.40	20	15	9.5	.27	.50	.88	14	6.5	4

Note: Rep. = Republican; S. Dem. = southern Democrat; N. Dem. = northern Democrat.

[a] Index is based upon the relative attractiveness of the committee in terms of the net number of members that transfer to it.

[b] Dissolved in the 94th Congress.

Source: Data for 80th–91st Congresses are from Bullock (1973, p. 94); Data for 92d–96th Congresses are from Parker and Parker (1985).

reassignments, and Veteran Affairs and Post Office are among the least desirable assignments. This table also reveals that some committees have grown in attractiveness while other committees have declined in prestige. For example, Government Operations has grown in attractiveness for Republicans, southern Democrats, and northern Democrats, while Public Works has lost some of its attractiveness. In other instances, committees have become more attractive to a certain subset of congressmen, but less attractive to other legislators. For instance, Agriculture became more attractive to Republicans and southern Democrats between the 92d and 96th Congresses, but less attractive to northern Democrats during the same period; conversely, Banking became less attractive for Republicans and southern Democrats between the 92d and 96th Congresses, but the Committee increased its attractiveness for northern Democrats during this period. Regardless of the differential attractiveness of committees among subsets of congressmen, there is an overwhelming consensus that the three exclusive committees are the most desirable, and this consensus is relatively stable over time.

Seniority affects the ability of members to transfer to other committees:

> As a congressman's seniority increases, his opportunities for transferring expand. Seats on the highly-prized, exclusive committees—Appropriations, Rules, and Ways and Means—are largely unattainable by congressmen who have not served an apprenticeship. For other committees, House experience, while not essential, may enhance one's position vis-a-vis any other claimants, although there is no certainty that it will do so. (Bullock, 1973, pp. 89–90)

While seniority may enhance the probability of gaining a better committee assignment,[2] members remain reluctant to relinquish the rank and perquisites that go along with long committee tenure. "Leaving a committee involves costs: for example, sacrificing seniority and its rewards, terminating working relationships with committee members and staff, and perhaps writing off time and effort invested in learning the subject matter of the committee" (Bullock, 1973, p. 90). As a member's investment in a career in a committee increases, the motivation to transfer declines precipitously (Bullock and Sprague, 1969). Gary Copeland (1987) concluded after analyzing committee transfers between the 96th and 98th Congresses that it was indeed rare for anyone in either party to sacrifice their investment in one committee to transfer to another. "Only about 5 percent of Democratic transfers are accounted for by those with more than three terms. Republicans transfer a little longer before settling into their committee assignments, but only about 1 percent of all Republican transfers are by those with more than four terms of service" (pp. 560–561). The attraction of seniority is indeed strong: Fewer members now transfer assignments, and even members initially assigned to less attractive committees are less willing to switch committees than in the past (Ray, 1982)!

Is There a Political Life Cycle? The significant investment that incumbents make in their congressional careers might lead some to suspect that members let their constituency responsibilities slide as they attain positions of legislative power. With seniority comes power, influence, and broader legislative interests; the zero-sum nature of a member's own time (Fenno, 1978) means that some obligations suffer. As seniority increases, so do party and institutional responsibilities. Leadership positions require greater attention to the time-consuming duties associated with policy formation and coalition building. Further, positions of legislative power require attention to nation-wide groups and causes that also detract from the amount of attention that can be spent in cultivating constituents. Under these conditions, the first demand on a member's time that is likely to be reduced is the personal time spent in the district or state. Simply put, time spent on constituent affairs might be expected to decline as seniority accumulates and legislative responsibilities multiply. There is some empirical evidence to support such a political life-cycle hypothesis.

We can find examples of life-cycle effects in the behavior of congressmen, especially with respect to constituency-related activity. Richard Born (1982), for instance, examined the utilization of personal staff and district offices by House incumbents between 1960 and 1976. He concluded that the differences in the utilization of staff and district offices among congressmen were a function of seniority:

> Thus, after about three terms, new generation members no longer demonstrate any of the special aggressiveness that characterized their initial freshman period of service. Instead, there actually is a rather rapid relaxation in their labors as seniority accumulates. Cohorts of the new and old generation, then, chiefly are distinguished by differences in the intensity of constituent-directed activity arising during the first term of incumbency. (p. 357)

Similarly, Albert Cover (1980) uncovered a life-cycle pattern to congressional mailings. Analyzing the number of mass mailings distributed by a sample of congressmen to their constituents, he found that the level of communication was related to seniority. He suggested the following explanations for these seniority effects:

> Perhaps senior members require a less aggressive communications effort because their views are sought out by local or national media. Or perhaps they feel that their constituents have learned enough about them over time to make a vigorous effort relatively profitless. After several terms in Congress, members may assume that they are well-acquainted with constituency opinion, thus reducing their incentive to send out questionnaires soliciting

information from constituents. Of course, senior members may simply be too busy with other matters to worry very much about mass mailings. As members move into positions of influence in the House, they almost inevitably withdraw some of their time and attention from constituents. ... (p. 131)

A major implication of a political life cycle is that constituents suffer, at least in terms of the personal attention of their representative, when an incumbent assumes a position of institutional leadership. If such a cycle exists, it could create a widespread and persisting problem of representation since the attainment of positions of congressional leadership is a goal harbored by most members of Congress, and a large number of congressmen already hold leadership positions. If, after attaining positions of committee power, legislators find it increasingly difficult to maintain previous levels of constituency attention, then constituent-legislator linkages are weakened as members neglect constituent responsibilities for legislative ones.

If a political life cycle ever existed, it no longer survives due to the widespread adoption of attentive home styles during recent decades. The

TABLE 5-2 Mean Number of Days Spent in the District Per Congress By House Committee and Subcommittee Chairs: 1963-1980

			Mean Days for Cohort Elected[a]			
Congress	Years	Mean days for All Members	Before 1958	1958–1965	1966–1973	1974–1980
88th	1963–1964	17.7	18.4 (66)	12.5 (8)		
89th	1965–1966	41.1	41.6 (58)	38.1 (9)		
90th	1967–1968	79.8	79.5 (50)	80.3 (22)		
91st	1969–1970	99.5	93.4 (45)	110.4 (25)		
92d	1971–1972	103.6	97.5 (41)	111.7 (35)	90.0 (2)	
93d	1973–1974	134.8	129.3 (37)	135.5 (49)	150.2 (11)	
94th	1975–1976	154.6	139.3 (31)	147.2 (41)	189.9 (22)	
95th	1977–1978	180.9	140.4 (28)	169.2 (49)	220.9 (39)	197.6 (9)
96th	1979–1980	212.7	188.5 (20)	213.0 (41)	211.9 (33)	229.9 (29)

[a]Numbers in parentheses indicate the number of members of that cohort who chaired a committee or subcommittee during that Congress.

Source: Travel vouchers submitted to the clerk of the House of Representatives. Excludes members from Delaware, Maryland, and Virginia and members who did not complete a full term of service.

uniform *conversion* to more attentive home styles on the part of congressmen and senators has actually increased levels of personal attention to constituent affairs. Table 5-2 presents the appropriate data for analyzing the over-time changes in the attentiveness of House committee leaders. The figures in this table represent the mean number of days that House leaders spent in their districts between 1963 and 1980. These data are organized by Congress (rows of the table) and cohort classes (columns of the table) that are collapsed into eight-year periods, except for the last cohort (1975–1980), which represents a six-year period due to the time span of the analysis. As the table illustrates, House committee leaders have increased significantly the amount of time that they spend in their districts. In 1965–1966, committee leaders and subcommittee leaders more than doubled the time spent in the district during the 88th Congress, and the trend continues, so that by the 96th Congress (1979–1980) they had spent more than 10 times the amount of time that they had spent during the 88th Congress (1963–1964).

There is also no evidence in Table 5-2 that seniority effects are present: in each cohort, House leaders increase, rather than decrease, the amount of time they spend in their congressional districts. This conclusion is bolstered by the fact that the oldest cohort of House leaders (those elected before 1958) exhibit significant increases in attentiveness as their tenure increases. This generation is one that might be expected to respond to seniority effects, and the *increased* attention among members of this cohort serves as a sharp contradiction to what we would expect if a political life

FIGURE 5–1   Time Spent in the District and Committee Responsibilities (Source: Travel vouchers filed with the Clerk of the House, 1963–1980.)

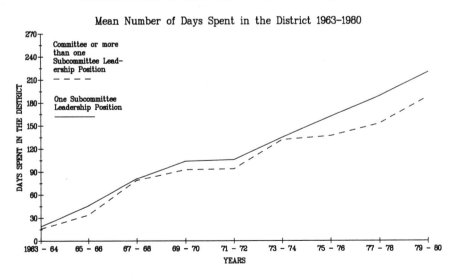

Mean Number of Days Spent in the District 1963–1980

cycle were present. Contrary to the predictions based on a political life cycle, House leaders have actually increased rather than decreased the time they spend with constituents.[3] And there is no evidence that time spent in the district decreases as committee responsibilities multiply. In Figure 5-1 the data from Table 5-2 are categorized in terms of the number of committees and/or subcommittees chaired by House members. While members with more than a single subcommittee chairmanship, and/or the chair of a full committee, are less attentive to their districts than those with less responsibilities, the differences are largely insignificant.[4]

THE INSTITUTIONALIZATION
OF CONGRESSIONAL CAREERS

These patterns in the pursuit of positions of power and leadership can be explained by the institutionalization of Congress. Nelson Polsby (1968) identifies three characteristics associated with institutionalization:

> 1) It is relatively well-bounded, that is to say, differentiated from its environment. Its members are easily identifiable, it is relatively difficult to become a member, and its leaders are recruited principally from within the organization. 2) The organization is relatively complex, that is, its functions are internally separated on some regular and explicit basis, its parts are not wholly interchangeable, and for at least some important purposes, its parts are interdependent. There is a division of labor in which roles are specified, and there are widely shared expectations about the performance of roles. There are regularized patterns of recruitment to roles, and of movement from role to role. 3) Finally, the organization tends to use universalistic rather than particularistic criteria, and automatic rather than discretionary methods for conducting its internal business. Precedents and rules are followed; merit systems replace favoritism and nepotism; and impersonal codes supplant personal preferences as prescriptions for behavior. (p. 145)

Movement to positions of party leadership reflect the institutionalization of Congress: Leadership succession patterns are routinized, transcending political and personal considerations to an unusual degree. Basically, one attains a position of leadership in the party because of prior occupation of the penultimate position leading to it. The decrease in politically related departures by party leaders is further evidence of the institutionalization of leadership careers.

Career patterns in the committee system are also structured by the congressional seniority system, an aspect of institutionalization that is characteristic of the movement away from discretionary practices and toward universally applied principles. "Seniority is not a 'rule' to be adopted or repealed, but a habit, a way of life, and a means of resolving conflict" (Price, 1971, p. 24). The seniority system makes continued service in Congress more attractive by guaranteeing automatic advancement and predictability. The stability and survivability of congressmen—increases in tenure and declines in turnover—make seniority attractive to a membership comprised primarily of careerists; a highly junior membership, subject to large and frequent influxes of new congressmen, could hardly be expected to support a system where longevity is prized.

The Senate could be called the incubator of the present-day seniority system, and for good reason. "The chamber has a continuous existence, only one-third of the members come up for reelection every two years, and it lacks a powerful presiding officer who might dominate appointments or use them for bargaining as in House speakership contests" (Price, 1975, p. 14). Table 5-3 provides a chronology of the establishment of the seniority system in the Senate. From 1789 to 1846, Senate committee chairs were selected by ballot or appointed by the presiding officer—the vice president or the president *pro tempore* of the Senate. Neither committee leaders nor members were selected on the basis of seniority. The seniority system in the Senate was born during the second session of the 29th Congress (December 7–17, 1846) with the defeat of a motion to entrust the appointment of committees to the vice president. With the defeat of this motion, the Senate began balloting for chairmen in accordance with its 1826 rule. After six chairs were elected, a long debate ensued over the method of choosing the remaining committee leaders and members. The Democratic floor leader then presented motions which arranged the names of committee members according to seniority and ensured the majority's succession to chairmanships that might become vacant. This event marked the origins of the seniority system in the Senate, but the birth of the seniority system

TABLE 5-3   Selection of Senate Committee Chairmen: 1789–1846

Years	Selection Procedure
1789–1823	Senator with the greatest number of votes is selected chairman.
1823–1826	Presiding officer named chairmen.
1826–1828	Elected by separate ballot of the Senate (Ezekiel Chambers Rule).
1828–1833	President *pro tempore* appointed chairmen.
1833–1837	Elected by separate ballot of the Senate as in 1826.
1837–1841	Appointed by the presiding officer.
1841–1845	Appointed by the president *pro tempore*, as presiding officer.
1845	Appointed by vice president or presiding officer in March; elected to positions in December.
1846	Selection by caucus (beginning of the seniority system).

Source: Packwood (1975, p. 65).

was largely a matter of convenience structured by the exigencies of the times:

> The Senate in 1846 did not "back into" the seniority system for any of the high-sounding reasons advanced by its defenders today for its retention. Instead, the Senate turned to the seniority system over a century and a quarter ago in desperation. The Senate was tired of balloting for weeks to choose chairmen and fill the committees. It distrusted the Vice President. It wanted to assure that members of the majority party would be in line for succession to the chairmanship in case of the chairman's absence or withdrawal. The seniority system enabled the parties to rapidly organize the Senate and assured succession to the chairmanship on the basis of party. (Packwood, 1975, p. 68)

In the late nineteenth century House, chairmanships were won or lost as a side product of the bargaining involved in the persistent scrambles for the speakership. While the same members normally hung on to their committee posts, each and every position was always available for negotiation. This pattern continued so long as membership, party, and leadership turnover was high. Strict seniority, which meant little in the selection of House leaders in the early 1900s, came to meet almost everything in naming committee leaders and ranking members by 1920.

There are at least two interpretations of the events leading to the establishment of the seniority system in the House. Nelson Polsby, among others (Abrams and Cooper, 1968), attributes the rise of the House seniority system to the 1910 "revolt" against Speaker Joseph Cannon and his arbitrary use of his appointment powers:

> Cannon's problem seems to have been that he took over a relatively unified party and had little need at first to build a special supportive coalition. When the party began to split apart in his third term, he responded by attempting to maintain a workable coalition by dumping insurgent chairmen and rewarding loyal Republicans with chairmanships. In so doing he deprived more incumbents and chairmen of major and semi-exclusive committees than had previously been done in the House. Cannon also resorted disproportionately after his first term to the strategy of demoting chairmen or jumping over potential chairmen, rather than moving them to other committees. ... It seems likely then, that it was not the sheer number of his seniority violations that earned Cannon his notoriety as the House's most ruthless Speaker, but how and when they occurred. (Polsby et al., 1969, p. 801)

H. D. Price offers a different explanation for the rise of seniority as a guiding principle in the distribution of legislative influence. According to Price, since relatively few members had substantial seniority in the House due to the high turnover in membership and the frequent alteration of party control, there was really no seniority influence to buck. "For the House there could be no question of modern-type 'seniority' until membership turnover was reduced to a level such that there was substantial continuity of committee service. Such *de facto* stability tends to generate demands for *de jure* seniority" (Price, 1975, p. 14). Membership turnover declined as a result of the 1896 realignment, which reduced the number of competitive House districts and resulted in a steady increase in the number of committed careerists. As tenure increased, members wanted their waiting to count for something and their positions on the committee ladders protected.

While Polsby and his colleagues (Polsby et al., 1969) see the seniority system as making service in the House more attractive to its members, Price (1975) views declines in turnover as preceding rather than following the emergence of the seniority system in the House. Whatever the reason for the emergence of the seniority system, there is little doubt that the custom has shaped career patterns in the parties and in the committees. Seniority provides the rule for most appointments to the most powerful and attractive committees and often influences the ability of congressmen to transfer to better committees. Seniority may be violated in some instances, but it remains the major way to allocate power and influence among members.

POLICY CONSEQUENCES

Congress is unusually accommodative to the needs and interests of its members. David Mayhew (1974a) has argued that the structural units in the House and Senate (committees, parties, congressional offices) are arranged to meet the electoral needs of their members. Other accommodations are equally salient: The legislative schedule has been adjusted to conform to the demands on members to keep in touch with their constituents; the perquisites of office have eased the task of serving constituents, promoting popular images, and electioneering; and the staff allocated to each office help members to run their campaigns, serve constituents, and promote the legislative interests of their bosses. The seniority system is also accommodative to the interests of congressmen:

> What the congressional seniority system does as a system is to convert turf into property; it assures a congressman that once he initially occupies a piece of turf, no one can ever push him off it. And the property automatically appreciates in value over time. (Mayhew, 1974a, pp. 95–96)

To accommodate the personal legislative goals of its members, Congress has increased the number of subcommittees, expanded the size of the leadership corps, and permitted members multiple committee assignments. Structural reforms of the committee and subcommittee system have had the widespread effect of increasing the availability of committee leadership positions. This has occurred as a result of two major institutional changes: House reforms that limited the number of subcommittee leadership positions that could be held by a single congressman and the expansion of leadership positions. Both of these changes resulted in the expansion of committee leadership positions, but the expansion of the subcommittee system seems far more important. Norman Ornstein (1975) suggests that the subcommittee reforms served to open the subcommittee system to new members by increasing the number of new chairs and spreading the power to younger, less senior members: "The reform-aided chairmen had an average seniority in 1971 of 7.3 years; the men they replaced 17.8 years" (p. 102). Many new leaders also gained their positions as a result of the expansion of the number of subcommittees in the House; the number of subcommittees is largely a decision made by the parent committee. There was a net gain of 13 subcommittee positions, for example, during the 94th Congress—the largest net gain in leadership positions since the 84th Congress (Smith and Deering, 1984). The absolute number of subcommittees increased from 120 during the 92nd Congress (1971–1972), to 151 in the 94th Congress (1975–1976) (Ornstein et al., 1982), and the number of members who assumed a committee or subcommittee leadership position for the "first time" (between 1965 and 1980) peaked during the 94th and 95th Congresses (Parker, 1986a). The expansion of the subcommittee system enabled many members to help satisfy their legislative goals of power and influence. "By opening up a large number of subcommittee chairs and power-committee slots, the House acted, as it often does, to satisfy the desires of its members—in this case for a piece of legislative turf" (Loomis, 1984, p. 190).

In a similar vein, the parties have increased the number of positions of party leadership.[5] While the objective of this expansion of the leadership corps may have been to help party leaders cope with an increasingly independent membership, the expansion also provided a vehicle for members to realize personal career goals of power and influence in Congress. For example, the whip system was quite limited before 1970, but after that point, the number of whips appointed by party leaders increased dramatically:

> In the 1970s the whip system expanded as the number of whips appointed by the leadership increased. The deputy whip position was divided into two positions in 1970. In 1972 the position of chief deputy whip was created and the number of deputy whips grew to three. Three new appointive positions, called at-large whips, were added in 1975. Women, blacks, and freshmen were demanding inclusion in the whip system, and these new positions were created in response. ... When Tip O'Neill became Speaker in 1977, he increased the number of at-large whips to ten. In 1981 a fourth deputy whip position was created and the number of at-large whips rose to fifteen. (Sinclair, 1983, pp. 55–56)

Other organizational units have also been added or reconstituted during the 1970s, such as the Democrat's Steering and Policy Committee, which was revitalized during the 1970 reforms. Undoubtedly, party leaders have been helped by expanding the number who assist them in their leadership functions, but we should not ignore the fact that these increases in the size of the leadership corps also enhanced the opportunities for congressmen to realize their more ambitious career goals—to exercise influence in Congress.

Another example of the expanding opportunities to exercise policy influence is the decline in the percentage of incumbents with a single committee assignment. Louis Gawthrop (1966) first called attention to the growth in multiple committee assignments between 1947 and 1965. He noted that the decline in single-committee assignments was due to the "steadily increasing size of most House committees" (p. 371). Extending Gawthrop's categorization of House committees in terms of the percentage of members with more than a single committee assignment reveals that there has been an even greater decline in the number of members with single committee assignments since 1965. For instance, the number of committees with more than two-thirds of their members with single assignments has declined from 7 in 1959 to 3 in 1979, and the number of committees with between 33 and 66 percent of their members with single committee assignments declines from 7 in 1969 to zero in 1979 (Parker, 1986b). Some of this growth in multiple committee assignments between 1949 and 1979 can be explained by the establishment of new committees like Small Business, Budget, and Standards of Official Conduct, but the vast majority of the increase cannot be explained in this way. It seems more likely that additional seats were created under pressure by members to serve on committees on which there were no existing vacancies.

Louis Westefield (1974) contends that House leaders expanded the number of committee seats in order to manufacture resources that could be bartered for vote support. This is a reasonable proposition; however, if these assignments were not highly desired by members *already*, the value of such additional assignments in inducing party support would be miniscule. That is, multiple committee assignments would not serve the needs of party leaders if members were not already interested in expanding their policy responsibilities. Increased policy responsibilities provided the types of opportunities that members could exploit to develop legislative power and policy influence.

In sum, the career motivations and objectives of incumbents have created pressures for greater opportunities to realize these goals. Congress has responded to these needs by creating more positions of party and committee leadership and by expanding the number of committee assignments that a member could hold. These accommodations enabled members to realize their legislative goals.

One consequence of these increased opportunities to exercise leadership has been the further decentralization of influence and power in Congress. "Not all in the leadership can actively lead. One upshot of this devaluation may be that members will use leadership positions much as they use their subcommittees and personal offices: They will employ their slots to gain publicity (advertise), claim credit, and take positions—and thus add to, not reduce, the body's fragmentation" (Loomis, 1984, p. 198). In creating additional centers of power within the parties and Congress, party leaders have relinquished some of their influence. Power has been decentralized and widely dispersed, allowing many incumbents to gain dominance over specific policy domains. "The resulting dispersion of power within Congress, and the refusal to allow strong centralized leadership, ensures that congressional decisions on major policy matters (unless aided and pushed by an outside leader) will be incremental at best, immobilized and incoherent as a norm" (Dodd, 1985, p. 496). Since seniority protects each committee's membership from removal and largely determines who will chair each committee, committee members are free to follow their personal policy predilections and to alter any legislation that falls within their committee's jurisdiction. Thus, as Congress accommodated to member needs for power and policy influence, it dispersed influence and thereby weakened centralized political leadership.

SUMMARY

I have tried to demonstrate that a major characteristic of Congress is that its members follow well-traveled routes in the pursuit of personal goals; I have termed these *career paths*. The structure of the political parties and the committee system provide career paths for members to follow in attaining personal goals, such as wielding power or legislative influence. A distinct succession pattern tends to define movement through the hierarchy of offices within the political parties in both the House and Senate, and, once in office, party leaders can expect long careers.

In the committee system, movement to positions of committee leadership is largely a function of seniority, despite the establishment of procedures for electing committee chairmen in the 1970s. Seniority—the practice of ranking committee members in each party according to years of consecutive service on a committee—is a tradition that has the force of law; it encourages members to establish careers on their assigned committees, since the most senior member of a committee is likely to succeed to the chairmanship when it becomes vacant. While the requirement that committee leaders must be elected has resulted in the rejection of three committee leaders, the normal practice is for the parties to reaffirm the selections of committee leaders that would result from adherence to the seniority rule (i.e., the most senior member gains the chairmanship). Similarly, rule changes in the House that required subcommittee leaders to be elected by the majority party members of the committee have failed to alter the effects of the seniority system on the selection of subcommittee chairman: Seniority remains the dominant criterion.

These career paths persist because of the institutionalization of Congress. That is, movement to positions of party leadership (succession patterns) have become routinized and appear to transcend political, partisan, and personal considerations. Occupation of the penultimate position leading to a higher office within the party is usually the requirement for attaining the next higher position of party leadership. The seniority rule is a creature of institutionalization since it is characteristic of the movement away from discretionary practices and toward automatic, universally applied rules. As Congress has attempted to accommodate the demands of its members for "wider career paths" so that more members can realize their goals, it has expanded the number of party and committee leaders. For example, Congress expanded the subcommittee system so that more members could gain access to these positions of committee power. As a result, influence within Congress has been further dispersed, thereby weakening the potential for centralized leadership.

NOTES

1. Larry Dodd (1985) suggests that members' transfers to committees follow stages in their careers. In the early stages of their careers, members concentrate on shoring up their electoral support in their constituencies; hence, they seek assignment to constituency-oriented committees such as Public Works or Interior. In the second stage, members feel electorally secure enough to pursue appointment to key policy committees such as Education and Labor or Commerce. In the third stage incumbents seek assignment to "power" committees like Appropriations, Rules, Ways and Means, and the Senate Finance and Foreign Relations Committees.

2. David Rohde and Kenneth Shepsle (1973) present evidence that the control of seniority in committee assignments is considerably less today than in the past, since freshmen appear to have a greater probability of receiving a requested assignment than nonfreshmen. This may occur because nonfreshmen are more likely to request appointment to a highly attractive committee, like Ways and Means, than freshmen who rarely request such assignments because of the low probabilities of obtaining them. Thus the ambitious nature of nonfreshmen requests for committee reassignment may reduce their probabilities of success.

3. The behavior of House committee leaders is not a function of their party identification (Democrats) since there are no statistical differences in the levels of attention exhibited by Democrats and Republicans over time (Parker, 1986a).

4. The two categories are: (1) members with a single subcommittee leadership position, and (2) members who chaired a committee or at least two subcommittees. None of these differences are statistically significant at 0.01 level.

5. Burdett A. Loomis (1984) points out that the number of leadership positions within the House Democratic Party rose from 61 in the 87th Congress to 103 in the 97th Congress, and the number of legislative leaders rose from 22 to 100 during the same period.

Chapter Six
BARGAINING PROCESSES

Bargaining is a ubiquitous feature of the legislative process, yet few texts on Congress devote more than a page or two to its discussion, and most fail to even reference "bargaining" in their indexes. This lack of distinct attention to bargaining reflects the widespread belief that bargaining is endemic to the legislative process. You can't get anything done in Congress without striking a bargain or two: Congressmen are unable to get pet bills passed without striking bargains, perhaps "rolling a log" or two (trading favors) in the process, and party leaders frequently barter with members for their votes. Sometimes congressmen bargain in their own self-interest, as when they negotiate with party leaders for committee assignments. Normally, congressmen bargain as agents for constituents, groups, committees, institutions, and/or federal agencies. Bargaining occurs whenever one congressman, preoccupied with his own distinctive agenda, seeks to bring another member around to his position, though this other member is preoccupied with his own particular agenda. The result is normally a sequence of moves and countermoves of a highly interdependent nature and recognized as such by those involved. Bargaining describes the various symmetrical manipulations that occur among congressmen.

Probably the most cited example of bargaining in Congress is logrolling. Woodrow Wilson's description (1956) of logrolling remains a classic one:

"Log-rolling" is an exchange of favors. Representative A is very anxious to secure a grant for the clearing of a small water course in his district, and representative B is equally solicitous about his plans for bringing money into the hands of the contractors of his own constituency, whilst representative C comes from a sea port town whose modest harbor is neglected because of the treacherous bar across its mouth, and representative D has been blamed for not bestirring himself more in the interest of schemes of improvement afoot amongst the enterprising citizens of his native place; so it is perfectly feasible for these gentlemen to put their heads together and confirm a mutual understanding that each will vote in Committee of the Whole for the grants desired by others, in consideration of the promise that they will cry "aye" when his item comes on to be considered. (p. 121)

Most vote trading takes place covertly and is seldom a matter of public record, although floor leaders occasionally acknowledge the need to appeal to specific voting blocs for support. "Trades of one specific item for another are not often made. But if a senator helps another senator, he anticipates that when he needs help at some future time he will be able to obtain it from the person he is presently helping. Most senators keep no detailed accounts on these trades, but a man soon establishes a reputation for being either helpful or unhelpful on legislative matters" (Ripley, 1969, pp. 175–176).

Bargaining can assume different forms. Normally, bargaining involves the exchange of conditional threats and promises: "If you do this for me, then I will do this for you," or "do this, or else...." A congressman, for example, might promise to vote for another member's bill on the floor, or to support that member's amendment in committee, in exchange for similar support at present or in the future. This is probably the simplest way in which bargaining occurs, but there are other forms of symmetrical manipulation: partisan discussion, compensation, and reciprocity.

When a congressman attempts to bring a colleague around to his preferred position on an amendment or bill by showing that member how his preferred position *also* satisfies the interests of the other member, partisan discussion has occurred. No coercion is involved in calling another member's attention to the ways in which a specific policy does or does not serve that member's particular interest. "Often such a discussion identifies inconsistencies in the preferences or preference statements of the participants, or brings information to bear on a participant's estimate of the costs of achieving an objective. Sometimes, however, X simply tries to make vivid and concrete Y's perception both of his own preferences and of the relevant facts" (Lindblom, 1965, p. 69).

The distinction between partisan discussion and bargaining is sometimes difficult to make since congressmen frequently practice both simultaneously. The significant difference is between adding to the obstacles that stand in the way of the adoption of a policy favored by another (bargaining) and changing that member's estimate of how many and how severe those obstacles will be (partisan discussion). Thus, while bargaining alters consequences, partisan discussion exchanges information about unaltered consequences.

Members also enter into bargaining relationships when one member *compensates* another for his support by a promise of gratification or when both members make conditional promises to each other. President Franklin Roosevelt's attempt to pack the Supreme Court with his own appointees is an example of the use of compensation as a tool for inducing support:

> He is thought to have offered Senator Wheeler the privilege of nominating some new justices; he promised leaders of the farm organizations that he would revive AAA legislation; he used patronage heavily; he held out hopes of generous relief and public works projects in the states of Senators whom he wished to sway; he proposed to manipulate labor leaders by offering wage and hour legislation; and he called in Senators to discuss with them "problems of their states." (Lindblom, 1965, p. 73)

Finally, bargaining relationships exist when some form of *reciprocity* occurs among congressmen: when a congressman makes a concession, knowing that it places an obligation to reciprocate on the part of another, or when he obtains the support he needs from another because of an existing obligation. In both cases, a congressman's request for support is acceded to because that accommodation creates an obligation that can be redeemed at a future time. Reciprocity often marks the passage of pork-barrel legislation as support is exchanged among those with claims on the federal budget, and most members can boast of such claims. Vote trading of this nature is probably limited to short periods of time, perhaps a month or two, and rarely beyond a single legislative session. Since legislators operate in the here and now, they are more willing to settle for a single vote delivered today than wholesale support on a series of measures later in the session. Moreover, it is always hazardous to bank votes against future contingencies, since favors are sometimes forgotten or the repayment is not of comparable value because of intervening factors that deflate the value of the initial favor.

In these ways, then, congressmen manipulate one another to achieve their goals—through bargaining, partisan discussion, compensation, and reciprocity. These decision-making processes permeate all aspects of the legislative process and characterize the interactions among congressmen federal agencies, congressional committees, and between institutions (House and Senate).

WHERE AND HOW BARGAINS ARE MADE IN CONGRESS

Budgetary Politics. One legislative issue that attracts the interest of a diverse set of political actors is the federal budget. Agencies, constituents, groups, congressional committees, party leaders, presidents, and individual members all have a stake in how the government spends money. This fact alone brings these legislative actors into contact with one another and fosters different processes of bargaining. For example, budgets are critical to the survival and prosperity of agencies, and bureaucrats strive to protect and increase the size of the budget allocation assigned their agencies. Agencies, therefore, attempt to convince congressmen of the value of programs and the necessity of continuing and increasing support for them. By engaging in such partisan discussion, bureaucrats influence the perceptions and evaluations of agency programs held by influential congressmen.

Two bureaucratic strategies that entail partisan discussion are the attempts of administrators to protect their budgets against cuts by arguing that if a cut is made, an entire program will have to be scrapped, or that the budget is so "tight" that performance will necessarily suffer (Wildavsky, 1984). Partisan discussion is more prevalent when bureaucrats seek to increase the size of their budgets. "Since appropriations for new programs are particularly difficult to obtain, agencies are motivated to claim that what they want to do is just what they have been doing. The funds requested are said to be part of the agency's base, its continuing program, rather than some new way to spend money" (Wildavsky, 1984, pp. 108–109). Perhaps the surest way of expanding an agency's budget is for the agency to introduce new programs. As in the instances of protecting the agency's budget or increasing the base, bureaucrats attempt to influence the perceptions of these new programs held by relevant congressmen, usually those who control the agency's budget. Often this is accomplished by convincing these congressmen that the budgetary increase is a "temporary adjustment to a passing situation" (Wildavsky, 1984, p. 11) or that it is so small as to be eminently justifiable, especially when compared with other costs. If it can be demonstrated that new projects are integral components of those already in the agency's budget, then the implied obligation to continue existing programs passes on to the new project. Or increases in expenses can be presented as the inevitable result of the expansion in the tasks performed. Sometimes budget increases are defended by claiming that the more you spend now, the less you will have to spend in the future! In short, bureaucrats cleverly structure their presentations so that added costs and programs are not perceived to increase the budget.

Compensation is also a feature of the budgetary interactions between agencies and committee members. Bureaucrats support some programs because they are the "pet rocks" of powerful committee members. The inefficiency or lack of cost effectiveness may be less important considerations when bureaucrats decide which programs to ax than how many influential congressmen will be offended by the action. Bureaucrats see agency support of these programs as a way of compensating congressmen for their help in protecting agency budgets and advancing the interests of the agency in Congress. Such bureaucratic support, in turn, is compensated in the budgetary process: Agencies gain decision-making authority and budgets expand. "So long as the bureaucracy accommodates congressmen, the latter will oblige with ever larger budgets and grants of authority" (Fiorina, 1977, p. 49).

Compensation is also characteristic of bargains struck between committees, especially when the committees are from different institutions. For instance, House and Senate committees sometimes reach agreement because one side is compensated for its support. Such a situation arose between the House Budget Committee (HBC) and its Senate counterpart (SBC) over funds for a summer school food program:

> ...the House rushed through a bill already approved by the Senate providing funds for a school food program. The Senate version had a "backdoor" provision which provoked a standard objection from HBC. With summer approaching, however, supporters of the backdoor provision feared that a requirement that funds be provided through the appropriations process would effectively kill the program. Accordingly, a deal was arranged to remove the backdoor provision in exchange for a firm commitment to expedite the funds through the appropriations process. (Schick, 1980, p. 395)

In fact, the reforms that gave rise to the present-day budgetary process reflect a bargain that featured compensation. "In order for existing committees to accept the new rules, they had to get some concrete gains to compensate for the risk of future losses" (Schick, 1980, p. 79). While most committees successfully exacted some compensation for their support, the benefits were not distributed equally:

> The Appropriations Committee got half of the loaves they wanted. New contract and borrowing authority was placed under their jurisdiction and they gained a limited role with regard to entitlements. These committees did not succeed in establishing a deadline on the enactment of authorizing legislation, but they got a deadline on the reporting of authorizations. The tax committees achieved their primary objective, a legislative procedure for limiting federal expenditure. They also secured a second advantage, some alleviation of the political onus for periodic legislation raising the statutory limit on the public debt. Authorizing committees gained some opportunity to influence budget outcomes before the Appropriations Committees have acted. (Schick, 1980, p. 79)

Reciprocity occurs in budgetary decisions in at least two ways. In some instances, members support the pork-barreling efforts of colleagues in anticipation that at some future time the debt will be repaid. House Appropriations Committee members, for example, believe senatorial "backscratching" is a major cause of the tendency for the Senate to increase appropriations:

> Someone on the other side will say, "Senator so and so wants this project or Senator so and so is interested in this item." That senator isn't even on the committee and hasn't attended the hearings, but he wants something and the rest look out for him. He isn't physically in the conference room but he's in there just the same. It's a club and they are trying to help him out. Maybe he just spoke to the chairman or the clerk and said, "I want this in," and they'll fight for him in conference. (Fenno, 1966, p. 628)

House members may have a point since the Senate's habit of doing favors on a face-to-face, personal basis produces considerable sympathy for amending the budget on the floor of the Senate to include a fellow senator's projects (Fenno, 1966, p. 607). Reciprocity also can occur among subcommittees involved in budgetary decisions, as each subcommittee supports the budgetary recommendations of the other subcommittees. This occurs quite frequently among Appropriations subcommittees and as a result, the recommendations of these subcommittees rarely are altered in the full committee.

Conference Committees. The conferences between the House and the Senate that occur when different versions of the same bill pass each are ideal institutional settings for bargaining. Conference committees are appointed to resolve the differences between the House and Senate over a particular policy issue, and although only about 15 percent of all legislative bills go to conference, important legislation typically requires one. Conference committees are usually composed of a few senior members from the relevant committees and subcommittees in each house (committee or subcommittee with jurisdiction). Both political parties are represented on conference committee delegations, and decision making is by agreement of the majority of each of the two delegations. The reconciliation of the differences between the House and Senate produces an environment conducive to bargaining:

> It is expected that the delegations from each house will "fight to win" in any disagreements between the two contingents. However, it is also assumed that disagreements will have to be compromised so that a final bill can be produced that will be acceptable to both houses. Thus the conferees know that they will have to bargain and cannot expect to win all points in dispute. (Ripley, 1983, p. 191)

Writing about the Appropriations Committees, Fenno makes a similar point:

> Faced with the twin prescriptions that they win and that they write a bill, the conferees can only achieve these goals by compromising their differences. In the broadest sense, then, the maintenance expectations of both chambers and of the managers themselves prescribe a bargaining process in which each team of negotiators should yield something of its position to the other side.

> Every House–Senate conference is expected to proceed via the methods of "give and take," "trading back and forth," "pulling and hauling," "horse-trading and compromise," "splitting the difference," etc. (Fenno, 1966, p. 620)

Normally, conferees possess significant leeway in striking bargains, though they are limited by certain procedural constraints. For instance, conferees may not go beyond the scope of the bills agreed to in the House and Senate, they only can consider the points of disagreement between the two houses, and they cannot reconsider provisions in agreement between the houses (in the original versions of the bill). Within these constraints, partisan discussion, compensation, reciprocity, and "pure" bargaining shape conference committee decisions.

One way that partisan discussion is exhibited in conference committees is when conferees try to persuade their counterparts from the other house that they risk defeat of a bill if further concessions are made. By convincing their "opponents" that " 'even if we did surrender, our house wouldn't accept the bill,' a group of conferees can gain a powerful bargaining advantage" (Pressman, 1966, p. 67). Sometimes conferees try to convince members of the other delegation that a conference bill that includes certain amendments, such as nongermane amendments, would be subject to a point of order that would doom the legislative measure:

> In the 1966 Demonstration Cities conference, House conferees objected to the Senate's seasonal housing measure. The Senate's Demonstration Cities provisions were contained in two bills, whereas there was only one House bill. Because the seasonal provisions were not included in the Senate bill under consideration in conference, a point of order could be made against adding the seasonal housing provisions to the conference bill. The turning point in conference interaction, however, came when the Speaker indicated that he would sustain such a motion. Senate conferees then agreed to drop the provisions from the conference bill. (Vogler, 1971, p. 102)

Conference committee deliberations also reveal the use of compensation: One delegation promises to support a conference bill, or particular provisions of that bill, in return for the deletion of a provision in a bill or for some other action within the purview of the conferees. For example, a Senate conferee explained his acquiescence to the demands of House conferees in these terms:

> I have signed the conference report on the District of Columbia crime bill primarily because the bill has been a stumbling block to other District legislation. The House District Committee has made agreement on a crime bill a sine qua non of mutual accommodation between the two Houses of Congress on other District matters. (Vogler, 1971, p. 100)

Sometimes the process deteriorates from bargaining to logrolling as House conferees agree to certain Senate-passed provisions in order to gain acceptance of House-passed provisions that are strongly supported in their own chamber. When conferees make conditional promises of this nature, "bargained compensation" best describes the dynamics (Lindblom, 1965, p. 34). Finally, conferees trade support in ways that demonstrate reciprocity: One delegation will make concessions because it knows that this places an obligation on members of the other delegation to do likewise. Thus, conferees sometimes achieve agreement by merely swapping items in dispute (Wildavsky, 1984).

Which institution, the House or the Senate, maintains the upper hand in conference deliberations? There is some rather convincing evidence that the Senate has been more successful than the House in having its provisions adopted. With respect to appropriations decisions, for example, the Senate was far more victorious than the House:

> The difference between the number of Senate and House victories seems, despite the limitations of the data, to be a significant one. It is certainly not—especially if one includes splits—overwhelming. Still, a Senate victory is the modal pattern, and it occurs in over a majority of the cases. And if one considers only the 288 cases where a victory was won, the Senate conferees defeated the House conferees by the significant margin of 65 percent to 35 percent, or nearly 2 to 1. (Fenno, 1966, p. 663)

In another study of five Congresses between 1945 and 1966, David Vogler (1971) found that the pattern of Senate domination of conference committee outcomes extended over a diverse set of policy areas (appropriations, national security, public works, general government, and agriculture).

Some scholars suggest that these senate conference victories may indeed be hollow ones. Gerald Strom and Barry Rundquist (1977) point out that the chamber acting second on a bill may have an advantage in gaining agreement on the specifics of the bill, but this edge may be more than offset by the influence implied by acting first and thus setting the agenda for eventual compromise. On all appropriations bills, and on many other important pieces of legislation, the House acts first; hence, the Senate is frequently in the unenviable position of amending and reacting to a House-structured agenda. Thus, the Senate may "win" more frequently in conference when matched against the House, but the victories are of questionable significance.

Leader–Follower Relations.   Bargaining has always been a major element of leader–follower relations, but it is far more central to those interactions in the present Congress than in past ones. Changes in the congressional environment, some of which are related to electoral politics (Cooper and Brady, 1981), have forced contemporary legislative leaders to rely heavily upon their bargaining skills in eliciting the cooperation of other members. For example, changes in House rules that have granted subcommittees considerable autonomy have made the legislative environment less predictable for party leaders. "The number of significant actors is larger. There is more taking place, and it is taking place in more arenas" (Sinclair, 1982, p. 6). One of the clearest expressions of the increased dependence upon bargaining on the part of congressional leaders is the growth in the use of unanimous consent agreements for organizing Senate business.

If the Senate were to strictly follow its own rules, the institution would become mired in a bog of parliamentary intricacies. The business of the Senate is expedited, however, by setting aside the rules of the Senate with the unanimous consent of its members. Once accepted, unanimous consent agreements are as binding on each senator as any standing rule, and they can only be modified by the unanimous consent of the Senate. The fundamental objective of unanimous consent agreements is to limit the time it takes to dispose of controversial issues in an institution where debate is unlimited. Since the system of unanimous consent would collapse if even a single senator were habitually mistreated, Senate leaders find it necessary to negotiate these agreements among the widest number of interested parties. The majority and minority leaders consult with one another, top assistants, other senators, party members, committee leaders, and committee staff in determining the scheduling of Senate business. Again, this is not really a question of equity but of necessity, since Senate rules provide ample opportunities for a disgruntled senator to frustrate the legislative process. For example, the Senate filibuster is the time-honored way for senators to bring business to a halt. Not only are unanimous consent agreements "costly" for leaders to negotiate because of the large number of individuals involved, but the increased use of these agreements has added to these costs: Unanimous consent agreements now are issued more frequently, affect more legislative measures, and contain more specifics (Oleszek, 1984).

Congressional leaders seem to make partisan discussion their stock and trade as they seek support from party members. For example, they frequently alert their members to the relevance of a bill to the party's cause and its legislative and electoral success by taking and disseminating official party positions on proposed legislation. Sometimes the appeal is more specific as party leaders justify their legislative preferences in terms of how they accommodate important group, regional, constituent, or national interests.

Leaders have little trouble in finding members who are willing to engage in some sort of bargaining since there is widespread recognition that party leaders can help members. As one southern Democrat noted with respect to the Speaker:

> Every member needs the help of the Speaker. The Speaker must be on your side to get recognition, to have a bill called up, to get a bill scheduled, to see

to it that a bill gets assigned to the proper committee, to get an appointment to the Interparliamentary Union, to get a good committee assignment, to help you in the Rules Committee. These are the areas in which you need the Speaker's friendship to further your career. (Ripley, 1967, p. 152)

Clearly, members perceive that tangible benefits can result from supporting party leaders. A large number of representatives, for instance, feel that party leaders "use their control over specific legislation that might involve funds for the district, private bills, or small pieces of general legislation to reward the loyal and punish the disloyal"; many also perceive party leaders as capable of rewarding or punishing members through committee assignments (Ripley, 1967, p. 150). Party leaders can, in fact, use their control over these resources to compensate members for following the wishes of their leaders. Senator Russell Long (D-La.), former chair of the Finance Committee, became one of the leading Senate power brokers because of his control over tax legislation. At one time or another, almost every senator wants a tax break for some constituent or group, and Long was normally willing to accommodate. Whether explicitly stated or left unsaid, he always exacted a price, and the price was often unwavering support for some bill that he (Long) favored. Compensation was also an invaluable tool for party leaders in earlier Congresses, since leaders frequently compensated members who were skipped over for committee chairs by "reimbursing" them with other attractive committee assignments (Polsby et al., 1969). In short, compensation is a recognized way for leaders to gain the cooperation of followers.

Legislative leaders like to accumulate obligations ("chits") from their members that can be called in when necessary. By doing a favor for a member, leaders place that individual under an obligation to reciprocate at some future time. This gives leaders access to votes that may play a critical role in leadership strategies and success. Senator Lyndon Johnson (D-Tex.) was probably the quintessential leader in terms of his penchant for promoting conditions of reciprocity:

> He apportioned office space in the Senate office building with an eye toward the level of cooperation a senator had displayed in the past or might be encouraged to display in the future. He willingly helped cooperative colleagues secure banquet speakers, locate additional staff assistance, or attend overseas conferences. Scarcely any aspect of senatorial life, however routine and seemingly removed from the formulation of national policy, escaped Johnson's watchful eye or his uncanny talent for translating these activities into resources which could be used in running the Senate according to the Johnson formula. (Stewart, 1971, p. 66)

Building credit with party leaders is good business for most members since you can never tell when you will need their help. "When you do things for the administration or leadership it is like putting money in the bank.

You build up a reservoir of good feeling and friendship. Eventually you will need some favors from them" (Ripley, 1967, p. 154). As one subcommittee chair described the reciprocal relationship between him and his party's legislative leaders: "I try to cooperate with them in those particular areas where they need help; and they cooperate with me when I need their help" (Fenno, 1966, p. 425). By creating obligations, and eventually calling them in, legislative leaders practice reciprocity in their bargaining relationships with party colleagues.

Bargaining in Committees. Congressional committees are natural settings for bargaining. In many cases the decisions made in congressional committees are ratified on the floor of the House or, to a lesser extent, the floor of the Senate; hence, to wait until a bill reaches the floor before striking bargains is to wait too long. And Congress expects its committees to bring bills to the floor that reflect agreement among contending interests. Committees that are unified with respect to a piece of legislation maximize their influence on the floor, gaining passage of the legislation in a form recommended by the committee. For example, Donald Matthews (1960) found that the degree of committee unity was closely related to committee success on the floor of the Senate, and James Dyson and John Soule (1970) reported that from 1955 to 1964 a majority in the House voted with a majority of a committee's members on 90 percent of the bills reported.

Perhaps the most obvious opportunities to engage in bargaining are the mark-up sessions that committees conduct in rewriting and amending legislation. During these sessions, pending legislation is read section by section for approval by a committee majority. Details are ironed out and compromises are made in an effort to meet the objections of committee members. By limiting the scope of legislation, paring the cost, or adding provisions sought by specific interests, the marked-up bill is designed to accommodate and pacify potential opponents. If committee members have performed this task adequately, the committee's version of the bill will sail through its chamber relatively unchanged. If, on the other hand, the committee fails in this regard, their revised bill is probably doomed to defeat or, at the very least, substantial modification on the floor of the House or Senate.

Prior to the mark-up, most committees conduct hearings on the legislation. While there is no guarantee that a bill will receive a hearing, only rarely is a bill approved without one. Hearings provide committees with one of the best means of obtaining information, and those testifying before committees are expected to supply such information and facts. What normally transpires during such hearings is partisan discussion: Interested groups and individuals present their viewpoints, perceptions, and most of all their *versions* of the facts to committee members. Individuals testifying before committees attempt to influence the perceptions that committee members harbor about the value and impact of policies or changes in those policies. Bureaucrats try to gain support for their programs by convincing members of the benefits to individual constituencies associated with their preferred policies. Groups and constituents alert committee members to the adverse consequences of some policies and the beneficial prospects of others.

Moving bills through the committee and to the floor of the House or Senate requires the mobilization of a coalition of supporters that is numerically capable of deciding the issue. To accomplish this often necessitates other forms of bargaining: compensation and reciprocity. For instance, a committee member's support of a bill might be rewarded by including a provision that diverts federal funds to the constituency represented by such a pivotal member. Perhaps the bill in question provides for the establishment of regional offices or pilot projects; a member's support might be gained by offering to place a regional office or pilot project in his district or state. Compensation of this tangible nature may be quite effective in attracting support among committee members.

Reciprocity may be even more ingrained in committee procedures than compensation. For example, Senator John Tower (R-Tex.), former chair of the Armed Services Committee, sought to reduce the pork in the defense budget by asking senators to identify military programs and installations that could be trimmed. Only 6 of the 99 senators offered any suggestions, and not one dime involved a military installation in their own state or that of another senator (Fitzgerald and Lipson, 1984). One of the best examples of reciprocity is the logrolling that is historically associated with tax legislation: Tax exemptions and restrictions are added to such legislation to satisfy the demands of members and to ensure its passage. These reciprocal accommodations are viewed by congressmen as a natural and rational response:

> In many cases the congressman considering a special tax provision may not realize that tax fairness is at all involved. He sees only the problem of the particular constituent or group concerned. ... The congressman may therefore not even appreciate that arguments of over-all fairness and equity have any relation to the question, or he may very well think them too intangible and remote. ... He is not a tax technician and he may view the proposal in isolation rather than perceive its relationship to the intricate technical structure of the revenue code. The proposal, so viewed, becomes merely a "little old amendment" which helps a constituent and does no harm. His brother congressmen are quite willing to be good fellows and go along, especially if the congressman urging the proposal is well-liked. After all, they too from time to time will have "little old amendments" to propose. (Surrey, 1973, p. 207)

It should be clear that most bargaining situations entail the use of partisan discussion, compensation, *and* reciprocity. Some of these forms of bargaining are used in conjunction with one another, while in other situations a specific form of bargaining may dominate. Participants also may simultaneously or sequentially rely upon different forms of bargaining. The conceptual distinctions between these various forms of bargaining may be easier to make than to isolate in any particular bargaining situation. Bargaining is not unique to Congress; it appears to affect decision making in many political institutions. What is unusual about bargaining in Congress is that it permeates so much of the life of the institution. "The very essence of the legislative process," writes David Truman (1951, p. 368), "is the willingness to accept trading as a means." But why is bargaining so pervasive in Congress?

FACTORS PROMOTING BARGAINING

There are undoubtedly a number of forces that indirectly or unintentionally promote bargaining in Congress. For example, the prior experiences of congressmen—many have served as state legislators or are lawyers by trade—may equip members with favorable attitudes toward negotiation and compromise. Former state legislators have already realized the virtues of bargaining as a result of their experience in the legislature; hence, they may be more predisposed toward bargaining than others with less bargaining experience. Similarly, lawyers are involved in negotiating contracts and agreements and representing the interests of clients; such occupational experiences also equip them with positive attitudes toward bargaining processes. It would be difficult, indeed, to catalog all the factors that promote bargaining since it is so basic to Congress and the behavior of its members, but three of the most important forces are the weakness of party leaders, the existence of norms supportive of bargaining, and the decentralization of Congress.

Weakness of Party Leaders. There is little doubt that bargaining skills have always been high on the list of attributes associated with successful party leaders. Such interpersonal skills, however, are far more important to party leaders in present congresses than past ones. In early congresses, party leaders possessed many prerogatives that gave them considerable influence over legislative outcomes, especially in the House of Representatives. For instance, the Speaker held the power to appoint committees, and absolute discretion over the recognition of motions for unanimous consent and suspension of the rules. Members of committees were disposed to cooperate with these czarist Speakers of the past not only because of their control over committee assignments but also because of the vast array of rewards and sanctions that the position bestowed.

> For example, the Speaker could provide access to the floor by granting a rule or recognizing a motion to suspend the rules; he could lend invaluable assistance in getting a project included in a bill or in getting a bill out of committee. Moreover, if all the rewards and sanctions at the disposal of the Speaker still proved to be insufficient, there was yet another factor that discouraged opposition at the committee stage. The plain fact was that to oppose the Speaker would in all probability be fruitless. (Cooper and Brady, 1981, p. 412)

With the reduction in the formal powers of the Speaker between 1909 and 1911, party leaders lacked the influence over individual members that they possessed under Czar rule. Party leaders found it necessary to behave more as brokers and middlemen, and less as commanders of stable party majorities. These tendencies intensified with time to weaken the power and position of party leaders. One lasting consequence has been an ever increasing emphasis on bargaining between leaders and followers in the contemporary Congress:

> In sum, by 1940 the role and power of the party leadership had been substantially altered. Though the leadership retained responsibility for and continued to provide overall guidance and direction in the conduct of the House's business, it now had to operate within a far harsher set of constraints than in 1910. At the floor stage, the leadership usually had no choice but to engage in the painful process of assembling shifting majorities behind particular bills through bargaining and maneuver. At the committee stage, the leadership was often forced to engage in intricate and prolonged negotiation with committees and committee chairmen. Indeed, the leadership was now placed in a position where inability to accommodate an organizational unit would mean failure to pass party legislation, unless it was able to organize a majority of such strength and intensity that it could force a vote on the floor through the pressure of opinion in the House or the use of a mechanism such as discharge. The result was that by 1940 the personal, political skills of the leadership, rather than its sources of institutional power, had become the critical determinant of the fate of party programs. (Cooper and Brady, 1981, pp. 419–420)

Party leaders now sought to gain the support of their followers by doing favors for members that might ease their lives in Washington, enhance their sense of personal worth, and advance their political and legislative careers. By nurturing friendships and creating obligations, today's party leaders try to accomplish the tasks that in past congresses could have been accomplished at the discretion of these same leaders.

Conditions and developments during the 1970s may have weakened party leaders still further, and increased their dependence upon bargaining in organizing partisan majorities. The democratization of congressional rules and procedures have permitted the rank and file far greater participation in legislative decision making. For example, the reactivation of the Democratic Caucus during the 1970s provided dissatisfied members

with a means for influencing legislative outcomes: the Caucus could in-
struct committees to report certain legislation with specific provisions.
Curtailing the power of committee chairmen and making them responsible
to the party for their reappointment may have reduced the countervailing
power of committee leaders, but it also made committee decisions more
responsive to the views of individual members, not necessarily party
leaders. Declining adherence to norms, such as apprenticeship, during the
1960s and 1970s meant that members could more actively participate in
their committees and on the floor without fear of violating norms or offend-
ing senior members. In such an environment, party leaders find it imperative to do "favors" for their members to ensure future support:

> ...the leaders both make themselves available to rank-and-file members and
> provide services to the membership collectively...and individually, by be-
> stowing a variety of favors. By thus meeting member expectations, the
> leaders contribute not only to their own job security but also to party main-
> tenance; they accumulate "chits" that can be used in coalition building; and
> they gain information that is vital to the effective performance of both of their
> primary functions. (Sinclair, 1982, pp. 87–88)

In short, the weakened position of party leaders in terms of their command
over resources and the expectation of participation in decision making that
characterize congressional cohorts entering Congress during the 1970s
and 1980s have made bargaining an essential characteristic of the legislative process.

Decentralization of Congress. Another reason for the persistance of bargaining is the decentralized organization of Congress: Power and influence
in Congress are widely dispersed over a number of positions of legislative
authority. Legislative power resides in the hands of committee leaders,
subcommittee leaders, and spokesmen for regional and informal voting
blocs, in addition to party leaders. This wide decentralization of legislative
power supplies the occupants of these positions of influence with vantage
points to counter the legislative influence of others and to foster bargaining and exchanges of mutual benefit. The movement of legislation through
Congress requires that party leaders engage in extensive bargaining to
overcome potential opposition since there are so many actors involved in
decision making and because these actors possess the necessary influence
to disrupt their plans. Such hindrances may be small individually, but collectively they could sabotage the plans of leaders.

Beginning in 1971, the Democratic Caucus passed a series of reforms
that had the effect of distributing positions of influence more widely and
shifting power to more organizational units: Each Democrat was limited
to chairing a single committee or subcommittee, and subcommittees eventually gained guarantees of staff, funds, and jurisdictional responsibilities.

This greatly expanded the number of legislative actors involved in decision making and fostered an even greater need for leaders to broaden the number of bargaining partners. I will have more to say about decentralization in the next chapter when I discuss it as a characteristic of Congress. Let it suffice at this point to note that the decentralization of Congress is linked to the persistance of bargaining among congressmen.

Norms Supportive of Bargaining. There are at least two congressional norms that appear to promote bargaining: compromise and reciprocity. The norm of compromise is central to the bargaining system that operates in Congress: No individual or group ought to expect to get exactly what it wants from the process; each is expected "to give a little and take a little." Since each member expects to sacrifice something for the sake of agreement, the conditions are ripe for bargaining. This is not to deny that most bargains within Congress have definite winners and losers; I would only argue that the outcomes of the negotiations are rarely zero-sum in nature.

The norm of reciprocity—that assistance or favors rendered by another congressman should be repaid in kind—is also supportive of bargaining. Most of the time, we associate reciprocity with the trading of votes, but reciprocity is not confined to such practices. Donald Matthews (1960, p. 100) refers to reciprocity as "a way of life in the Senate," and to many members, reciprocity merely means helping a colleague:

> A lot of time if a particular project is of great significance to a friend of mine, sure, I'll vote for it just because I like the guy, but not because I want him to support me on something else.
> If a Senator wants something for his state, everybody's automatically pretty sympathetic, because we all have states we want to represent and we want to be helpful, whether it's a Republican or Democrat—and you respect a man who's fighting for his state; after all, that's one of your functions. (Rohde et al., 1985, pp. 174–175)

Like the norm of compromise, reciprocity benefits most members of Congress, which may explain its durability over time (Rohde et al., 1985).

The norm of reciprocity extends to committees, and in some cases to subcommittees. In order to minimize intercommittee disputes over legislation, jurisdiction, or appropriations, "committees negotiate treaties of reciprocity ranging from 'I will stay out of your speciality if you will stay out of mine' to 'I'll support your bill if you will support mine' " (Fenno, 1965, p. 73). Declining adherence to the norms of apprenticeship and of deference to senior members, however, may have undermined the norm of committee reciprocity in the House, if not the Senate: "The reciprocity norm is weaker now and there is a greater tendency to 'mark-up' bills on the floor. Younger members are simply not willing to defer to the committee" (Sinclair, 1983, p. 10).

The classic example of the existence of reciprocity among subcommittees is the House Appropriations Committee:

> Members of each subcommittee are expected to observe reciprocity with respect to the recommendation of every other subcommittee. When a subcommittee brings its appropriation recommendations to the full committee—that is to say, to the other subcommittees—for approval and legitimation, the full committee could choose to reargue the recommendations *de novo*. But it is not expected to do so. In accordance with the norm of reciprocity, it is expected to defer to the subcommittee which has specialized in the area, has worked hard, and has "the facts". "It's a matter of you respect my work and I'll respect yours." "You don't go barging into another man's field unless something is patently wrong." (Fenno, 1966, p. 163)

While it is difficult to know the extent to which reciprocity governs the relationship among subcommittees, there is evidence that subcommittees may indeed trade support: Subcommittee leaders vote together in several House committees, such as Agriculture, Appropriations, Government Operations, House Administration, International Relations, and Science and Technology (Parker and Parker, 1985).

The pervasiveness of these norms—compromise and reciprocity—promotes an atmosphere in Congress that is conducive to bargaining. Members expect to receive less than a "whole loaf" and to repay favors in terms of an equivalent currency. These expectations bring legislative actors together in the hope of reaching mutually beneficial accommodations. The persistance of the bargaining system in Congress suggests that, more often than not, legislative actors are able to reach such accommodations.

POLICY CONSEQUENCES

The pervasiveness of bargaining has both positive and negative consequences for the formation of public policy. On the positive side, bargaining minimizes conflict within Congress that might incapacitate the institution and coordinates decisions and decision makers. The legislative process attracts the attention and pressure of contending interests within society, since all societal groups, such as labor and business interests, seek governmental intervention at one time or another. In many cases, these groups cannot reach agreement among themselves, which may be the rationale for bringing the issue to the attention of Congress (Lowi, 1968). Furthermore, there is intense disagreement among congressmen, as well as groups, over a whole range of values; liberalism and conservatism are just two categories of values and attitudes that create strong adversaries among groups and congressmen. And all sources of division are, of course, overlaid with partisanship. Historical images and policies are not the only matters that separate the two major parties. Electoral antagonisms, produced by defeating an opponent from the other party, reinforce antipathies toward the opposition, even among members whose attitudes might incline them to support the opposition party's programs. Bargaining provides a mechanism for reducing the potentially disruptive effects of these conflicts:

> Conflict is the very life blood of a decision-making body in a free society. Yet it is amazing how much of the time and energy of House members is devoted to the business of avoiding conflict. The reason for this is simple. Excessive conflict will disrupt and disable the entire internal structure. In the interests of stability, therefore, a cluster of norms calling for negotiation and bargaining is operative at every point where conflict might destroy the institution. In view of the criticisms frequently pointed at bargaining techniques—"back scratching," "log rolling," "pork barrelling," "vote trading"—it should be noted that these techniques are designed to make majority-building possible. (Fenno, 1965, pp. 75–76)

Another positive aspect of bargaining in Congress is that it achieves an element of coordination among policy makers and legislative decisions.[1] The attempts of congressmen to influence each other through some sort of manipulation are familiar processes for coordinating decision makers:

> That negotiation is a method of coordination is obvious. Of all the methods of partisan mutual adjustment it is in the highest repute. Anyone can call up examples including cases in which, as in tripartite commissions, negotiation is very deliberately chosen as a decision making and coordinating process, as though it were obvious that for some circumstances there were no better way to take account of the complexities of the policy problem than to bring the various interested parties together, to let them explore each other's partisan views, and to arrive at a settlement satisfactory to all concerned. One sees coordination, sometimes of a high order, emerging in such a situation because a wide variety of factors in the decision are brought into a considered relationship to each other and because the final settlement is not agreed to until the policy intentions of the various partisans are reconciled in some more or less satisfactory way. (Lindblom, 1965, p. 68)

Such coordination may be essential in light of the disjointed nature of policy making in Congress and the fragmentation of institutional power.

On the other hand, bargaining entails some negative effects: it slows the legislative process and it may produce inefficient expansion of the federal budget. Simply put, bargaining takes time. On most legislative issues a consensus must be reached, not only on the objectives of the legislation but also on the appropriate means for achieving those objectives. Even those who can agree on the need to maintain a strong national defense, for instance, might disagree as to whether nuclear or conventional weaponry can best serve this goal. Similarly, the reduction of poverty might be an objective of welfare legislation that gains a sympathetic ear from many members of Congress, but the best way to achieve that objective—increase welfare payments or force welfare recipients to earn a portion of the dole—is likely to divide these same members. Furthermore, each congressman who sponsors or manages legislation (on the floor) must take into account the views of other members who might interfere with, or facilitate, the passage of a given legislative measure. The normal path is to pursue compromise: find a common denominator that a majority of members can support. To do so, however, fosters delay and slows the legislative process. Bargaining, then, is a major cause of the lack of alacrity that we often associate with the legislative process and the congressional response to societal problems (Huntington, 1965).

Finally, the emphasis on reciprocity, and perhaps compensation, are apt to increase the size of the federal budget. While compromise is a useful way of reaching agreement, logrolling is equally effective. Instead of accommodating the interests of contending legislative actors by forcing each "to give in a little," decision making may proceed by merely aggregating the divergent interests. Each interest gets what it wants as the policy or program is expanded to satisfy demands. "In giving out particularized benefits where the costs are diffuse (falling on taxpayer or consumer) and where in the long run to reward one congressman is not obviously to deprive others," writes David Mayhew (1974, p. 83), "the members follow a policy of universalism." Universalism means that every incumbent, regardless of party or seniority, has a right to share in the benefits of congressional action. That such logrolling increases the federal budget is evident in the role of universalism in distributing interior projects (Fenno, 1973), tax benefits (Manley, 1970; Fenno, 1973; Surrey, 1973), urban renewal projects (Plott, 1968), and projects in appropriations bills (Fenno, 1966, 1973).

SUMMARY

Bargaining describes the symmetric manipulations that occur among congressmen. In its "purest" form, bargaining involves the exchange of conditional threats and/or promises, but it also includes partisan discussion, compensation, and reciprocity. Partisan discussion describes the efforts of congressmen to influence the decisions of others by convincing them that their interests are best served by a particular policy; such manipulation often involves exchanges of information and perception. Bargaining also occurs when one member is compensated for his support or makes a concession to another because the accommodation creates an obligation that can be redeemed at a future time (reciprocity). These bargaining processes permeate every aspect of legislative life. Bureaucrats engage in partisan discussion, for example, to influence the perceptions and evaluations of agency programs held by influential congressmen, and they compensate congressmen for their support by expanding their favored programs. The unilateral raids on the budget that are constantly executed by individual congressmen would come to naught without the widespread expectation of mutual gain through reciprocity. Bargaining is the recognized way for resolving differences in conference and standing committees and is essential to the relationship between party leaders and their members.

Three of the most important factors promoting bargaining are the weakness of party leadership in Congress, the existence of norms supportive of bargaining, and the decentralization of power in the House and Senate. Party leaders lack sufficient resources to *command* the allegiance of their members; instead, they must bargain for support. The situation is exacerbated further by the expectation of participation in decision making on the part of recent congressional cohorts. The wide dispersal of power in Congress supplies the occupants of positions of influence with vantage points to counter the legislative influence of others and fosters bargaining situations. The legislative norms of compromise and reciprocity also promote bargaining since each member expects to sacrifice something for the sake of agreement and favors are expected to be repaid in kind.

Bargaining is important because it reduces the intense antipathies associated with the formation and passage of public policies and achieves an element of coordination in a largely disjointed legislative process. Aside from these positive attributes, bargaining also entails negative effects. Since bargaining takes considerable time, it slows the legislative process, delaying congressional response to societal problems. Finally, the emphasis on reciprocity may be at least partially responsible for inefficient expansion of the federal budget: Vote trading can disintegrate into logrolling as specific interests are aggregated rather than compromised. Each interest gains what they desire most as agency programs and budgets are expanded to incorporate *all* demands.

NOTES

1. Although the notion that coordination can be achieved through bargaining is familiar to most legislative scholars and conspicuous in congressional decision making, bargaining is probably not the dominant form of coordination: "If one could imagine a frequency count of uses of negotiation and other adjustments, negotiation—for all its prominence—would certainly be found less often turned to than parametric adjustment, which is a coordinating element in every decision; and, as for manipulated adjustments, the frequency of an X's negotiation with Y is much less than that of his indirect manipulation of through third parties" (Lindblom, 1965, pp. 68–69).

Chapter Seven
DECENTRALIZATION: THE FRAGMENTATION OF CONGRESSIONAL POWER

Decentralization describes the wide dispersal and fragmentation of power within Congress, an aspect of American politics with strong historical roots. Since 1910 in the House, and since 1915 in the Senate, the overall trend has been toward a weakening of centralized leadership. The restoration of seniority in the Senate and its rigidification in the House have contributed—along with various congressional reforms—to this dispersion of power. "The net effect of the various changes of the last thirty-five years in the power structure of the House of Representatives has been to diffuse the leadership, and to disperse its risks, among a numerous body of leaders" (Galloway, 1962, p. 128). Decentralization can be structurally induced through the establishment and proliferation of autonomous subunits, like congressional committees. Pressures and precedents may also lead to wide dispersals of power. For instance, legislative leaders might be forced to relinquish some of their influence because of pressures from significant segments of their parties or due to the existence of norms. The decentralization of Congress is evident in the autonomy of congressional committees and subcommittees and the existence of policy-oriented groups within and between the parties.

COMMITTEES

By the end of the nineteenth century, power in Congress had become concentrated in the hands of a relatively small number of congressmen, normally the Speaker in the House and the majority party leader in the Senate. These leaders possessed authority for organizing committees, appointing committee members and leaders, and for guiding the passage of the majority party's legislative program through congressional committees and on the floor of the House and Senate. The powers of these legislative leaders helped to ensure that the majority party's program would be passed. A new order emerged after 1910: The speakership was stripped of many dictatorial powers in the revolt in the House against Joseph Cannon, the patronage power of senators declined, and the popular election of senators replaced their appointment by state legislatures.

While congressional committees have always existed as arenas where hearings were held and legislation drafted, most merely served as arms of the party leadership. But after party leaders were stripped of important prerogatives, committee members and leaders quickly filled the void as committees became increasingly autonomous in their own policy areas (jurisdictions). The seniority system and the two informal rules associated with it—committee assignments cannot be retracted, and choice assignments and committee leadership positions are determined according to seniority—replaced the discretionary power that strong party leaders had exercised in organizing committees in earlier eras.

As we noted in Chapter Four, members of Congress found legislative service attractive in the late nineteenth and early twentieth century partially because of the increased power of the national government and the enhanced role of the House and the Senate in the formation of national policy. Service in Congress offered an accessible way to gain political influence and mold policy, but once in Congress, members found power so concentrated that their ability to influence policy and exercise influence was negligible. One solution was to disperse congressional power to the already existing committees, thereby giving each congressman a better opportunity to influence policy and to gain some measure of power. There may have been few incentives in the early congresses to disperse power since most members of Congress were not interested in congressional careers and served for relatively limited periods, but the incentives were considerably greater once careers developed and longevity of service increased. Committee government offered an attractive avenue through which individual congressmen who were interested in congressional service and power could gain influence.

While committee government may be satisfying to most congressmen, party leaders have lost rather than gained from it. Formerly, the Speaker of the House and the Senate's majority leader possessed sufficient power to forcefully push the majority party's legislative programs through Congress. As power became dispersed among hundreds of committees, subcommittees, special committees, and joint committees, numerous members gained authority over particular policy areas. More congressmen had to be consulted and persuaded to go along with the decisions of their leaders. In the absence of mechanisms for disciplining members, committee leaders and members gained bargaining leverage and independence from their party leaders. Since a committee's members can stop any legislation that falls within the committee's jurisdiction, no matter how widespread the support for the legislation in Congress or the country, committees are a subject of concern to party leaders.[1]

One of the best examples of the extent to which an autonomous committee can impose its will on the leadership is the House Rules Committee. In earlier eras, the Speaker controlled the Rules Committee and could neutralize the power of the committee to block the consideration of the majority party's programs, or he could use his influence over the committee to block legislation that he opposed. As the Rules Committee gained autonomy, like other House and Senate committees, the wishes of the Speaker and the majority party remained just that—wishes. Party leaders found it difficult to discipline committee members without stirring the wrath of most party members, who feared that to allow them to do so would undermine the seniority rule which protected *every* congressman's individual interests.[2]

The committee system was strengthened further by the 1946 Legislative Reorganization Act. The Act embodied the efforts of many members of Congress to reorganize the legislative process along lines more amenable to coherent policy formulation and aggressive policy oversight. The 1946 Reorganization Act had the major objective of streamlining and modernizing the committee system. To accomplish this aim, the Act reduced the number of committees by dropping inactive, minor committees and by merging committees with related functions; it also specified more clearly the jurisdiction of each committee, authorized the hiring of committee staff, and regularized committee procedures for meetings, maintaining records, reporting legislative measures, conducting committee deliberations (presence of a committee quorum as a condition for committee action) and hearings.

The Act forced some painful sacrifices on the part of members: Some had to give up cherished committee assignments while others lost leadership positions on committees or subcommittees that were consolidated or abolished. The Act did little, however, to alter the fundamental design of committee government. If anything, the 1946 Reorganization Act refurbished the committee system, bolstering its autonomy and removing its most glaring shortcomings. The Act may have reduced the number of committees, but no effort was made to reduce the autonomy of the remaining committees. The new committees, by virtue of broader jurisdictions and increased staff resources, were actually stronger; with the clarification of jurisdictional lines, there existed even less opportunity for party leaders to bypass an obstinate committee by maneuvering a bill into another more responsive committee.

Committee Members as Voting Cues. The committee system serves to decentralize influence within the House and Senate in another way: The specialization of committee members that comes from long committee service creates cadres of experts. As policy experts, committee members provide "direction" for those unfamiliar with a particular policy area. For the non-committee member, reliance upon the judgments of experts is an efficient and rational way to make decisions in policy matters beyond one's area of specialization. "Members pride themselves on producing, through specialization, a home-grown body of legislative experts to guide them in making their decisions and to serve as a counterweight to the experts of the executive branch" (Fenno, 1965, p. 54). Members are likely to defer to a committee when the issues are unusually technical and complicated, when large segments of Congress are not personally involved in the policy decision, and/or when the committee is united in support of the legislation as it is reported to the floor. The authority of committees rests on the belief that committee members devote more time and possess more information on the policy matters within their committees' jurisdiction than do other congressmen. One consequence is that legislative leaders cannot monopolize the flow of information and advice to their colleagues—a major source of their legislative influence. Committee members serve as alternative sources of information and guidance, sometimes contradicting the directives issued by party leaders to their members. This means that the advice of party leaders and their instructions to their members must compete with the information and interpretations supplied by committee members and leaders. Even if the voices of party leaders are normally heard above those of committee leaders or members, committee members are still sufficiently vocal and visible to shape the decisions of many members on the floor of the House and Senate.

Committee members frequently perform this role by serving as voting cues for other members of Congress. "When a member is confronted with the necessity of casting a roll-call vote on a complex issue about which he knows very little, he searches for cues provided by trusted colleagues who—because of their formal position in the legislature or policy specialization—have more information than he does and with whom he would probably agree if he had the time and information to make an independent decision" (Matthews and Stimson, 1975, p. 45). This makes it possible for most congressmen to vote in a rational manner and to do so on the basis of a paucity of information. Outside the area of his own policy specialization, a congressman need only decide which cue-giver to follow on particular issues, and this information can be accumulated rather rapidly through experience and observation. Donald Matthews and James Stimson found that 86 percent of the congressmen they surveyed mentioned committee members as sources of voting cues: "No one knows any more about a piece of legislation than those who heard the arguments in committee," commented one of the congressmen in their study (1975, p. 89). In the same study, 45 percent of the House incumbents they interviewed identified committee leaders as cue-givers. Ranking minority members serve as cue-givers among members of their own party, but they do not obviously serve as frequent cue-givers for majority party members.

Budgetary Process. Congressional committees also serve as decentralizing influences on money decisions, though budget reforms have centralized decision making in this area to some degree. Congressional spending decisions are made through a multistep process: Spending decisions involve both authorization and appropriation. First, a law must be passed establishing a program or agency, specifying the objectives served and in many cases setting a maximum amount for financing the functions of the agency or program. The periods covered by authorizations vary: Some are indefinite, others are for a specified number of years, and still others are for a single year. Authorizing legislation is handled by the legislative committee in each chamber with jurisdiction over the program or agency involved. Subsequent to the passage of authorizing legislation, the appropriations stage is initiated to grant the actual monies that have been authorized. The House and Senate Appropriations Committees have jurisdiction over the granting of budgetary authority to agencies to operate their programs. As with authorizations, budget authority can be granted for varying periods. In many cases, budget authority must be voted annually; in other cases, such as appropriations to pay the interest on the national debt, Congress has provided permanent budget authority so that annual legislative action is unnecessary.

Under annual appropriations, the congressional power of the purse resides in the Appropriations subcommittees, but multiyear authorizations reduce whatever centralization these subcommittees might bring to spending decisions. For example one form of "backdoor spending" occurs with respect to "mandatory entitlements." These are payments to persons or to state and local governments that the federal government is obligated to make when the legal requirements for receiving payment are fulfilled. For programs of this nature, spending decisions are a function of eligibility requirements, economic conditions, and administrative efficiency rather than decisions made by Appropriations subcommittees. Sometimes such "backdoor spending" occurs by linking payments to various indexes. For instance, retirement benefits can be attached to shifts in the cost of living:

program costs adjust automatically as the consumer price index changes. Thus the authorizing committees, by sponsoring legislation that establishes an automatic increase in payments or benefits under various programs, can evade effective review and centralization by the Appropriations subcommittees. Such situations fragment spending decisions and mitigate against centralizing these decisions.

Prior to 1974, Congress lacked a procedure for coordinating authorizations, appropriations, and revenue decisions. Under PL 93–344, the Congressional Budget and Impoundment Control Act, Congress enacted a number of important procedural and organizational changes to bring coherence to the budgetary process and to coordinate expenditures, revenues, and authorizations. New Budget Committees were established, and a congressional budgetary organization that parallels the functions of the Office of Management and Budget in the executive branch was created (Congressional Budget Office). In addition, the fiscal year was changed and a fiscal-year timetable was established for congressional consideration of the budget; other provisions of the act dealt with backdoor spending and impoundments.

In the first stage of the new process, Congress spends about three months (January to March) gathering and evaluating information for planning the federal budget. Congress is assisted by the Congressional Budget Office (CBO) and the House (HBC) and Senate (SBC) Budget Committees, which collect information from various congressional committees as well as the president. This information includes estimates of economic growth, inflation, employment, and details about the programs that various authorization committees expect to report to the floor. The compilation provides the Budget Committees with an idea of the budget alternatives confronting Congress. These alternatives include the president's proposed budget and those prepared by important members of the Budget Committees and party leadership. These competing budgets will normally differ on the level of spending and taxing proposed and in the deficit or surpluses that they project. The alternative budgets arise from contrasting philosophies about federal spending, varying estimates about the nature and direction of the economy, and differing beliefs regarding national priorities.

In the second stage, Congress makes decisions about spending priorities. This occurs as the Budget Committee in each chamber reports its decisions to the appropriate house in the form of a budget resolution. By May 15, both houses are expected to have agreed to a set of budgetary guidelines: a series of statements specifying how much money Congress is prepared to spend; how the money is to be distributed among different policy areas and programs; how these programs will be financed; and the level of budget surplus or deficit that would result from the implementation of the pending budget. This May 15 statement, termed the First Concurrent Budget Resolution, must be passed in an identical form by both the House and Senate. This resolution establishes *targets* for authorizations, appropriations, and revenues to guide subsequent congressional budget decisions.

The third stage of the new budget process is marked by the actions of congressional committees in reporting legislation and the actions of Congress in approving or rejecting that legislation. Since the budget resolution only sets broad programmatic goals rather than narrow program specifications, committees still retain considerable latitude in the type of legislation they send to the floor; hence, committees can construct any type of program they want. Similarly, revenue committees (House Ways and Means and Senate Finance) are assigned general revenue goals, but they maintain a wide range of choices as to how to meet those revenue targets.

During the fourth stage of the budget process, Congress reassesses the legislation it has passed and the programs it has established. CBO provides Congress with information on the extent to which legislative activity has violated the targets established in the first budget resolution; it also provides updated figures on the state of the nation's economy—information necessary for evaluating the accuracy of the initial budget resolution and accompanying economic assumptions. The Budget Committees review this information and report a second budget resolution that details the mandatory levels of spending and revenue that the committees believe should be adopted by Congress; if accepted by both houses, Congress commits itself to abiding by the figures set in that resolution. Since these are mandatory figures, committees may be required to redraw previously passed legislation in a way that will bring spending or revenue items into line with the requirements of the Second Budget Resolution. Once this resolution is approved and all spending legislation is reconciled with the resolution, the budget has been completed for that fiscal year.

Clearly, the new budget process provides Congress with a mechanism for establishing priorities in spending decisions and for coordinating spending and revenue decisions. In other ways, however, the budget process has failed to centralize budget decisions. "The provisions affecting backdoor spending and entitlements are relatively weak and do not place these and other forms of uncontrollable spending under strict, centralized control. There is also some question about Congress' willingness to use the budget system to curtail overall spending increases and deficits" (Ippolito, 1978, p. 119). Thus, despite the centralizing mechanisms in the new budget process, crucial aspects of spending decisions continue to be made in a relatively decentralized political environment.

Committee Factions. While congressional committees are influential forces that decentralize power within Congress, power within committees is also fragmented: Power is exercised by committee factions and staff.

Committee factions operate in a coordinated fashion to influence commit-tee decisions because, in most committees, power resides in groups or fac-tions rather than in the hands of individual members. This is not to deny that some members wield significant influence over certain policies within a committee. Clearly, subcommittee leaders exercise greater influence in guiding subcommittee deliberations than other subcommittee members, and the same is true of committee leaders. Rarely, however, can a single member consistently influence committee decisions over a whole range of issues. More frequently, groups of members or factions act to influence policy decisions within a committee, serving to further fragment power. These factions materialize as members who are pushed in the same policy directions by the interplay of committee pressures join forces. Factions rep-resenting similar attitudes, policy orientations, or loyalties—factions that represent mutually accommodative interests—tend to coalesce. Some-times, a majority of members form a large faction that dominates commit-tee decisions; at other times, several factions representing mutually accommodative interests join forces to create a coalition capable of control-ling committee outcomes.

The ways in which members align into voting blocs or factions reflect the pressures within the committee's decision-making environment. The environments of congressional committees are composed of the major for-ces that shape legislative behavior: parties, ideologies, constituencies, presidents, agencies, policies, and groups. These influences push and pull committee members in different policy directions, thereby creating factions within the committee and cross-pressures on its members. Factions, there-fore, are not cohesive groups: Members maintain a primary allegiance to a single committee faction, but they also maintain varying commitments to other factions within the committee. Leadership and organization may underlie the emergence of factions in some congressional committees, but members can act in a coordinated fashion to form voting blocs without such explicit direction.

Influences in a committee's environment operate in at least three ways to create cleavages, and therefore factions, within committees: through sub-jective identification, through interpersonal communication, and through shared interests. The desire on the part of congressmen to gain acceptance of, and to maintain a satisfying relationship with, other individuals or groups is the motivating factor behind the conformity that is induced by identification. For example, labels like "conservative" or "hawk" and sym-bols of identification can induce partisans to close ranks behind a party, con-stituency, administration, or other group-identified position on an issue. Compliance occurs when an individual adopts certain behaviors because there are specific rewards or punishments associated with conformity. This mechanism is evident when political actors such as interest groups or ex-ecutive agencies lobby, promise, cajole, and generally attempt to persuade committee members to support preferred positions on legislation before the committee. Finally, some behavior occurs because it is congruent with a congressman's attitudes, values, and beliefs. Where these predispositions are shared by a number of committee members, some form of unconscious "cue voting" may materialize as committee members with similar interests coalesce. Thus, members form factions because they identify with other members, because they comply with the pressures operating on them in order to secure specific benefits or to avoid punishments, or because they share certain predispositions with other committee members.

Cleavages found in the House committee system during the 1970s are listed in Table 7-1. These cleavages define the voting blocs or factions within committees—they reflect the environmental pressures on committee members. Four types of cleavages can be identified in the House committee system: partisan, ideological, constituency, and administration. These cleavages reflect differences between Democrats and Republicans,

TABLE 7-1   Cleavages Within House Committees: 1973–1980

Congressional Committee	Party 1973 –1976	Party 1977 –1980	Ideology 1973 –1976	Ideology 1977 –1980	Administration 1973 –1976	Administration 1977 –1980	Constituency 1973 –1976	Constituency 1977 –1980
Agriculture	X	X	X	X			X	X
Appropriations	X	X	X	X	X	X		
Armed Services			X	X	X	X		
Banking, Finance and Urban Affairs	X	X	X	X			X	X
Budget	X	X	X	X				
Education and Labor	X	X	X	X			X	X
Foreign Affairs			X		X			
Government Operations	X	X	X	X				
House Administration	X	X	X	X				
Interior and Insular Affairs	X	X	X	X				X
Interstate and Foreign Commerce	X	X	X	X				
Judiciary	X	X	X	X				
Merchant Marine		X		X				X
Post Office and Civil Service	X	X	X	X	X	X		X
Public Works	X	X	X	X				
Rules	X	X	X	X				
Science and Technology	X	X	X	X				
Standards			X					
Ways and Means	X	X	X	X	X	X		

Source: Parker and Parker (1985, p. 249).

liberals and conservatives, members with a constituency interest in a policy issue and those without one, and pro- and anti-administration foes. The most prevalent cleavages are those associated with party identification and political ideology: Ideological cleavages are found in every House committee, and only three committees lack evidence of partisan cleavages.

The legislative jurisdictions of committees help to determine the types of cleavages that will arise in particular committees. For example, committees with jurisdictions that touch upon important executive functions such as foreign affairs, national defense, taxes, and expenditures exhibit factions supporting and/or opposing the president and individual administrative agencies; some jurisdictions, for example Rules, are explicitly partisan in their duties and responsibilities. Jurisdictions also determine which committees will have to deal with some of the most ideologically controversial issues within society. For instance, the Education and Labor Committee in the House cannot avoid large doses of ideological conflict, since its responsibilities cover divisive issues like labor–management rights. Since committee jurisdictions are relatively stable, so are the cleavages and factions that they promote within committees.

Committee Staff. Staff also exercise power within committees, adding to the existing sources of fragmentation within committees. Committee staff are actively involved in drafting legislation, planning investigations, providing information, and seeing lobbyists; such activities are inextricably linked to the making of public policy. In fact, committee staff seem to be more involved in policy-making duties than the clerical functions they are assigned! For example, staff of House and Senate committees spend a greater proportion of their time participating in committee hearings, writing floor speeches, and working with other committees and interest groups than researching legislation, supervising clerical staff, responding to requests for information, or conducting oversight (Fox and Hammond, 1977). The involvement of staff in these policy-making activities may have become a necessity since members are spending more time in their constituencies than in the past—a relationship that persists even among committee and subcommittee leaders. Faced with such competing obligations, many members become more dependent upon committee staff for legislative direction and evaluation; constituency duties require the congressman's physical presence in the district or state, but many committee activities can be conducted adequately by staff members while committee members attend to other responsibilities. Thus, committee staff exercise considerable influence in committee deliberations because committee members need their services.

Subcommittees. In 1965, Richard Fenno had reason to conclude that the "decisions of the House for the most part are the decisions of its committees" (p. 53). To keep this statement relevant to the House in the 1970s and 1980s, we need to add that the decisions of its committees are now more than ever the decisions made in subcommittees. Prior to the 1970s, most subcommittees were dominated by their parent committee and its chairmen. Committee chairmen like Senators Carl Hayden (Appropriations), Richard Russell (Armed Services), Arthur Vandenberg (Foreign Relations), and Representatives Clarence Cannon (Appropriations), Carl Vinson (Armed Services), and Howard Smith (Rules) dominated their committees, if not their respective chambers. Talent was not the sole basis for the power of committee chairman, though many were subject-matter experts who had mastered the technical aspects of legislation within their committee's jurisdiction. Even these committee barons did not shy away from the use of the formal prerogatives assigned them.

Chairmen controlled the flow of legislation through the committee, hired staff, monopolized time in hearings, and manipulated the organization and workload of their subcommittees. Chairmen were always aware of the potential decentralizing effects of an independent subcommittee system; hence, they frequently took action to ensure that such independence was not exhibited by their own subcommittees. "Strong chairmen retained the most important issues in full committee and discouraged the development of subcommittees, either eliminating them altogether (as did Mills in Ways and Means) or keeping their jurisdictions tightly constricted (as did Vinson in Armed Services). Even when subcommittees were employed, the committee chairmen molded them by appointing their members and chairmen" (Davidson, 1981, p. 104).

This situation changed as subcommittees began to play a larger role in the movement of legislation through committees. Larry Dodd and Richard Schott (1979) suggest that this evolution occurred in three stages. In the first wave, committees placed a greater reliance upon their subcommittees, though Senate committees were less disrupted by this change than were House committees. Committee power in the Senate is not as concentrated in the hands of committee chairmen because of the smaller size of the Senate and its less hierarchical organization. The Senate, therefore, relied on subcommittees from the outset of the postwar years, but in the House the control of committee chairmen was far more absolute. One indicator of the effect of this increased reliance upon subcommittees is the growth in the percentage of committee hearings held in subcommittees. "Although between 60 and 65 percent of all Senate hearings were held in subcommittee, only between 20 and 30 percent of all House hearings were held in subcommittee. Starting in the 84th Congress (1955) the figure jumps to 50 percent in the House, increasing to 60 percent by the 88th Congress and to 70 percent by the 89th Congress. In approximately twenty years the proportional use of subcommittees to conduct committee hearings thus doubled in the House, which joined the Senate in predominant reliance on subcommittees" (Dodd and Schott, 1979, p. 109). In making greater use of subcommittees, committee chairs gave up some control over legislation since hearings and the mark-up of legislation were the province of subcommittee chairs which was more often than not someone other than the committee chair. This served to disperse authority more widely and gave more members an opportunity to influence committee outcomes.

The second stage of power dispersion is characterized by the expansion of the subcommittee system. In the past, enlargement of the subcommittee system was somewhat idiosyncratic; moves to expand a committee's subcommittees were largely committee-by-committee battles. But even when subcommittees were increased, committee chairs still retained control over most of the key prerogatives of subcommittee rule such as the hiring of staff and subcommittee budgets. The growth in the number of subcommittees has been quite dramatic since that time: "In the House in the early and middle 1950s, the number fluctuated between 80 and 85; by the middle of the 1970s, it had grown to approximately 140. In the Senate, the number increased from around 110 in the 1950s to 140 in the 1970s" (Dodd and Schott, 1979, p. 111). This expansion increased the number of new committee leaders, and those who gained a subcommittee chairmanship sought to protect the existence, independence, and authority of their subcommittees. Subcommittee members and leaders had a hard time realizing these goals since committee chairs maintained sufficient control over subcommittee prerogatives, therefore ensuring their subservience. In the final stage, moves to formalize the autonomy and authority of subcommittees and to ensure their responsiveness to the full standing committee rather than committee chairs were undertaken. These three stages resulted in an institutionalization of subcommittee government, especially in the House:

> In the three decades following the 1946 reforms, Congress had moved to proliferate subcommittees for legislative work, to guarantee a relatively equal spread of committee and subcommittee chair positions among members, to establish rules and procedures that allowed a greater disciplining of committee chairs through a slightly modified system of committee seniority, to establish clearer jurisdictional responsibilities for subcommittees, and to give the chairs of subcommittees greater autonomy and authority. (Dodd and Schott, 1979, p. 124)

The proliferation of subcommittees appears to have subsided, due in part to the ceiling on the number of subcommittees established by House Democrats in 1981. The rule limited standing committees to eight subcommittees (an exception is made for the Appropriations Committee); committees with more than 35 members and fewer than six subcommittees could increase the number to six or, with the approval of the Steering and Policy Committee, seven subcommittees. This cap on subcommittees forced some committees, like Agriculture and Banking, to reduce the number of subcommittees; the 97th and 98th Congresses were the first since 1947 in which the number of subcommittees failed to increase. The Senate limitation on the number of subcommittee assignments and chairmanships that a senator could hold helps to account for the decline in the number of subcommittees from 127 to 90 between 1973 and 1979.

Within committees, therefore, legislative initiative has tended to pass to the subcommittees. Subcommittees are the leading drafters of legislative measures and reports. Few committees deliberate *de novo* on legislation; more frequently, they simply review their subcommittee's decisions or simply pass the subcommittee's product to the full chamber. Furthermore, most legislation is now managed on the floor by subcommittee chairs, whereas most bills were previously managed by full committee chairs; scheduling, control of time during debate, coalition building, and other issues of strategy and tactics are now almost completely in the hands of subcommittee chairs (Deering, 1982). Leadership involvement in subcommittee activities rarely involves more than the scheduling of legislation once it has cleared the full committee.

Until the 1970s, many committee chairmen eschewed the referral of legislation to subcommittees in order to retain control of legislation they opposed. But since 1975, subcommittees have gained a stronger foothold in committee deliberations: More legislation is being referred to subcommittees and more than three of every four bills referred to a House subcommittee is reported to the floor; in the Senate, however, most referred and reported legislation fails to receive subcommittee treatment (Smith and Deering, 1984). Furthermore, nearly all House hearings, and a majority of all committee meetings at which substantive policy decisions are made, are held in subcommittees. In the Senate, the pattern is a consistent one: Hearings are held in subcommittees but legislation is marked up in the full committee. Despite the recent expansion of the subcommittee system in the Senate, subcommittee government is less institutionalized than in the House, at least in terms of such indicators of subcommittee activity as meetings and hearings. Simply put, Senate subcommittees are generally less significant than House subcommittees in committee decision making.

The inability of subcommittee government to dominate decision making in Senate committees as it does in House committees is at least partially due to the fact that senators are less dependent upon their committee memberships as avenues of participation. The ability of senators to propose amendments or to filibuster on the floor, the absence of rules guiding consideration of legislation on the floor of the Senate, and the practice of permitting individual senators to place a "hold" on pending legislation grant senators more strategic options to influence legislation outside of their committees. Senators are also less dependent on their subcommittees since they have nearly twice the number of subcommittee assign-

TABLE 7-2   Party Committees in the Senate and House

Committee	Democrats	Committee	Republicans
		Senate	
Policy	formulates and coordinates recommendations for party positions on legislation and assists leaders in scheduling bills for floor consideration	Policy	defines Republican positions, researches procedural and substantive issues and drafts policy alternatives
Steering	assigns Democrats to committees	Committee on Committees	assigns Republicans to committees
Campaign	furnishes campaign assistance	Campaign	furnishes campaign assistance
		House	
Steering and Policy	assigns Democrats to committees, discusses and endorses party policy and strategy	Policy	discusses policy alternatives and seeks to promote consensus among Republicans
Campaign	furnishes campaign assistance	Campaign	furnishes campaign assistance
Personnel	oversees patronage appointments among Democrats	Personnel	oversees patronage appointments of Republicans
		Research	conducts research for Republican members
		Committee on Committees	assigns Republicans to committees

ments. Further, the greater number of committee and subcommittee assignments means that Senate committees often neglect to hold subcommittee mark ups because members do not have the time to attend them; gaining a quorum sufficient to take formal action in Senate committees is therefore more of a problem for subcommittees in the Senate than the House. The smaller size of Senate committees provide senators with more opportunities to influence deliberations at the full-committee level than representatives enjoy. Fragmented decision making, however, thrives in the Senate even though subcommittees lack the power of their House counterparts.

In short, Senate subcommittees are generally highly permeable to outsiders, and their permeability reduces the incentives to demand greater independence for them. Subcommittee independence is of little value when full committees themselves lack autonomy. In fact, subcommittee independence is counterproductive to the participatory individualism of senators. For these reasons, then, subcommittees are less important decision-making arenas in the Senate than in the House.

POLITICAL PARTIES

Party Organization. Like many organizations, the distribution of power within political parties is not an overlay of organizational structure. This is not to suggest that congressional leaders at the upper levels of the party possess no influence over those lower in the hierarchy. While party leaders may not be able to dictate all of the terms of the agreements they reach with those at the lower rungs of the party organization, they undoubtedly get their way more often than not. The decentralized nature of party leadership in the House and Senate (Figures 7-1 and 7-2), and within the congressional parties produces layers of party committees and legislative leaders. This serves to fragment the power of centralized leaders by forcing them to share party resources with lower-level leaders.

Granted, in many cases these resources amount to very little, rarely rivaling the resources held by top party leaders. Nevertheless, in an institution of equals any small increment of prestige, power, or influence can bring immeasurable pleasure to many members. What these low-level positions and committees provide, then, are alternative channels for realizing goals. The mere existence of these layers of party and legislative authority serves to satisfy an important member goal—the exercise of power—no matter how limited the range of influence. Further, the ability of lower-level leaders to aid other members in realizing certain goals (e.g., espousal of policy interests, reelection support) builds credit with those they assist. Since the obligation is owed to a minor leader rather than the top party leaders, the latter cannot benefit from that obligation unless, of course, the interests of the lower and top leaders coincide. The existence of layers of party and legislative leadership not only fragments power by broadly dispersing authority within the parties, but it also means that the resources for inducing cooperation are shared with more individuals. This deprives top party leaders of a monopoly over resources that help members to realize their legislative goals. Decentralizing the political parties may make the organizational tasks of

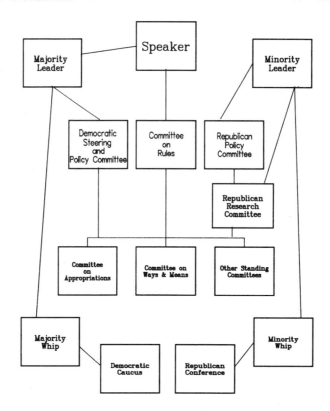

FIGURE 7–1   Organization of the House of Representatives [Source: Davidson and Oleszek (1981, p. 180).]

top party leaders more manageable, but it also diminishes their control over resources that might induce greater cooperation from their members.

Top party leaders exercise some control over those in lower leadership positions because of their appointment powers and prerogatives, but the increased individuality of members and the expanded workload that confronts leaders at the highest levels of the party guarantee lower-level leaders a large measure of discretion. This makes the job satisfying to the occupant and enables him to use this discretion to build "chits" among colleagues. In short, party leaders continue to accumulate credits from party members as in the past, but what has changed is that the debts are owed more frequently to members beyond the party's central leadership corps.

Informal Groups.   Informal groups, coalitions, clubs, blocs, and cliques are not new to Congress. What distinguishes present informal groups from those of the past is "their number (more than 70 by 1981); diversity (there are partisan, bipartisan, and bicameral groups, for example); institution-

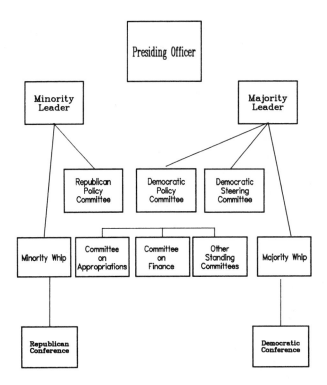

FIGURE 7–2 Organization of the Senate [Source: Davidson and Oleszek (1981, p. 180).]

alized character (many have paid staff, office space, dues-paying members, bylaws, and elected officers); and capacity to monitor federal activities that affect their interests" (Davidson and Oleszek, 1981, p. 352). House Republicans took the lead in forming a variety of clubs after World War II that were based on mixtures of congeniality, geography, committee assignment, and cohort that primarily served social functions.

The growth and institutionalization of these informal groups is due to at least three factors: sponsorship by regional or economic-based interest groups, the need to coordinate related legislative interests, and the electoral benefits that can be derived from membership in an informal group. Some interest groups are instrumental in the formation of informal legislative groups because they see their interests so closely tied to that of certain congressmen that they seize the initiative in fostering the organization of congressmen sympathetic to the group's cause. The economic decline of certain regions and industries has also incited congressmen to form groups protective of the interests of their region, and each move to protect one region's interests spurs a countermove; hence, the Sun Belt Caucus of southern congressmen was established in response to the operation of the Northeast–Midwest Coalition. Informal groups also help to coordinate the activities of members with similar policy and political interests. Finally, informal groups have grown because they enable congressmen to gain political strength back home and leverage in Washington. Membership in an informal group can be cited as evidence of a member's concern for his constituents and the plight of his district or state. Sometimes informal groups even supply campaign and fund-raising support.

There are a wide variety of informal groups (Table 7-3), but three of the most legislatively active are the Democratic Study Group, "Boll Weevils," and "Gypsy Moths." The Democratic Study Group (DSG) began initially as a loose alliance of liberal Democrats in the House in 1957 but has become institutionalized since that time with an elected chairman, staff, budget, and its own whip organization. The DSG issues reports on legislative issues, summaries of projected legislative activities, and analyses of bills and votes. The DSG whip organization performs functions similar to that of regular party whips, though its main task is to ensure turnout for important votes. The DSG is a remarkably cohesive voting bloc on the floor of the House, which gives its leaders leverage in dealing with formal party leaders. The cohesion is largely a result of the ideological agreement among members, which is a basis for a self-selected membership.

A group of conservative Democrats, popularly called the "Boll Weevils" and named after the southern pests that are destructive to cotton, have met with some regularity to discuss legislation and to formulate group positions. Until 1981–1982, Democratic leaders in the House were basically unwilling to negotiate with the "Boll Weevils," most of whom they believed to be uncompromisingly opposed to the party's policies. With the election of a conservative Republican president in 1980, however, the significance of this bloc as a pivotal coalition partner increased, and Democratic party leaders could no longer ignore the "Boll Weevils," who had now adopted the less offensive title of Conservative Democratic Forum. The improved position of this conservative group is evident by their increased representation on important party and legislative committees.

In 1981, a shifting and informal group of moderate and liberal Republicans from the upper midwest and northeast began meeting because of the disproportionate impact of Reagan budget cuts on their constituents. Like the "boll weevils," who were destructive to the fabric of life in the old south, these deviants from the conservatism of congressional Republicans were named "Gypsy Moths," after the pests that attack the foliage of shade trees in the North. And also like their Democratic counterparts, the "Gypsy Moths" have become an important voting bloc that has been able to exact a price for its support of Republican policies.

It should be clear that informal groups fragment congressional power by their ability to supply alternate sources of information and voting cues.

TABLE 7-3 Informal Groups In Congress

HOUSE

Democratic

Conservative Democratic Forum
Democratic Research Organization
Democratic Study Group

New Members' Caucuses for
95th, 96th, and 97th Congresses
United Democrats of Congress

Republican

'Gypsy Moths'
Republican Study Committee

Republican Clubs for 95th,
96th, and 97th Congresses
Wednesday Group

Bipartisan

Ad hoc Congressional Committee
for Irish Affairs
Alcohol Fuels Caucus
Auto Task Force
Congressional Ad hoc Monitoring
Group on South Africa
Congressional Arts Caucus
Congressional Black Caucus
Congressional Coal Caucus
Congressional Port Caucus
Congressional Shipbuilding
Coalition
Congresswomen's Caucus
Domestic Energy Supply
Coalition
Export Task Force
Fair Employment Practices
Committee

Federal Government Service
Task Force
Great Lakes Conference
Hispanic Caucus
Industrial Innovation Task Force
Metropolitan Area Caucus
Missing in Action Task Force
Mushroom Caucus
New England Congressional Caucus
Northeast-Midwest Economic
Advancement Coalition
Rural Caucus
Steel Caucus
Suburban Caucus
Sun Belt Caucus
Textile Caucus

SENATE

Democratic

Midwest Conference of
Democratic Senators

Moderate/Conservative
Democrats

Republican

Republican Steering Committee

Wednesday Club

Bipartisan

Coal Caucus
Concerned Senators for the Arts
Copper Caucus
Export Caucus

Freshman Senators
Northeast Midwest Coalition
Rail Caucus
Steel Caucus
Western State Coalition

BICAMERAL, BIPARTISAN

Children's Lobby
Coalition for Peace
Through Strength
Congressional Clearinghouse
on the Future
Environmental and Energy Study
Conference
Friends of Ireland
High Altitude Coalition

Jewelry Manufacturing Coalition
Members of Congress for Peace
Through Law
North American Trade Caucus
(Pentagon) Reform Caucus
Pro-Life Caucus
Solar Coalition
Tourism Caucus
Vietnam Era Veterans in Congress

Source: Davidson and Oleszek (1981, p. 354).

Informal groups have assumed, in some cases, "a leading role in performing functions historically associated with the party and committee systems: calling attention to problems which need to be addressed, developing
substantive and procedural expertise among members and promoting the
integrated consideration of policy proposals" (Stevens et al., 1981, p. 428).
Further, the cohesiveness of most of these groups promotes the formation
of voting blocs on the floor, which gives groups greater leverage with their
leaders, who often equate the ability to deliver votes with legislative power.
Thus, groups that can deliver large blocs of votes will normally have the
greatest influence on congressional leaders. The independence of these informal groups and the ties that bind their members to group causes further fragments power in Congress.

   State Party Delegations.   State party delegations supply their members
with information about legislative issues and voting cues, but it is probably the latter that is most influential in fragmenting power. When leaders
have to contend with alternative sources of legislative "advice," their ability
to structure voting outcomes diminishes significantly. There are several
reasons why members accept cues from members in their own party from
the same state. First, an individual may be highly respected among congressmen from the state; hence, he may serve as a reliable voting cue in
any number of situations. Second, voting as a bloc is a protective
mechanism since "sticking together" discourages criticism from being
focused on any one member—it diffuses criticism. Finally, most state
delegation members realize that they can enhance their bargaining position in the House if they exhibit a high degree of unity in floor voting. Not
all state delegations behave the same, nor are they all able to maintain
high levels of cohesion:

> State delegations can be grouped into four broad types. The first type rarely
> meets, discusses only local issues (for example, new federal installations or
> the performance of federal programs in the state) at meetings, and explicit-
> ly does not seek unity in voting on the floor. The second type also meets rare-
> ly, but discusses national as well as local issues, and does seek floor unity.
> The third type meets often, discusses national and local issues, and seeks
> floor unity. The fourth type meets often, discusses only national issues, and
> does not seek floor unity. (Ripley, 1983, p. 248)

   The existence of such groups within Congress has served to fragment
congressional power. "The communication networks of congressmen are
infinitely complex and, in the absence of two party hierarchies capable of
making policy, all of these less formal sources of consultation become consequential for policy making" (Fenno, 1965, p. 66). The existence and institutionalization of policy-making groups within Congress, and within
and between the parties, illustrate the high degree of fragmentation that
characterizes Congress and the legislative process.

FORCES PROMOTING THE FRAGMENTATION OF POWER

There are a large number of factors that help to explain the fragmentation of power in Congress, but three of the most important are: The changes produced through congressional reforms, the persistence of norms supportive of decentralization, and the existence of member goals that are best realized within a decentralized power structure. These three factors have encouraged and sustained the decentralized nature of congressional power by strengthening the autonomy of subunits within Congress and by spreading legislative "action" more widely among congressmen.

Congressional Reforms. In a number of ways congressional reforms have strengthened the positions of centralized leadership within Congress, especially in the House. For example, reforms have streamlined the Senate committee system by consolidating or abolishing several committees, thereby reducing the number of positions of legislative power (committee chairmanships) in the Senate. Moreover, the power of individual senators has been constrained by changes in the rule of unlimited debate (Rule 22): The rule for ending Senate filibusters (cloture rule) has been revised so that continuing debate—filibusters—can be ended if supported by a three-fifths majority of the Senate rather than a two-thirds majority of those present and voting. In the House during the same period, the Speaker gained significant powers; for example, the authority to make appointments to the Rules Committee with the approval of the Democratic Caucus and to refer bills to more than a single committee. At the same time that congressional power was being centralized, however, it was also being subjected to centrifugal pressures by other congressional reforms.

House reforms helped to fragment power in the institution by strengthening committees, institutionalizing subcommittee government, and in general ensuring the wide dispersal of legislative power. Subcommittees have certainly gained power in the House at the expense of committees, but reforms also have increased the power of committees by broadening their privileges and powers, such as subpoena power. The real beneficiaries of congressional reform, however, are the subcommittees. The adoption of a so-called "subcommittee bill of rights" in the House forced committee leaders to share their authority with their subcommittees: Each committee's majority caucus (Democratic members of the committee) was granted authority to select subcommittee chairs, define subcommittee jurisdictions, set party ratios on the subcommittees, and establish a subcommittee budget; subcommittees were authorized to hold hearings, set meeting times, and were guaranteed the referral of legislation by the committee chairman within two weeks of its referral to the committee.

The forces of subcommittee government were bolstered further by Democratic reforms in the House in 1975. For example, the reforms introduced by the Hansen plan in 1974 required the establishment of at least four subcommittees in committees with more than 15 members (increased to more than 20 members by the Caucus in 1975); in 1975 subcommittee leaders (chair and ranking minority member) were each permitted to hire one staff person to work directly with them. Subcommittee members also were given authority in 1974 to determine the number of subcommittees their committee would have, but House Democrats subsequently amended this rule by limiting the number of subcommittees and committee subunits that could be established by the standing committees. Other congressional reforms served to spread power among an even larger number of congressmen: In 1971, House Democrats restricted members to chairing a single subcommittee, and later extended (in 1975) this rule to the chairing of standing, select, special, or joint committees.

Congressional reforms have had less of an impact in further fragmenting power in the Senate since the institution is far more open to member influence than the House, and power is more evenly distributed among senators than representatives. Senate debate is unrestricted, floor amendments are easily attached to pending legislation, and most senators can boast of a position of leadership. Still, Senate reforms also have spread power among more and more senators. For instance, 1975 changes in Senate rules enabled junior senators to hire up to three staffers to work in their committees; in the past, committee staffs were tightly controlled by senior senators. The Senate, like the House, has also adopted rules that limit the number of leadership positions (committee or subcommittee chairmanships) held by a single senator. In sum, congressional reforms have promoted and sustained the fragmentation of congressional power by strengthening the positions of subunits within Congress and by dispersing authority and power more widely.

The Specialization Norm. The fragmentation of congressional power is also sustained by the persistence of the legislative norm of specialization.[3] Specialization of tasks is probably essential in a modern legislative institution that is forced to deal with complex tasks in a limited period of time. As I have noted, congressmen are expected to specialize in those matters that are of particular interest and importance to their constituents or committees. Such expertise enhances the influence and effectiveness of individual members:[4] "If a man be a specialist on a subject, if he knows more than the ordinary congressman knows or can hope to learn by mere dabbling, then he can compel Congress to listen to him, and he rises to be a power" (Silverman, 1954, p. 188).

Specialization may be a more powerful norm in the House than the Senate since House incumbents (more than senators) are required to develop an area of expertise to be maximally effective. For example, senators "do not specialize as intensively or as exclusively in their committee work as House members do" (Fenno, 1973, p. 172). There are far fewer rewards for specialization in the Senate: Decision making is less committee-centered, committees are more permeable to the influence of non-committee members, and senators by necessity hold more committee and subcommittee assignments than representatives. This is not to suggest that senators do not specialize in their committees; they do, but they see this as a matter of necessity, not the expectations of others. Clearly, there is widespread recognition among senators that they are expected to attend to their committee obligations and to develop expertise in these matters. A junior Republican senator described the "pull" of specialization in these terms:

> I don't know if you're expected to [specialize] as much as you're almost forced to because of the wide range of activity that takes place and just the constraints on your time that don't give you the opportunity to delve into other committee areas as much as you might like. I find that it's all I can do just to keep up with my own committee work, let alone get involved in something that's going on in another committee. So you do become dependent on members of other committees whom you learn to respect for their judgement as time goes on. (Rohde et al., 1985, p. 178)

The maintenance of alternative voting cues based on expertise, the independence of committees and subcommittees, and the division of labor within the political parties are aspects of the fragmentation of congressional power that are supported by the norm of specialization. Because they have gained expertise by specializing in a policy area, many members serve as voting cues for those less familiar with a particular policy area or legislative issue. The value of specialization in dealing with complex issues enhances the authority of committees and subcommittees over narrow policy matters, and the specialization of functions within the party—scheduling, committee assignments, campaign and patronage assistance—ensures an elaborate, decentralized party organization.

Member Goals. The fragmentation of congressional power also persists because it helps members realize personal legislative goals. Congressmen exploit their access to small islands of power within Congress ("turf") to satisfy their interest in particular policy questions or to exercise power. In short, decentralization serves the objectives of members quite well. Even proposed efforts to centralize power among the most powerful leaders (e.g. committee leaders) were not perceived to be viable alternatives to a decentralized power structure. "The persons least enthusiastic about a policy committee made up of committee chairmen probably were the committee chairmen themselves, who had no wish to trade sovereignty for a vote in council" (Huitt, 1961b, p. 335).

Positions in the party hierarchy or positions of committee leadership are obvious opportunities for members to influence policy and exercise power, subcommittee rule has increased these opportunities for less senior members. The organization of factions within committees and the political parties also serves the needs of members to exercise power since an individual member can have more influence on a legislative measure or maintain a greater bargaining edge when he joins with other members to form a cohesive voting bloc. The influence of a voting bloc may even outweigh its size if the cohesiveness of the faction is high. Decentralization of congressional authority, then, is especially conducive to the realization of policy and power goals:

> Each member wants to exercise power—to make the key policy decisions. This motive places every member in a personal conflict with every other member: to the extent that one member realizes his or her goal personally to control all key decisions, all others must lose. Given this widespread power motive, an obvious way to resolve the conflict is to disperse power—or at least power positions—as widely as possible. One logical solution, in other words, is to place basic policy-making responsibility in a series of discrete and relatively autonomous committees and subcommittees, each having control over the decisions in a specified jurisdictional area. Each member can belong to a small number of committees and, within them, have a significant and perhaps dominant influence on policy. (Dodd, 1985, p. 491)

In short, members of Congress want to call the shots and gain the psychological satisfaction that comes from exercising power or influencing policy. It is simply not sufficient to be electorally secure or a member of the ruling majority. Those already in possession of positions of power cling tenaciously to them, while those who lack such positions of influence struggle to obtain them. Decentralizing power is an easy way to accommodate the desires of members to exercise influence without inducing turnover in existing leaders (and the conflict that such revolts create).

POLICY CONSEQUENCES

Decentralizing legislative authority has contributed to the incremental and disjointed nature of policy outcomes and the time-consuming nature of policy making. The dispersion of authority in Congress means that a large number of actors are inextricably involved in the formation of public policy; further decentralizing trends that have strengthened committees and subcommittees have in some instances doubled or tripled the number of legislators who are involved in the formation of public policies. With such a large number of *independent* actors involved, most policies reflect marginal or incremental changes to existing policies. That is, the necessity of securing the cooperation and agreement of a large number of political actors not only taxes the resources of legislative leaders but forces them to focus on areas of consensus, which are generally quite narrowly defined. The policies that are most likely to gain the assent of such a broad decision-making group are those that make only marginal changes in the status quo—the existing agreement among political actors. Thus, the fragmentation of legislative authority contrives to promote incremental policy outcomes rather than comprehensive policies.

I should also point out that policy outcomes are not only incremental: The fragmentation of legislative power also promotes disjointed policy outcomes. That is, the division of congressional authority into islands of legislative power restricts the likelihood that comprehensive policies will emerge from legislative deliberations because decision makers will concern themselves only with those problems directly in their own purview. The result is that policies are not only incremental but also may bear little relationship to policies formed in other independent subsystems. This does not mean that policies are totally uncoordinated because of the fragmentation of congressional authority. The fragmentation of legislative power may, in fact, contribute to coordinating policies. Decisions can be viewed as coordinated in at least a weak fashion if the adverse consequences of any one decision for other policies are avoided, reduced, counterbalanced, or outweighed. With a multiplicity of policymakers, such coordination can be achieved:

> ...decision makers mop up the adverse consequences of each other's inevitably imperfect decisions, multiple decision makers will, in addition, compellingly call to others' attention aspects of the problem they cannot themselves analyze. Moreover, just as the single decision maker will sometimes anticipate adverse consequences that he must nevertheless treat as separate problems for fear of making his existing problem unmanageable, so also other decision makers can anticipate what they either cannot anticipate or cannot attend to. (Lindblom, 1965, pp. 151–152)

Since decision making is incremental and disjointed, more rather than fewer policy makers facilitates coordination. Where policy making is dispersed over a large group, as in the present Congress, their very numbers afford the possibility of coordination. The possibilities are even greater if these policy makers have different interests and specializations and look at problems differently. "If numbers sometimes create a problem of coordination, it is only traditional bias that causes us to overlook the contribution numbers can make to its solution. A multiplicity of energies, interests, and intelligences can itself be exploited to achieve coordination" (Lindblom, 1965, p. 157).

Finally, the decentralized nature of the legislative process ensures ample amounts of delay. The large number of decision makers involved in policy formation, and their independent sources of authority (such as their expertise), forces legislative leaders to engage in time-consuming negotiations. Party leaders must "touch base" with an even larger assortment of decision makers in the present Congress than in past ones. This slows legislative response to societal problems—a stigma associated with Congress and the legislative process. Thus, the proliferation of independent centers of power within Congress and the political parties has added to the obstacles confronting centralized leadership: They find themselves engaged in negotiations with a large number of decision makers, and they cannot seem to gain sufficient consensus among these decision makers to make sweeping and comprehensive changes in public policy.

SUMMARY

This fragmentation of congressional power is evident in the autonomy and influence of subunits, like committees, in the House and Senate and the capacity of committee members to serve as alternative sources of information and advice; hence, legislative leaders cannot monopolize information—a major source of their influence. As policy experts, committee members provide "guidance" for those congressmen unfamiliar with a particular policy area, often serving as cue-givers because of their expertise. The multistep nature of the budget process and the ability of committees to make multiyear authorizations add to the decentralizing influence of congressional committees. Even the power of congressional committees is itself subject to decentralization: Power within committees is exercised by committee factions, staff, and subcommittees. Voting blocs, or factions, frequently form to control committee decisions, and congressional staff play an active role in these decisions (e.g., drafting legislation, planning investigations); in addition, subcommittees have gained influence over committee decisions. Decentralization is also evident in the layers of party committees and legislative leaders in Congress. This fragments power by forcing top party leaders to share party resources with lower-level leaders while at the same time dispersing legislative authority. Informal groups and state delegations fragment power within the parties even further by supplying party members with alternative sources of information and voting cues.

Congressional reforms have helped to fragment power by strengthening committees, institutionalizing subcommittee government, and dispersing legislative power widely. For example, committees and subcommittees have gained influence as their prerogatives were expanded by congressional reforms. The persistence of the specialization norm also helps to explain the fragmentation of legislative power. The value of specialization in dealing with complex legislative issues enhances the authority of committees and subcommittees, and the specialization of functions within the party ensures an elaborate, decentralized organization. Finally, the fragmentation of congressional power persists because it helps members realize personal legislative goals: legislators exploit their access to small islands of power within Congress to satisfy the desire to exercise legislative influence.

As a consequence of the decentralization of congressional power, a larger number of actors are involved in the formation of public policies. Such a large number of independent actors ensures that most policies reflect only marginal or incremental changes in existing policies: The policies most apt to gain the approval of a large number of decision makers are those that make only marginal changes to the surviving political bargain (i.e., the status quo). This also promotes disjointed policy outcomes since legislators concern themselves only with those problems directly in their own purview. While the multiplicity of decision makers resulting from decentralization promotes incremental and disjointed policies, it also facilitates coordination. The more decision makers involved in a policy decision, the greater the likelihood that adverse consequences of that policy will be anticipated and remedied. Finally, decentralization fosters legislative delay since it forces party leaders to "touch base" with a large assortment of decision makers, and such time-consuming negotiations slow the legislative process.

NOTES

1. The power of congressional committees consists of their gatekeeping functions, advantage in access to information, and their capacity to originate legislation. Kenneth Shepsle and Barry Weingast (1987) call attention to another aspect of committee power: ex post veto power. Committees that are empowered to withdraw a proposal after it has been modified on the floor or that can modify further, or reject such proposals in some other forum (for example, a conference proceeding with its counterpart in the other chamber) possess *ex post veto power.* "A committee with only the power to move first—by opening the gates or keeping them closed—essentially possesses only blocking power. Once it opens the gates almost anything can happen, and the committee is virtually powerless to alter the subsequent path. In contrast, a committee with powers at subsequent stages, especially the penultimate stage i.e., conference committee decisions, not only affects the subsequent outcome but also influences the antecedent actions of others by conditioning their beliefs and expectations" (Shepsle and Weingast, 1987, p. 91).

2. It is interesting to note that Democratic House leaders made the Rules Committee more responsive to their appeals during the 1960s by enlarging the size of the committee rather than disciplining recalcitrant members by removing them from the committee. For an excellent study of this decision see Peabody (1963).

3. There has been a notable increase in the extent to which decision making occurs on the floor of the House and Senate. This has raised doubts about the survival of the specialization norm:

   Between the 1950s and the 1980s, the number of amendments offered to pending legislation in each Congress more than tripled. The percentage of all legislation subject to floor amendment more than quadrupled. The number of members offering amendments almost doubled. The norms of specialization, committee reciprocity, and apprenticeship met their demise during the 1960s and 1970s. ... (Smith, 1986, p. 1)

This increased activity, and the success of noncommittee members in amending legislation (Smith, 1986, pp. 15–17), are interpreted as evidence that specialization has declined: if specialization persisted, legislation from committees would not be subject to amendment with such regularity; moreover, non-committee members should be far less successful in their attempts to amend committee legislation. This is a reasonable interpretation, but it seems to ignore the distinction that Rohde and his colleagues (1985) make about the two "sides" of the specialization norm. In one sense, the specialization norm is nothing more than the expectation that members will work hard in their committees to develop expertise on those policy issues that their committees deliberate. On the other hand, the specialization norm entails the expectation that members confine their attention almost *exclusively* to the matters considered in their committees. In this book, the specialization norm refers to the expectation that members will develop policy expertise, rather than the expectation that involvement is to be *restricted* to those policy areas where a member has developed that expertise. There is evidence that the expectation that members specialize survives, but there is no evidence that there is any adherence to the other side of the specialization norm—that members should *restrict* their activity to policy areas in their committees, and defer to others on legislation outside of their committees (Rohde et al., 1985).

4. Barbara Sinclair (1987) argues that Senate committees have become even less autonomous. "The floor has become a more active decision making arena. More decisions are made on the floor and these are consequential not symbolic decisions. Committees can no longer expect their decisions to be accepted by the chamber without question. Attempts to alter committee decisions through floor amendments are now routine and are often successful" (p. 15).

Chapter Eight
CONSTITUENCY REPRESENTATION

It should come as no surprise that the representation of constituency interests is an important characteristic of Congress. Even if none of the original framers of the Constitution foresaw the professional (Price, 1975) and institutional evolution of Congress (Polsby, 1968), they recognized that the legislative process was an appropriate arena for the representation of the diverse interests within society, as parochial as they might be. Often, when we think of constituency representation, our attention focuses on the legislative voting of senators and representatives. The question of representation in Congress is usually addressed in terms of the degree of congruity between the consensus within a constituency (district or state) with respect to a particular policy and the legislator's vote on that issue. The argument is usually made that the greater the congruence, the stronger the representational ties between the legislator and his constituents. This is an obvious area for constituency representation to occur; some might argue that it is a critical element in constituency representation.

While policy agreement is a natural way for representational obligations to be fulfilled, floor voting is only one way to represent constituency interests. Constituency representation also occurs in the frequent bureaucratic intercessions that congressmen make on behalf of constituents. For instance, congressmen seek to remedy the effects of an adverse agency regulation (or ruling) or to gain some benefit for the constituency or individual constituents by exploiting their influence with specific agencies. Constituency interests are also represented within congressional committees: Congressmen select their committee assignments with an eye toward how the assignment might further the interests of their constituents; this relationship is evident in the tendency for congressmen to gravitate toward committees that deal with issues vital to constituency interests. Thus, constituency representation occurs in major decision-making arenas: the bureaucracy, the congressional committees, and on the floor of the House and Senate.

ARENAS OF CONSTITUENCY REPRESENTATION

Bureaucracy. When citizens have grievances over bureaucratic action, they contact their senator or, more frequently, their representative without hesitation. Whether it is a missing social security check or a bureaucratic decision that adversely affects an industry, constituents bring their problems to their legislators. As I have noted, one reason why congressmen are frequent sources of contact for such problems is because of their self-proclaimed notoriety for resolving them to the benefit of constituents. For example, rarely will a constituent newsletter fail to mention the congressman's successful intervention in some sort of bureaucratic decision. Perhaps congressmen too often take credit for changes in bureaucratic rulings that they really never influenced. On the other hand, no one on or off Capitol Hill doubts the success of members in pressuring agency officials for decisions that are beneficial to their districts and states.[1]

No matter how large or small the issue may be, you can bet that if district or state interests are involved, congressmen will get involved. For example, when the Forest Service wanted to consolidate and close the Oconee ranger district in Georgia in 1982, thereby saving a mere $20,000 a year, Senator Mack Mattingly (D-Ga.) had language introduced into a House appropriations bill that prohibited such action; Senators Lee Metcalf (D-Mont.) and Frank Moss (D-Utah) executed the same ploy in 1972 to prevent the closing of regional Forest Service offices in their own states (Fitzgerald and Lipson, 1984). Similarly, when the Farmers Home Administration recommended reducing office hours in Oklahoma's Love and Coal counties to part-time status because of the lack of business, Wesley W. Watkins (D-Okla.), who represents these areas, was "persuasive" enough to have language adopted by the House Agricultural Appropriations Subcommittee (of which he is a member) directing Agricultural

Department officials to maintain full-service in these offices (Fitzgerald and Lipson, 1984, p. 44)!

Even when decisions are made that affect more than a single constituency, congressmen are sometimes able to force exceptions to bureaucratic rulings that favor their constituents. The case-by-case analysis that agencies engage in when evaluating exemptions (or exceptions) to agency rulings provides the type of opportunities that members can exploit to the advantage of their constituents. A congressman's argument that a constituent's or group's situation is unique and warrants an exemption to an agency's ruling is very persuasive with bureaucrats, who are often dependent upon the good will of the congressman for their budgets and programs. For instance, in a major cost-cutting effort, officials of Amtrak (a federally funded national railroad corporation) moved in 1981 to terminate the Cardinal along with a number of other money-losing, long-distance passenger trains. While several subsidized passenger trains did come to an end, the Cardinal remained, owing to the efforts of Senator Robert C. Byrd (D-W.Va.), who introduced language forcing Amtrak to continue rail passenger service between Washington, D.C. and Chicago via Cincinnati (Fitzgerald and Lipson, 1984, p. 66).

In addition to seeking preferential treatment for constituents, congressmen also try to further, as well as to protect, constituency interests. This effort promotes the type of symbiotic relationships that mark the "cozy triangles" described in Chapter Ten: Committees, groups, and agencies establish mutually rewarding relationships that feature electoral support for committee members, expansion and protection of agency programs, and favorable bureaucratic action toward committee members' constituencies. Since the nature of cozy triangles is discussed in Chapter Ten, I only note that congressmen are quite successful in ensuring the representation of constituent interests in bureaucratic decisions relating to the distribution of federal projects and contracts.

Congressmen normally intercede on an informal basis to further constituent interests, but they are not adverse to seeking legislative recourse. As I have noted, congressmen are willing to introduce language into appropriations legislation to protect programs that benefit constituents, and in some instances there is no question as to who or which districts will benefit from its passage. For example, in the 98th Congress several congressmen and senators introduced legislation that prohibited the sale of federal lands in their districts or states or that forced the national government to transfer federal land to state or local authorities. Congressmen can become involved, sometimes on a daily basis for several consecutive weeks, in mediating between the decisions of bureaucrats and the grievances of constituents. Most of the time, however, this mediation entails no more than a routine letter of inquiry or a telephone call to an agency official. Such rather minor intercessions, however, may be sufficient to alter the administrative course of bureaucratic rulings. Clearly, congressmen are vigilant over constituency interest, and their diligence often pays off handsomely in benefits for constituents and groups.

While the merits of each case are undoubtedly important in determining the vigor with which a congressman pursues a constituent's complaint, that is not always the case. Some congressmen no doubt realize that a constituent's complaint is without standing or merit, but this recognition does not preclude them from intervening on behalf of that constituent. As one representative explained:

> Many of the cases that reach my desk...are unmeritorious, and I know it. But undeserving or not, any request to my office is going to be passed along. It's a necessity for me, as a matter of public relations. (Gellhorn, 1966, p. 69)

Some even claim that congressmen are unfettered by the merits of a constituent's case. "They spring into action with uncritical zeal," writes Walter Gellhorn (1966, p. 71), "determined from the outset to win for the complainant because he is a constituent, not because his cause is known to be just." In any event, constituent interests are well represented in bureaucratic decisions: Constituent problems are referred to the appropriate official for quick action (which congressional requests normally receive), district and state interests are protected and furthered through legislative directives, and constituencies benefit from the distribution of federal monies in the form of grants, contracts, and government installations.

Committees. Constituency representation occurs within congressional committees in a number of ways. For instance, members use their positions on committees to ensure that their districts and states get a "fair share" of the benefits distributed through federal contracts, grants, and projects by agencies under the committee's scrutiny (jurisdiction). Committee members are vigilant over the constituency benefits derived from agency programs—they seek to protect and expand them. One example of the dedication of members to serving the interests of their constituents is the tendency for congressmen to gravitate to those committees that oversee programs beneficial to their constituents.

In Chapter One it was suggested that congressmen exercise considerable latitude in the selection of their committee assignments since there is no noticeable electoral pay off to particular assignments. Nevertheless, members choose assignments that benefit their constituents. The rise in multiple committee assignments enables congressmen to satisfy personal legislative goals without jeopardizing constituency interests, since incumbents are not forced to choose between realizing their own goals through prestigious committee assignments or subordinating these goals by serving on less attractive committees. Even if it is now easier to represent constituents because it doesn't detract from what congressmen want to do, this should not negate the fact that congressmen select assignments that benefit their constituents on their own volition.

Bruce Ray has shown that congressmen select committees based upon preexisting federal activity in their congressional districts. Ray analyzed federal outlays in congressional districts held by freshmen in 1970, 1972, and 1974 and their assignment requests. Ray found that there was "a tendency for members from districts with greater-than-average involvements in a committee's jurisdiction to be overrepresented among those seeking the assignment" (Ray, 1980, p. 498). This may account for the frequently observed overrepresentation on committees of certain constituencies that are beneficiaries of federal programs under the purview of those committees.

It is not too surprising that constituency representation occurs on committees closely tied to certain types of constituencies (Merchant Marine and Fisheries, Agriculture, Interior, Armed Services). Many of these committees directly influence programs, like agricultural subsidies, that affect constituent interests. Constituency interests, at least those that can be aggregated to the level of a state concern, are also consistently represented on the most powerful committees in Congress. This is evident in the long-term influence that states exercise over committee assignments: prescriptive seats (Bullock, 1971). Prescriptive seats reflect the propriety claims to committee representation that states have successfully and repeatedly defended in Congress. That is, many states have exercised virtual unaltered control over the naming of an occupant for a vacant committee slot.

States build claims to a committee seat through a variety of means. Sometimes freshmen members are assigned to committees that oversee important state interests but that are less attractive than other assignments. After a brief tour of duty, the newcomer is given a more attractive assignment, and his former position on the committee is assigned to a less senior member from the state's party delegation. In other instances, seats on some committees become regarded as the fiefdom of legislators from a specific district. For example, a congressman may successfully claim a seat on a committee by arguing that his predecessor used the assignment to build a winning coalition and that without that assignment his own political future would be short-lived. Large state delegations frequently argue that size alone entitles them to representation on certain committees. Charles Bullock reported that between 1947 and 1968 over one-third of the committee seats in the House were controlled by state delegations; if we exclude those committee seats occupied by the same individual during the period studied, 28 percent of the House seats were under the control of state delegations (Bullock, 1971, p. 532).[2] Further, about one-half of the committee slots on the most powerful committees in the House (Appropriations, Armed Services, Rules, and Ways and Means) fell under consistent delegation control (Bullock, 1971, p. 533); the pervasiveness of state delegation control on these powerful committees is not matched by the percentage of prescriptive seats on constituency committees. Thus, constituency concerns are pursued on *all* types of committees, even on those without a direct effect on the state. This continuous vigilance ensures that constituency interests are well represented in committee decision making.

Floor Voting. One of the clearest examples of constituency representation is the roll call voting of congressmen. While congressmen need not follow constituency opinion on every matter requiring their vote, two factors normally encourage such vote agreement: The intensity of constituent opinion and the saliency of the legislative issue. When a legislator feels strongly about an issue and his constituents are largely ambivalent, he voices his own opinion rather than that of his indifferent constituents; while his constituents may disagree with his opinion, they do not feel sufficiently intense about the issue to revolt against him at the next election. When a congressman, on the other hand, does not feel strongly about a particular issue but his constituents do, he generally goes along with them. "It is probably true that one rarely finds instances in which a congressman votes against the intense feelings of any significant group of constituents," John Kingdon observes, "and it is even rarer to find him voting against an intense majority of them" (Kingdon, 1973, p. 41). Sometimes members will oppose an intense subset of constituents if they believe that the intensity of feelings among these constituents will be a fleeting thing and that the situation will eventually quiet down.

Salient issues—those that stimulate attention and discussion inside and outside of Congress—tend to be those on which constituency intensity attains its highest levels, and these issues tend to strengthen the agreement between the votes of congressmen and the opinions of their constituents. On these votes "he subjectively considers constituents more important, and he votes more in accordance with their wishes, to the point that the predictive capability of a constituency position is really quite remarkable" (Kingdon, 1973, p. 44).

As in committees, congressmen are equally vigilant over constituent interests on the floor of the House and Senate. They are constantly on the prowl for legislation that reaches the floor embodying provisions with adverse consequences for their constituents:

> Many examples of this kind of protection for constituency industries can be found. For one congressman, it is agriculture: "I'm from an agriculture-producing area, and I'm concerned for farmers' welfare and will look out for them. If New England consumers are suffering, why the hell should I care?" For another, it is the oil industry; for another, insurance; for another, shoe

manufacturers' problems with foreign competition; for another, mineral interests. Every area has its important industry, and every congressman is expected as a matter of course to defend these interests. (Kingdon, 1973, p. 37)

One reason why congressmen may be so concerned about protecting industries within their districts is because they gain political advantage from it. Like casework, protecting an industry is "pure profit"—there is nothing to lose and everything to gain by defending it in Congress.

When congressmen do decide to vote against the wishes of their constituents, they normally have already prepared an explanation for justifying that action to voters. Some of the strategies available to congressmen for rationalizing their votes and "getting off the hook" include blaming the outcome (vote) on the way the issue was structured by parliamentary rulings, citing other votes or actions (constituency service, nonpolicy assistance for constituents) to divert attention, and noting the similarity between a congressman's position and that of another authority that is well respected by constituents. As effective as these strategies may be in disarming constituent opposition, congressmen pay a great deal of attention to the opinions of their constituents when deciding how to vote on the floor of the House and Senate.

Since constituents generally lack information about political issues and the roll-call behavior of their congressman, there may be little reason to expect congruence between constituent opinion and legislative voting. This lack of information ensures congressmen a large measure of latitude in their floor voting, and makes their explanations (of their roll-call votes) convincing. Moreover, most issues are either too remote or complicated for most constituents to promote the type of intense feelings that compel congressmen to strictly follow constituent opinion. Even when constituents feel intensely about an issue, the congressman can afford to give free expression to his own opinion and vote against his constituents from time to time: As long as members avoid a string of "wrong" votes, they can survive a few unpopular stands. Given these mitigating factors, any agreement between constituency opinion and the floor voting of congressmen might seem purely accidental. Nothing could be further from the facts.

There is little question that constituency attitudes and opinions are influential in determining the roll-call voting of congressmen; the magnitude of that influence is a more debatable issue. For example, Lynda Powell (1982) has demonstrated that substantial agreement exists between constituency opinion on several issues and their representative's positions on these same issues, and John Kingdon's study (1973) of the voting decisions of House incumbents also provides convincing evidence of a constituency connection:

> ...if a congressman perceives a constituency position on any given issue, the probability that he will vote according to that position is .76, considerably

better than a chance occurrence. The correlation between the perceived constituency position and the congressman's vote is .49. The only variable which noticeably reduces that correlation through partialing is the position of fellow congressmen, but even considering that powerful control, resilient constituency effects still show through to the extent that the congressman's informants among his colleagues come from similar constituencies. Furthermore, even fellow congressmen may represent constituency influence....In addition to this degree of agreement between constituency position and a congressman's votes, his constituency is also apparently much on his mind as he decides. Constituency was spontaneously mentioned 37 percent of the time, nearly as much as fellow congressmen and more than any other actor. It is also considered by the congressmen to be of major or determinative importance 38 percent of the time, again second only to the influence of freely selected colleagues within the House. (pp. 30–31)

Moreover, constituency influence appears to operate on a whole range of legislative issues. Aage Clausen uncovered constituency effects in several policy areas: constituency was the exclusive influence on civil liberties issues, and shared influence with the president and the political parties on social welfare, agricultural assistance, and international involvement votes. In short, constituency influence was evident in four of the five policy dimensions underlying congressional voting between 1953 and 1964 (Clausen, 1973).

The extent or level of constituency influence tends to be conditioned by several factors. Almost every study of legislative voting has demonstrated that constituency influence varies with the saliency of the issue. For instance, Warren Miller and Donald Stokes (1963) showed that constituency influence was greatest on civil rights issues but virtually nonexistent on foreign policy questions. They also suggested that the influence of constituency opinion was mediated by the congressman's perception of district opinion and his own attitude: Inaccurate perceptions of district opinion were found to be a major roadblock to agreement between that opinion and subsequent roll-call votes.

Constituency influence will also vary according to how we define constituency opinion: A legislator's policy positions are influenced more by the opinions held by voters in his reelection constituency than those held by citizens of the encompassing *geographic* constituency. The geographic constituency comprises the entire district or state represented by the representative or senator, but the reelection constituency only includes those voters who generally support him at election time. Since the geographic constituency includes both a legislator's supporters and his opponents, unchallenged representation of the opinions of the geographic constituency may be a little too much to ask of congressmen; it is far more reasonable to expect congruence when roll-call votes are compared with the opinions held by constituents in the congressman's reelection constituency. The rationale is simple: Legislators' policy positions should be influenced more by their reelection than their geographic constituency, since the latter includes the congressman's opponents as well as his supporters. This distinction between reelection and geographic constituencies helps to account for the differences in the roll-call behavior of senators elected from the same state (Bullock and Brady, 1983).

I should also point out that representation of constituent opinion can occur in the absence of a dyadic relationship between a specific congressman's vote and the opinion positions of his constituents. Robert Weissberg reminds us that institutions collectively represent shades of opinion within society even though misrepresentation may occur on an individual basis: "It may be impossible for one legislator to represent 400,000 people with any degree of accuracy; it may, however, be possible for 435 legislators to represent more accurately the opinions of 220,000,000 citizens" (Weissberg, 1978, p. 547). Weissberg demonstrates that there is a reasonable probability that such collective representation can occur, even if congressmen cast their votes in a random fashion:

> ...assuming random voting by legislators, a majority of constituency–representative dyads will be in agreement 41.2 percent of the time in a series of votes. If we combine this probability with the probability that exactly half of the constituency–legislator pairs will be in agreement (p=.176), the probability is approximately .588 that 50 percent or more constituencies will have their representatives vote "right" even if the representatives vote randomly. (p. 539).

Thus, there is considerable evidence that constituency interests are well represented on the floor of the House and Senate. Constituency influence, however, is conditioned by the saliency of the issue and the intensity of the feelings of constituents on the issue. Factors such as the accuracy of the congressman's perception of constituent opinion and the consensus among members of his reelection constituency also mediate the influence of constituency opinion on legislative voting. Despite the effects of such mediating forces and the lack of information on the part of constituents, congressmen appear to do a good job in reflecting constituency opinion in their voting decisions.

FACTORS PROMOTING CONSTITUENCY REPRESENTATION

Two of the major factors promoting the representation of constituency interests in the bureaucracy, in committees, and on the floor of the House and Senate are the internalization of attitudes conducive to representation and the existence of electoral mechanisms of constituency influence. Congressmen seek to protect and further the interests of their constituents because they believe that this is what their constituents expect them to do or because their political views and perceptions are identical to those held by a large majority of their constituents. That is, constituency opinion and interests are represented because congressmen feel they should represent those interests or because they have the same political orientations as their constituents. Supporting and perhaps generating these representational motivations is the electoral system: Elections are one of the best instruments available to constituents for promoting attention to district or state interests. Elections keep members "in tune" with the opinions and problems of their constituents. Elections may be less threatening to incumbents in the contemporary Congress than in earlier ones, but they remain one of the most potent mechanisms for ensuring the representation of constituency interests.

Attitudes Conducive to Representation. In 1977, a sample of representatives were asked to list "the major kinds of jobs, duties, or functions that you feel you are expected to perform as an individual member of Congress" (U.S. Congress, House, 1977). The list of expected functions is presented in Table 8-1. While there is near universal agreement that representatives are expected to perform legislative duties (87 percent), constituency service was cited almost as frequently as a job expectation (74 percent). The comments of two representatives make clear the significance that members attach to serving their constituents:

> Constituent work: that's something I feel very strongly about. The American people, with the growth of the bureaucracy, feel nobody cares. The only conduit a taxpayer has with the government is a congressional office.
> People turn to their congressmen or senator for help when the rest of the system fails. They don't vote for the Small Business Administrator, or the

TABLE 8-1   Representatives' Views of Functions Expected of Them

Function	Percentage of Representatives Mentioning Function
Legislative	87%
Constituency service	79
Education and communication	43
Representation of constituency interests	26
Political obligations	11
Oversight	9
Institutional responsibilities	7
Office management	6
No specific function; all functions	6
Other	4

Source: U.S. Congress, House (1977). Total weighted n = 146; multiple responses possible.

Farmer's Home Director, or the EDA Assistant Secretary. They probably never see them. They don't vote for the Social Security Administrator. They do vote for their congressman and senator. They see them, know them, touch them, talk to them, write to them. (Cavanagh, 1981, pp. 65–66)

Other expectations also promote attitudes conducive to the representation of constituency interests. For instance, representatives feel that they are expected to keep in touch with their constituents. As one representative observed:

Staying in contact with the people in my district. Answering the mail. That's my first priority, because it may well be their only contact with the office. You let them know you represent them....(Cavanagh, 1981, p. 66)

In addition, 26 percent of the representatives felt an obligation to represent constituent opinion. As one legislator observed,

...I have a collateral responsibility to the country as a whole, which my constituents are part of, but that's almost secondary. I'm supposed to be a spokesman for our constituency and our constituency point of view. (Cavanagh, 1981, p. 67)

Thus, congressmen believe that they are expected to protect, promote, and vote in support of the interests of their constituents. The internalization of these attitudes promotes the acceptance of the representational obligation (representation of constituency interests) that goes along with the job of congressman. Congressmen represent the interests of their constituents because they believe that they are expected to behave in this fashion. Perhaps members gain some psychological satisfaction from successfully promoting the interests of their constituents. A "successful intervention in a constituent's behalf does undoubtedly produce a glowing sense that humanity has prevailed over impersonality. The helpless have been helped. The defeated have become victors. The victims have been restored. The unorganized have gained a spokesman" (Gellhorn, 1966, p. 75).

The tendency for congressmen to be "home-town boys" also promotes the representation of constituency interests. Since many members have been born, raised, and continue to live in the same geographical area, they have probably absorbed or internalized the consensual attitudes within the community. The basic values of the constituency have been ingrained in the congressman practically from birth and are constantly reinforced through his frequent contacts at home. Hence, on some policy questions congressmen represent their constituents by voting their own opinions! As one congressman noted with respect to the problems faced by farmers, "I understand farm problems. I have one of the most heavily agricultural districts in the country. I grew up with these people and I guess I reflect their thinking" (Kingdon, 1973, p. 45). This may explain why congressmen rarely feel pressured by their constituencies: they are part of them. In fact,

John Kingdon found rather high levels of agreement between the attitudes of congressmen and their perception of the attitudes of their constituents:

> In the sample of voting decisions used in this research, the congressman's attitude on the matter before him and his perception of the constituency attitude agreed in 61 percent of the cases. In another 13 percent, the congressman saw no constituency position. Approximately three-quarters of the time, in other words, there was no conflict between constituency and attitude in the congressman's mind. (p.45)

In a sense, such representation is relatively unconscious: Congressmen need not make a voluntary, self-conscious effort to represent constituent opinion or interests.

> Representation of the constituency is involuntary in that it occurs without a conscious effort by the representative and is something over which the representative exercises little control, as in the case of breathing or the beating of his heart. The constituency orientations are an integral part of his being. They are operative in his personal political attitudes, in his cognition of the political environment, and in his views on a variety of non-political matters, some of which become intertwined with his politics. (Clausen, 1973, p. 132)

Thus, representation occurs because congressmen have internalized constituency values or because they feel that they should give expression to those values in the legislative process.

There are a number of forces that promote the internalization of these attitudes, such as the recruitment and candidate selection processes, but one of the most significant incentives is the electoral one. For example, Roger Davidson (1969) found that a representative's style of representation—whether the legislator accepts instructions from constituents (delegate), proceeds on his own (trustee), or acts as some mixture of these two roles (politico)—was related to the level of electoral uncertainty a representative confronted at the polls. "Among respondents from safe districts, 35 percent were Trustees, and only 11 were Delegates; while 19 percent of the marginal members were Trustees, and 44 percent were Delegates" (p. 127).

Elections as Mechanisms of Constituency Influence. There might be some question about the capacity of elections to promote the representation of constituency interest in light of the relative electoral security of incumbents (see Chapter Four). Although elections seem the obvious mechanism for ensuring constituency influence in Congress, Donald Stokes and Warren Miller's (1966) study casts doubt on the ability of the congressional voter to influence public policy. Miller and Stokes paint a picture of an abysmally ignorant constituent: "Although perceptions of individual candidates account for most of the votes cast by partisans against their parties, these perceptions are almost untouched by information about the policy stands of the men contesting the House seat. The increment of strength that some candidates, especially incumbents, acquire by being known to their constituents is almost entirely free of policy content" (p. 210). Despite this evidence, the representatives they interviewed refused to accept this unflattering view of congressional voters:

> Of our sample of Congressmen who were opposed for reelection in 1958, more than four-fifths said the outcome in their districts had been strongly influenced by the electorate's response to their records and personal standing. Indeed, this belief is clear enough to present a notable contradiction: Congressmen feel that their individual legislative actions may have considerable impact on the electorate, yet some simple facts about the Representative's salience to his constituents imply that this could hardly be true. (p. 368)

Is there any rationale for incumbents to have such a hardy respect for congressional voters?

One reason why members may tend to see the voter as a more knowledgeable, issue-oriented individual is because of the bias in the information reaching congressional offices. Most correspondence a congressman receives comes from an issue-oriented group of constituents. Even in their district or state visits, they are more apt to meet an active, issue-oriented subset of constituents. This may give them an exaggerated impression of the knowledge that voters use in casting their ballots. In addition, John Kingdon has uncovered a tendency for successful candidates to have a rather high opinion of the intellect of the average voter:

> ...winners develop complimentary beliefs about voters and losers develop rationalizations for their losses simply by virtue of the outcome of the election. Winners ...believe that the voters did a good job of choosing. Voters in their view are well informed about politics and vote according to the issues and the candidates, rather than blindly following their party. Losers, on the other hand, rationalize defeat by saying that voters are ill-informed and vote according to party label rather than the issues or the men who are running for office. Both winners and losers, in other words, rearrange their cognitions about voters to take account of the outcome of the election: winners congratulate the voters, and losers rationalize their defeat. (pp. 31–32)

In any event, congressmen might be expected to view their constituents as better informed about issues and their legislative records than the facts would reveal.

The major weakness in establishing representational linkages to elections is that voters fail to see the candidates in terms of political issues, especially House members, and that votes are cast only rarely in congressional elections on the basis of national issues. It is hard to refute this argument since there is little evidence of issue content in the images of representatives (though more issue content in the images of senators), and few congressional elections are decided on the basis of national issues. While these conditions enhance the relevance of elections as mechanisms of constituency influence over the formation of public policy, popular control of public policies can exist in the absence of these conditions.

Constituency influence over public policy exists if the opposing candidates for the same office differ significantly in their attitudes on various public policy questions and if the victorious candidates vote in accordance with their preelection attitudes: "If many candidates do not differ appreciably from one another, or if the winners fail to vote in Congress on their pre-election attitudes, there is little reason for voters to become familiarized with the issue positions of the candidates or to vote on the basis of these issue positions" (Sullivan and O'Connor, 1972, p. 1257). In the 1966 election—the only election where data of this nature have been analyzed and published—these conditions of popular control were met: Congressional voters, in the aggregate, were offered a substantively significant choice (Democratic candidates were invariably more liberal than their intradistrict Republican competitors) and the victorious candidates voted on subsequent issues as their preelection issue positions predicted (Sullivan and O'Connor, 1972). In short, the opportunity to influence policy existed even if most constituents resisted exercising the option.

Constituents may fail to exercise this option because there is little reason for them to do so: Congressmen may be so seemingly secure partly because they do a good job in representing the interests of their constituents. "One cannot fail to notice that even congressmen from safe seats spend a great deal of energy looking after constituents and taking account of them as they decide" (Kingdon, 1973, p. 61). In sum, the electoral safety of some members may be evidence of their success in representing constituent opinion in Congress. "They're safe because they vote that way," according to one legislative staffer (Kingdon, 1973, p. 61). Furthermore, electoral safety cannot always be construed as evidence that constituency interests will not be served. Warren Miller (1964), for example, presents data to suggest that incumbents from safe districts actually provided better constituency representation since they voted with their constituents more often than those from competitive districts:

> Legislative acts of Congressmen from competitive districts are associated almost exclusively with their own policy preferences rather than with their perceptions of district preferences. The behavior of Congressmen from safe districts reflects a more even balance between the two factors, but their perceptions of constituency policy positions are clearly more highly related to their roll call decisions than their personal attitudes. (pp. 375–376)

Longevity in office, then, may actually promote the type of linkage that maintains constituency representation.[3] Moreover, congressmen from safe districts may have more accurate perceptions of constituents' opinions than those from marginal areas, because it is easier to discern a constituency consensus in a more homogeneous district, and there is a tendency for homogeneous districts to be electorally safe (Fiorina, 1974).

One final point: Electoral competitiveness appears unrelated to policy moderation. What has been termed "the marginality hypothesis" assumes that a congressman strengthens his chances of reelection by taking moderate, middle-of-the-road positions aimed at pleasing a wide spectrum of his constituency. There is, however, little evidence to support this proposition. For example, Morris Fiorina (1974) finds no evidence that electoral competition exerts a moderating influence on roll-call voting:

> In agreement with traditional arguments, the theory indicates that a closely divided constituency puts the representative in a tight spot. But contrary to traditional arguments, both theory and data indicate that the representative does not gravitate to a spot between the two sides. Rather, he appears to go with one side or the other. (p. 122)

Thus, elections promote the representation of constituent interests in Congress, primarily because they provide opportunities for voters to exercise some control over public policy. Constituents may never exercise this option, but they may never need to since congressmen are responsive to constituent interests and intense constituency feelings. In fact, the longevity of congressmen may symbolize the satisfaction of constituents with the representation they are receiving in Washington. Even safe incumbents keep up the pace of attention. As one "safe" congressman observed, "I have to run the cocktail circuit and go back to the district every two or three weekends just to stay in office" (Kingdon, 1973, p. 61).

POLICY CONSEQUENCES

There are two obvious policy consequences of the representation of constituency interests: particularism in the distribution of federally supported projects and attention to citizen complaints. One way in which congressmen look after the interests of their constituents is by ensuring that their districts and states receive their "fair share" of the federal pork barrel. Within their committees, in their interactions with agency officials, and on the floor, congressmen seek opportunities to further the interests of their constituents in a material fashion; federal projects, contracts, grants, installations, and offices bring money and jobs to the district or state—two benefits that most constituents appreciate. Some may accuse congressmen of expending too much effort in raiding the federal pork barrel, but many congressmen believe that such activity is what their constituents want and expect. And, indeed, constituents do expect their congressmen to be on the watch for opportunities to further constituency interests. As a consequence, congressmen create and seize opportunities to benefit their constituencies:

> Not only do congressmen aggressively seek out opportunities to supply such benefits (little or no "pressure" is needed), they tend in framing laws to give a particularistic cast to matters that do not obviously require it. The only benefits intrinsically worth anything, after all, are ones that can be packaged. Thus in time of recession congressmen reach for "accelerated public works" bills listing projects in the various districts; presidents prefer more general fiscal effects. (Mayhew, 1974a, pp. 127–128)

A second policy consequence is that congressmen are very responsive to the complaints of their constituents. This does not merely mean that a polite acknowledgment is promptly sent in response to every constituent inquiry, question, or request, though this is a standard course of action in most congressional offices. Congressmen devote time and resources (staff) in addressing constituent problems, and they are quite effective in these efforts. Congressmen intervene between constituents and bureaucrats in a whole range of matters—disagreements over a regulation, delays in federal payments (e.g., welfare), absence of administrative action. In some instances, the congressman may actually serve as a lobbyist for special interests within his constituency vis-a-vis his committees and the federal bureaucracy. These "errand boy" activities, as they are unflatteringly called, are viewed by congressmen and constituents as basic elements of the job.

One result of this emphasis on pursuing constituent complaints is that oversight of the executive is provided on a continuous basis. As noted earlier, casework sometimes leads directly to formal oversight hearings or to the introduction of remedial legislation. Casework also offers a more continuous and instantaneous brand of oversight: Constituent reaction to agency programs and regulations may be the quickest way to alert agency officials and committee leaders to problems involved in the administration of a policy or program. The large number of constituents involved in an agency's program, or touched by its policies, provide the type of scrutiny that neither Congress nor its administration watchdog, the General Accounting Office (GAO), can supply. Since legislative goals are stated so vaguely in legislation, it is difficult to determine whether any violation has occurred unless some citizen or group registers a complaint; the large number of constituents affected by a program ensures that any violation that seriously harms an organized group will be identified. Such a system of decentralized "fire alarms" may efficiently counter the huge amounts of authority that Congress has delegated to executive agencies:

> Although Congress may, to some extent, have allowed the bureaucracy to make law, it may also have devised a reasonably effective and non-costly way to articulate and promulgate its own legislative goals—a way that depends

> on the fire-alarm oversight system. It is convenient for Congress to adopt broad legislative mandates and give substantial rule-making authority to the bureaucracy. The problem with doing so, of course, is that the bureaucracy might not pursue Congress' goals. But citizens and interest groups can be counted on to sound an alarm in most cases in which the bureaucracy has arguably violated Congress' goals. Then Congress can intervene to rectify the violation. (McCubbins and Schwartz, 1984, pp. 174–175)

I should also reiterate a point made in earlier chapters: Congressmen do not just respond to demands for their services; they also create such needs by encouraging constituents to bring their problems to them and by widely advertising their effectiveness in dealing with constituent complaints.

Another consequence of constituency representation is that a great deal of legitimacy is accorded the demands of constituents and groups. Groups and constituents are expected to seek a redress of their grievances through Congress and the legislative process—something of a norm in the American political system. While congressmen concede that the influence that some interests have in the administrative process may create problems, they prefer agencies and clientele groups maintain close relationships (Aberbach and Rockman, 1978).

Finally, constituency representation promotes "justifiable" policy voting. Congressmen are constantly called upon to explain to constituents why they voted as they did. They not only experience the discomfort of being called upon to justify a vote, but there is always the possibility that the situation will arise. Since explanations frequently precede voting (Fenno, 1978), congressmen seek legislative solutions that they "can live with." That is, legislative measures that they can support or oppose without entangling themselves in a web of justifications are likely to dominate legislative outcomes. Thus, the ease with which a vote can be justified may be an important consideration in mobilizing legislative support:

> Part of the process of building a coalition around a given piece of legislation, for instance, is providing potential members of the coalition with handy explanations that they can use in case the vote gives them trouble back home. They may not join the coalition without such an explanation. (Kingdon, 1973, p. 48)

Thus, some element of policy representation may be present in the voting behavior of congressmen because they dislike being called upon to account for their votes.

SUMMARY

Constituency interests are represented throughout the legislative process. Congressmen seek preferential treatment for their constituents in their intercessions with the federal bureaucracy. Constituent problems receive prompt attention within the congressional office and the relevant agency, constituency interests are protected and furthered through legislative directives to federal agencies, and constituents benefit from the distribution of grants and government contracts. In addition, congressmen select (and exploit) committee assignments that benefit their constituents. Members are equally vigilant over constituent interests when voting on the floor of the House or Senate; they are especially concerned about legislation that imparts good or harm to industries and groups within their constituencies. Finally, the voting behavior of congressmen is influenced by the attitudes and opinions of their constituents, although the relationship between constituent opinion and roll-call voting is conditioned by several important factors, such as the saliency of the issue and the accuracy of the congressman's perception of constituent opinion; despite these mediating forces, congressmen do a good job in reflecting constituent opinion in Congress.

Two factors promote the representation of constituent interests. First, the internalization of attitudes conducive to representation on the part of legislators creates representational motivations. Simply put, constituency opinion and interests are represented because congressmen share the same political views as their constituents or because they believe that this is what their constituents expect of them. The tendency of legislators to be "home-town boys" suggests that consensual constituency values have been internalized by many members; hence, on some political issues congressmen represent constituent opinion by voting their own opinions. Such representation may be involuntary or unconscious, but it is representation nonetheless. Representation of constituent opinion is also an obligation or expectation that most congressmen feel committed to honor.

Second, elections keep congressmen from taking too many political stands antagonistic to their constituents. Despite the evidence to the contrary, congressmen see their constituents as knowledgeable and informed; their behavior reflects the belief that someone is watching their every action. Therefore, a congressman may follow district opinion because he suspects that to do otherwise might become a salient issue to his well-informed constituents. Furthermore, elections provide voters with opportunities to influence public policy. Constituents may ignore this option regularly because they have no reason to exercise this type of electoral control: Incumbents do a good job in representing constituent opinion in their legislative voting.

The representation of constituency interests leads congressmen to seize and create opportunities to benefit their constituents. Within their committees, on the floor of the House and Senate, and through their interactions with bureaucrats, congressmen seek to benefit their constituents in some explicit material fashion (e.g., federal projects, government contracts, programs). Another policy consequence is that oversight of the executive branch is executed on a continuous basis: Constituent reaction to agency programs and regulations is one of the best ways to alert bureaucrats and legislators to problems involved in the administration of a policy or program. Furthermore, the large number of constituents involved in an agency's program provide a level of scrutiny that is unmatched by Congress, its committees, or its administration watchdog (General Accounting Office). Other policy consequences include an emphasis on resolving constituent problems and on formulating important legislative issues in terms that can be easily justified to constituents.

NOTES

1. John Johannes (1981) reports that the staff he interviewed believed a large proportion of the cases that required bureaucratic intercession were decided in favor of constituents (39.5 percent).
2. In an update of Bullock's initial study of prescriptive seats, David England and Charles Bullock (1986) report that state party delegations continue to control a large share of the committee seats: "Over a span of 18 congresses, 129 seats have been held by the same delegation with brief, if any interruptions, with 124 having passed from one member of a delegation to another" (pp. 499–500). England and Bullock also point out that there has been a decline in prescriptive seats. While there is some reason to believe that this decline may be more a product of measurement than any weakening of the norm (of state control), England and Bullock offer another interpretation:

   The decline in prescriptive seats is a response to subtle changes in power distributions in Congress. The decline in the apprenticeship norm and weakening of the positions of congressional leaders have resulted in fewer restraints on the ambitions of junior members. These legislators are less willing to defer to the wishes of their delegation deans and colleagues by accepting appointments to committees that hold little interest for them. Consequently, delegation control of seats on relatively unattractive committees lapses. (pp. 500–501.)

3. This conclusion is supported by Amihai Glazer and Marc Robbins (1985), who examined the changes in the conservative coalition scores of House incumbents in response to alterations in the composition of their districts resulting from the 1980 decennial reapportionment of the House of Representatives. They concluded that "senior congressmen respond more strongly to constituent changes than do their junior colleagues, who appear to follow constituency changes to a negligible degree" (p. 266).

Chapter Nine
LACK OF PARTY DISCIPLINE

One rather haunting characteristic of Congress is its lack of party discipline: Partisan majorities are difficult to organize and even more difficult to maintain for any length of time. Political scientists, in particular, have bemoaned this state of affairs. Perhaps the best example of their concern over the lack of party discipline (or cohesion) is the American Political Science Association's report on political parties, Toward a More Responsible Two-Party System (Committee on Political Parties, 1950). In that report, the Committee advanced the argument that our party system was woefully inadequate as an instrument for governing society because of its inability to maintain support for well-developed programs. The committee saw a need for parties to demonstrate sufficient internal cohesion to carry out their programs, and they cautioned that the continuation of this state of affairs could result in the disintegration of the two major parties and the emergence of extremist parties.

The notion of cohesive, program-oriented, disciplined parties, where candidates, campaign workers, and voters are recruited on the basis of loyalty to programs and policies is a conception of the American party system that is a far cry from how our parties actually operate:

...[The American party] system consists of parties which are moderate, eclectic, and somewhat opportunist in ideology. Organizationally such parties are decentralized and internally pluralized, containing factions and subgroups often in considerable conflict over programs (conflicts which are papered over often, but not resolved). These are open structures (some would say wide open) with great diversity in the characteristics and orientations of the working cadre of activists. Protest is tolerated, and the insurgents seldom expelled. There is much local autonomy, stratarchy, and respect for adjustment to local conditions. Such parties are presumably heterodox and adaptive structures—not consensual, not monolithic, not closed, nonhierarchical, and not rigid in control relationships. (Eldersveld, 1982, pp. 429–430)

This general description of the party system is easily applied to the behavior of political parties within Congress: parties exist as coalitions of factions and subgroups that exhibit only a minimum amount of loyalty to their congressional leaders. This lack of party discipline is evident by the weakened position of party leaders, the decline in party voting in Congress, and the regional fragmentation of the parties on a whole range of political issues.

EVIDENCE OF LACK OF PARTY DISCIPLINE

Weakened Party Leaders. If the powers of present legislative leaders are compared to those possessed by past party leaders, it is clear that present-day leaders operate at a distinct disadvantage. Barbara Sinclair (1983) succinctly characterizes the legislative plight faced by most party leaders in the twentieth century: "The current leaders lack both a strong intraparty policy consensus and resources sufficient to affect decisively members' goal attainment. They cannot count on members' goal directed behavior being conducive to party maintenance or coalition-building success; nor can they assure desirable member behavior by use of rewards and punishments" (p. 238). Near the turn of the century, however, party leaders were in a far better position to influence the goal attainment of their members and the legislative agenda in Congress. The powerful Speakers of the House who served during this period epitomize the strong party leaders of the past—leaders who were not the least bit timid about exploiting their powers to affect legislative outcomes. The parallel in the Senate to this era of powerful party leadership in the House of Representatives would probably be the period from the mid-1890s until the early 1900s; during this time, Nelson Aldrich (R-R.I.), William B. Allison (R-Ia.), and a small clique of Republican senators dominated the work of the Senate "by influencing the committee assignment process, the decisions made by the caucus, the decisions made by the principal standing committees, and the scheduling decisions made by the Steering Committee" (Ripley, 1969, p. 27).

As I have noted, committee assignments are a prized possession of most congressmen, and past House Speakers have exercised unusual influence over them. "Those who desired a change in assignment knew full well that their chances of advancement depended on the good graces of the Speaker. Conversely, since in this age seniority was far from sancrosanct as it is today, members were also aware that to alienate the Speaker was to risk loss of a chairmanship, an assignment, or rank on a committee" (Cooper and Brady, 1981, p. 412). During this period, then, to oppose the Speaker was to risk what members cherished most—projects and policies important to constituents (and therefore reelection) and committee assignments that provided avenues for realizing personal legislative goals.

The reduction in the formal powers of the Speaker between 1909 and 1911 had the expected effect of heightening the power and independence of the individual member and organizational units, such as congressional committees, and facilitating the expression of party factionalism. By 1940, the power of party leadership in the House had been altered significantly by placing a more severe set of constraints on these leaders than in 1910. Party leaders were forced to engage in the laborious and painful process of organizing shifting majorities behind specific legislation by negotiating with members for their votes and by bargaining with committees and their chairmen to gain their cooperation and support. "Denied the power they possessed over the individual member under Czar rule, party leaders began to function less as the commanders of a stable party majority and more as brokers trying to assemble particular majorities behind particular bills. Denied the power they possessed over the organizational structure under Czar rule or caucus rule, party leaders began to function less as directors of the organizational units and more as bargainers for their support" (Cooper and Brady, 1981, p. 417). As a result, party leaders made considerably more use of their own personal political skills to encourage party discipline rather than their now limited sources of institutional power.

Because of the effectiveness of the rewards and sanctions possessed by past legislative leaders, members had little choice except to follow their party leaders; to do otherwise was not even a viable alternative since past leaders possessed the type of resources that made legislative life worthwhile for many members. This factor alone probably made the arguments and pleas of party leaders quite effective with their members. As party leaders have, of necessity, come to depend almost entirely on personal skills for mobilizing party support behind legislation, the complusion to follow party leaders "or else" has also eased.

There is very little systematic evidence of the extent to which party leaders depend upon personal persuasion or pressure in their dealings with other members. One estimate of the reliance of party leaders on personal skills of persuasion is provided by Randall Ripley's study (1967) of party leadership in the House of Representatives. A particularly interesting aspect of his study dealt with the role of party in the House and member perceptions of the role of party leaders. Ripley asked a sample of 60 congressmen during the 88th Congress (1963–1964) to describe the kinds of appeals that party leaders use to achieve party unity. As a result of these interviews, Ripley identified four categories of appeals: personal ("I need you" or "the president needs your support"), party (loyalty to party or to its legislative program), merits of the issue (arguments dealing with the substance or impact of the legislation), and pressure (implicit rewards or punishments).

As we would expect, given the emphasis of present-day party leaders on persuasion and bargaining in their dealings with colleagues, the largest category of leadership appeals is personal: 86 percent of the Democrats and 48 percent of the Republicans interviewed mentioned personal appeals in describing the efforts of party leaders to elicit their support. Less than one-quarter of the congressmen mentioned pressure in the form of implicit rewards or sanctions (23 percent of the Democrats and 12 percent of the Republicans) (Ripley, 1967). This description is also appropriate to the Senate: "Party unity in the Senate is more the result of the correspondence of views of the senator and the actions of his party than the result of 'pressure' from the leadership" (Matthews, 1960, p. 145).

When pressure is applied, it is normally focused on the most recalcitrant elements of the party; hence, most members escape punishment not because they are necessarily strong adherents to the party's cause, but because party leaders prefer to subject only the most offensive members to pressure. Thus, Ripley found that southern Democrats and northeastern Republicans were more likely than other congressmen to associate the appeals of party leaders with pressure: 36 percent of the southern Democrats and 22 percent of the northeastern Republicans, mentioned rewards and punishments in describing how their leaders appealed to them to support the party (Ripley, 1967, p. 147). In sum, the weakness of present party leadership is evident in their emphasis on personal appeals to encourage party support and the relative lack of rewards and punishments as inducements for following the party line.

Perhaps a more pertinent question regarding the efficacy of the resources possessed by present party leaders is their effectiveness in promoting party support. Again, Randall Ripley's interviews with House members can shed light on this question. When asked, "what can the leadership do to you if you do not support their position," congressmen gave four basic responses: nothing (leaders have no leverage over members who refuse to go along with the party), isolation (psychological pressure), projects involving funds for constituents or small pieces of general legislation could be affected, and committee assignments might be withheld or opposed. The impoverished state of present House leaders is evident by the fact that more than one-third of those interviewed reported that their leaders were relatively powerless and could not exercise significant leverage on them (Ripley, 1967, p. 150).[1]

One reason why members who oppose their parties are free to do so is because party leaders are apprehensive about punishing members in any way. In short, party leaders are reluctant to "crack the whip" to induce party support. Not only do most party leaders prefer the "carrot to the stick," but they abhor using the "stick" at all. Part of the reason for the resistance to negative sanctions is that so few exist, but equally important is the fact that negative pressure (sanctions) may severely damage tomorrow's as well as today's efforts at coalition building. As one congressman observed:

> The theory behind that [resistance to the use of negative sanctions] is not only peace and tranquility and the "polite thing to do" but also "there's always tomorrow"; there's going to be another vote on another issue and you can't stay mad at anybody. If something happens and it doesn't work out, you may get mad momentarily but there's no percentage in staying mad. You need the guy tomorrow. It's a very practical aspect. There's always tomorrow. (Sinclair, 1983, pp. 89–90)

In addition to resisting the use of sanctions, party leaders are even unlikely to withhold rewards from those who oppose them. "Withholding favors from such members, the leaders believe, is likely to alienate them rather than produce leadership desired behavior" (Sinclair, 1983, pp. 238–239). Thus congressmen correctly perceive their leaders as unlikely to use coercion in promoting party unity, and the unwillingness of leaders to withhold favors from those who oppose party policies further weakens the incentives for following the dictates of party leaders.

This is not to ignore the resources available to present party leaders for affecting legislative outcomes. The powers of the Speaker of the House, for example, to determine the length of recorded votes and to set deadlines for reporting a bill referred to several committees—multiple referrals of legislation—provide him with strategic vantage points (Sinclair, 1983, pp. 35–36). Furthermore, party leaders can help members on an individual basis by intervening on their behalf in the affairs of other leaders and organizational subunits, like committees. An aide to former House Speaker "Tip" O'Neill described the utility of such interventions in these terms:

> "Tip" can't assure it, but he can talk to some people. Now, some of those people he talks to, even his friends on Appropriations, might say, "Tip, you don't want to ask me this; it's a stupid request, you know this thing ought to be cut out." And "Tip" will say, "the guy asked me to ask you." So he really hasn't done anything, maybe it will make a difference, and they ask. They

want to use his powers, members do, to get things done for their own districts or their amendments on the floor; they ask him all the time. He doesn't always do them; they may think he does. He may be effective and he may not be when you ask him. But they like him to try. (Sinclair, 1983, p. 38)

Despite these resources, party leaders are ill-equipped to demand any sort of party orthodoxy from their members. "Persuasion around here [the House of Representatives] is very soft. At best it involves evoking a sense of responsibility" (Sinclair, 1983, p. 89). Most resources are insufficient to affect member goals. For instance, party leaders can help members raise campaign funds, and some members may indeed benefit from such efforts, but most incumbents raise more money than they actually need in their campaigns (Goldenberg and Traugott, 1984). Furthermore, it is beyond question that party leaders would prefer to see the least loyal members of the party replaced with more supportive ones; however, party leaders realize that any attempt to withhold electoral support or assistance is only likely to damage the party's position in Congress. If the party deviant is reelected without the help of the party, his or her party loyalty is apt to plummet even further; if not reelected, his replacement is likely to be a member of the opposition party. There is no dilemma here: Rarely would a leader prefer a member of the opposition party to the most uncooperative party member.

Other member goals are equally resistant to leadership influence. Norms, for example, limit the discretion of leaders in making committee assignments and in appointing members to offices within the party. "By and large," Barbara Sinclair concludes, "the leadership can affect an individual member's goal achievement in only a peripheral or sporadic rather than a central and continuous manner" (Sinclair, 1983, p. 27). The more leaders can facilitate or prevent the realization of goals, the greater their influence over their members; their influence, however, also depends upon their willingness to use whatever resources they have toward this end. The inability of party leaders to significantly influence the attainment of important goals and their resistance to withholding rewards from party defectors demonstrate the weakness of present party leaders.

To complicate matters further, the interpersonal skills so central to the ability of leaders to mobilize partisan majorities are becoming less useful. The large number of new members entering Congress during the 1970s handicaps leadership efforts at persuasion since the development of the sort of personal relationships that serve as the foundation for effective persuasion requires considerable time and effort to build. Party leaders have weaker personal relationships with newer members because of the limited number of contacts and the large influx of these members. Old friends are gone and new ones must be made, but the logic is far simpler than the process for most party leaders.

Party leaders in the Senate fare no better than those in the House. In fact, Senate leaders are probably at an even greater disadvantage than their House counterparts in influencing the behavior of their members.

> The leaders of both parties in the present Senate play a limited role in restricting the options and choices of individual members. They clearly receive less deference and have a smaller impact on the members than the leaders in the House. Individual senators are content with this situation. They are willing to make changes in the leadership structure and operations if the changes will enhance their own position, but the members have almost no concern for the strength of their parties as such. Greater power in the hands of the leaders might mean diminished power in the hands of individual senators. (Ripley, 1969, p. 106)

Lack of Party Voting. Perhaps the clearest indication of the lack of party discipline is the rather low level of voting along party lines on legislative issues. If we compare the level of party voting exhibited by European legislatures with that displayed in Congress, it is evident that party voting in Congress falls woefully below the level exhibited by these parliaments. This may be an ill-conceived comparison since the party systems in the United States and Europe are so radically different and these differences alone might explain the contrasting levels of partisanship. Even if we eschew comparisons between voting in Congress and in European parliaments because of cultural and political differences in the party systems and compare voting over time in Congress, the conclusion remains the same: Party discipline in Congress is weak and perhaps getting weaker.

FIGURE 9–1   Party Voting in the House of Representatives 1886–1984 [Source: Brady et al., (1979, pp. 384–385) for data from 50th to 90th Congresses; data for 91st to 98th Congresses are from *Congressional Quarterly Almanac*, vols. 26–40.]

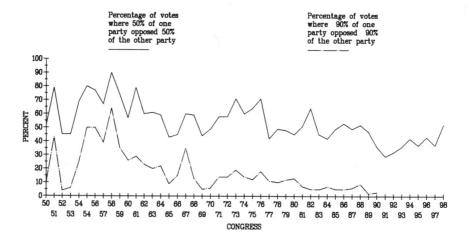

There are a number of ways to define party voting, but two of the most widely used classify party votes as those on which (1) 90 percent of one party opposed 90 percent of the members of the other party, or (2) 50 percent of one party opposed 50 percent of the members of the other party. Since the latter definition is obviously less restrictive than the former, party voting in Congress attains a more respectable level. Regardless of one's preference for either of these definitions of party voting, the trend in both reveal the same pattern: an over-time decline in party votes. In Figure 9-1, the percentage of party votes in Congress between 1886 and 1984 using both measures of party votes is shown.

The notion of "party government"—strong, disciplined, cohesive parties—best describes the period from the late 1800s to the early 1900s. From 1911–1940 party voting recedes, the decline interrupted only by the legislative effects of Warren Harding's landslide in 1920 and the emergence of the New Deal in the 1930s. During the mid-1960s and throughout the 1970s, party voting declined still further, but in the 1980s it rose slightly. Whether this upturn in party voting will continue or fade at the conclusion of the highly partisan Reagan presidency remains open to debate and speculation. Nevertheless, it is clear that party voting occurs less frequently today than in the past.

TABLE 9–1 Regional Fragmentation in the U.S. House of Representatives

Policy Dimension	Types of Issues	Time Period	Most Deviant Regions	
			Democrats[a]	Republicans
Government Management of the Economy	economic and national resources. Examples: public works, conservation, environment, energy legislation	1925–1938	Northeast (-)[b]	West North Central (+) Northeast (-)
		1939–1952	Solid South (-)	Pacific (+)
		1953–1960	Solid South (-)	East North Central (-)
		1961–1968	Solid South (-)	Northeast (+)
		1969–1976	Solid South (-) Border South (-) North(+)	Northeast (+)
		1977–1978	Solid South (-)	Northeast (+)
Agriculture	farm policies Examples: price supports, rural environmental assistance.	1925–1938	Northeast (-)	Northeast (-) West North Central (+)
		1939–1952		Northeast (-) West North Central (+)

TABLE 9–1 (con't.)

Policy Dimension	Types of Issues	Time Period	Most Deviant Regions	
			Democrats[a]	Republicans
		1953–1960	Northeast (-)	Northeast (-) West North Central (+)
		1961–1968		West North Central (+)
		1969–1976	Northeast (-)	Northeast (-) West North Central (+)
		1977–1978		Northeast (-) West North Central (+)
Social Welfare	aid to individuals and social welfare policies. Examples: labor law, minimum wage, aid to education, public housing.	1925–1938		West North Central (+)
		1939–1952	Solid South (-) Northeast (+)	
		1953–1960	North (+) Solid South (-)	Northeast (+)
		1961–1968	North (+) Solid South (-)	Northeast (+)
		1969–1976	North (+) Solid South (-)	Northeast (+)
		1977–1978	North (+) Solid South (-)	Northeast (+)
Civil Liberties	criminal justice procedures, black civil rights. Examples: busing, voting rights, regulation of subversive activities	1937–1950	North (+) Solid South (-)	
		1953–1960	North (+) Solid State (-)	Northeast (+) South (-)
		1961–1968	North (+) Solid State (-)	Northeast (+) South (-)
		1969–1976	North (+) Solid South (-)	Northeast (+) South (-)
		1977–1978	North (+) Solid South (-)	Northeast (+) Solid South (-)
International Involvement	nondomestic policy questions.	1937–1952		Northeast (+) Pacific (+) Interior (-)

TABLE 9–1 (con't.)

Policy Dimension	Types of Issues	Time Period	Most Deviant Regions	
			Democrats[a]	Republicans
	Examples: foreign aid, international involvement	1953–1960	North (+) Solid South (-)	Northeast (+) Pacific (+) Interior (-)
		1961–1968	North (+) Solid South (-)	Northeast (+) Interior (-)
		1969–1976	North (+) Solid South (-)	Northeast (+)
		1977–1978	North (+) Solid South (-)	Northeast (+)

Source: Sinclair (1982).

[a]Positive sign (+) indicates that regional grouping is more supportive of the particular issues falling on a policy dimension than most party members; negative sign (-) means that the specific regional grouping is less supportive of the policies associated with a particular policy dimension than other members.

[b]The regional categorization is as follows: Northeast: Connecticut, Maine, Massachusetts, New Hampshire, Rhode Island, Vermont, Delaware, New Jersey, New York, Pennsylvania; East North Central: Illinois, Indiana, Michigan, Ohio, Wisconsin; West North Central: Iowa, Kansas, Minnesota, Missouri, Nebraska, North Dakota, South Dakota: Solid South: Alabama, Arkansas, Florida, Georgia, Louisiana, Mississippi, North Carolina, South Carolina, Texas, Virginia; Border South: Kentucky, Maryland, Oklahoma, Tennessee, West Virginia: Pacific: California, Oregon, Washington, Alaska, Hawaii; North: all states except those in the solid and Border South; Interior: all states but those classified as Northeast or Pacific.

Regional Fragmentation. Another indicator of the lack of party discipline is the regional fragmentation of the two parties on most political issues and across time. Defections from the party do not occur in a random fashion; rather, they appear to be conditioned by long-standing regional differences among party members. Barbara Sinclair (1982) has identified several persisting policy dimensions and examined the regional voting patterns associated with these dimensions. Table 9-1 summarizes some of her findings regarding these regional alignments.

Clearly, regional divisions are salient on all issues and in most of the time periods Sinclair examined. The most persisting "deviant" regional groupings are southern Democrats and northeastern Republicans. Southern Democrats are consistently *less* supportive than other party members on issues associated with the government's management of the economy, social welfare, civil liberties, and international involvement; conversely, northeastern Republicans are consistently *more* supportive than other Republicans of these same issues and less supportive of policies associated with agriculture. In sum, regional factions within the major parties are powerful obstacles to party cohesion, and the persistance of these divisions over the whole range of political issues, over time, attests to the resiliency of these alignments.

WHY IS PARTY DISCIPLINE SO WEAK?

We can categorize many of the major factors that weaken party discipline as products of the institutional conditions that prevail in Congress and/or the decline in the electoral relevance of political parties. Two historical trends have fostered institutional conditions that weaken party discipline: the gradual decentralization of power in Congress and the emergence of automatic decision rules to replace discretionary ones.

I have already described the decentralization of power in Congress accomplished through legislative reforms. The resulting decentralization made the tasks of legislative leaders more difficult because of the larger number of congressmen involved in a single decision. Simply put, more bases now had to be touched:

> The leadership's task must have been infinitely less complicated in the days of Mr. Rayburn and Mr. McCormack. In Mr. Rayburn's days about all a majority leader or Speaker needed to do in order to get his program adopted was to deal effectively with perhaps 12 very senior committee chairmen. They, in turn, could be expected to influence their committees and their subcommittee chairmen whom they, in those days, appointed.... Well, now that situation is quite considerably different. There are, I think, 153 subcommittees. The full committee chairmen are not inviolable in their own precincts. They are not the great powers that they once were. They are dependent upon their own members for their election and for the support of their subcommittees for the program. And so, the leadership sometimes has to go beyond the committee chairmen and deal with subcommittee chairmen. We always try to work with the person who will have the responsibility of managing a bill on the floor. Increasingly, that is the subcommittee chair's appointment....[Therefore] we have to deal with a great many more people than was the case in Mr. Rayburn's day or Mr. McCormack's day. (Sinclair, 1983, pp. 19–20)

One way in which party leaders have adapted to this decentralized environment has been to include as many members as possible, on an ad hoc basis, in the making of decisions (Sinclair, 1983). This strategy of inclusion may be effective in carving out positions on issues that are not devastatingly divisive to party unity, but it also places legislative power in the hands of those outside of the party's formal leadership corps. Like most members, "coopted" ones must also be convinced or persuaded to follow party objectives. Decentralization, then, weakens the political position of party leaders and reduces the incentives for party voting.

Indeed, the periods when a high degree of power can be concentrated in the hands of party leaders, the result is not only to insure that the full potential for voting on the basis of party will be realized, but also to make it possible to artificially extend or exaggerate such voting. In contrast, when leadership power is decentralized, it becomes difficult to realize the potential that does exist and the sheer political skill of party leaders becomes of critical importance in providing the bare margins needed for victory. (Brady et al., 1979, p. 395)

The adoption of automatic decision rules also reduced the power of political leaders to dispense favors and reward or discipline members. What at one time or another fell firmly within the range of discretion associated with the prerogatives of party leadership have now become matters of rights. Office resources are automatically given to each member and the formula is beyond the manipulation of party leaders. Appointment to committees have become routinized to the point that most members can realize their preferred assignments after very short terms in Congress. Finally, seniority transforms an appointment on a committee into "turf" and the protections associated with longevity in office. These automatic decision rules mean that most members in the present Congress can "get along" without "going along," depriving leaders of important leverage over their members.

In addition, many of the factors that enhance the success of party leadership are largely beyond their control. For instance, Lewis Froman and Randall Ripley (1965) suggest that party cohesion is most difficult to maintain on controversial and/or salient issues—exactly the types of issues that are of central concern to party leaders. The factors promoting the saliency of an issue are also largely beyond the influence of party leaders. Presidents, groups, mass media, and enterprising congressmen are just some of the potent forces that elevate the saliency of political issues, and all are generally beyond the effective control of party leaders. Policies promoted as part of a president's legislative program, advanced by national groups, and/or extensively debated in the mass media, attain saliency with or without the aid of party leaders, and the pervasiveness of these conditions precludes effective party leadership. In fact, one of the major factors influencing the fragmentation of the congressional parties is the nature and change in the legislative agenda (Sinclair, 1981), an agenda that is not necessarily "set" along the lines desired by party leaders.

The decline of political parties also helps to explain the lack of party discipline. The weakened role of political parties within the electorate deprives leaders of a major incentive for mobilizing party coalitions. When the interests of the party are not coterminous with those of individual members, the cooperation and support of party members is practically impossible (or costly) to obtain. If parties have little hold on the sympathies of voters, can we expect congressmen to heed partisan appeals with any regularity? That is, if party is of relatively minor importance to the vote decision in congressional contests, we can hardly expect those elected to have any heartier devotion to their parties:

> If it is true, then, that centralized power ultimately rests on the willingness of party members to vote on the basis of their party affiliation, it is also true that such inclinations do not arise out of thin air. Rather, the ability of party to motivate members to sacrifice their independence and flexibility for the purpose of attaining collective goals and to legitimize such sacrifices rests on similarities in policy orientation and interest among party members; these, in turn, rest on similarities in basic values and goals among the electoral coalitions that elect them to office. (Brady et al., 1979, p. 395)

The rise in split-ticket voting and the decline of presidential coattails as an electoral force provide evidence of the distinction that voters frequently make in casting their ballots for congressman and president. Since voters seem unwilling to select congressmen politically in tune with the views of the presidential candidate they (the voters) support, congressmen feel free to oppose party policies and directives with immunity.

Party cohesion appears to attain high levels following elections where intense differences separated the parties and partisanship determined most votes. Such elections, frequently described as "realignments," produce legislative majorities that are unusually responsive to partisan directives. Unfortunately for most party leaders, realigning elections are anomalies. Party just isn't a critical factor in the election of most members in the present Congress: Incumbents have developed electoral coalitions that are loyal to them personally rather than the party that nominates them. Not only do incumbents survive without the help of their parties, some may even thrive because of it. The recognition a member receives for "bucking the party" on legislative votes or adopting a bipartisan (or nonpartisan) approach to political issues may win over supporters of the opposition party and strengthen election margins. If they are not dependent upon the party for their electoral survival, congressmen have less of an incentive to follow the dictates of party leaders.

SOME POLICY EFFECTS OF WEAK PARTY DISCIPLINE

Three major policy consequences stemming from the lack of strong party discipline in Congress are familiar ones: lack of party programs, policy entrepreneurship, and legislative delay. Without incentives to support the party, leaders cannot formulate party programs with any reasonable chance of success. Policies designed to promote the goals and preferences associated with the political parties require cohesive partisan majorities but the lack of party discipline poses obstacles to the realization of these party programs. Legislative programs must be modified in significant ways to produce any sort of party loyalty; issues are ignored, delayed, or the legislation is "watered down" to achieve a modicum of party cohesion. In the absence of extensive policy initiatives on the part of the parties and their congressional leaders, individual effort largely replaces organized party activity in the formation of public policies.

The lack of party discipline also means that leaders have to engage in protracted negotiations in mobilizing support behind party policies.[2] "The present distribution of power results in a segmented legislative process in which there is no consistently dependable central element that can guarantee a steady flow of outcomes or determine the nature of those outcomes. A constant formation of coalitions for and against specific legislative actions marks Senate and House activity. No single coalition remains in existence for long and none is a reliable winner on more than one or a few issues" (Ripley, 1969, p. 160). The effort and time required to create such coalitions fosters the kind of delays we normally associate with the legislative process.

SUMMARY

Congress is characterized by a lack of party discipline—partisan majorities are difficult to organize and maintain for any length of time. Rather than disciplined parties, congressional parties represent coalitions of factions and subgroups that exhibit only a minimum amount of loyalty to their leaders. Empirical indicators of the lack of party discipline include the weakened position of present party leaders, the decline in party voting in Congress, and the factionalization of the political parties. Party leaders appear to exercise less influence on their members today than in the past because they lack the resources to influence goal attainment, and because they are apprehensive about punishing members in any way. In fact, party leaders are even unlikely to withhold rewards from those who oppose them. Furthermore, the level of party voting exhibited by many congressmen is insufficient to maintain a disciplined corps of party members. Finally, long-standing regional differences among members are destructive of party loyalties and create obstacles to party leadership and discipline.

Several factors conspire to prevent strong party discipline from materializing in Congress. The decentralization of power in Congress has made the tasks of legislative leadership more difficult since a greater number of congressmen must now be included in any policy decision. Congressional leaders also have been weakened by the gradual adoption of automatic decision rules for distributing office resources and committee assignments. These nondiscretionary decision rules mean that members in the present Congress can "get along" without conforming to the demands of their party leaders; this deprives leaders of important resources for dispensing favors and gaining leverage over those dependent upon these resources. Party discipline is also difficult to maintain because congressmen are not dependent upon their political parties for their electoral survival; without the electoral motivation, congressmen have no incentive to follow the directives of party leaders.

This lack of party discipline results in the absence of party programs, legislative delay, and policy entrepreneurship. Policies designed to promote the goals and preferences associated with the parties cannot survive without the persistent support of cohesive partisan majorities. And the effort required to mobilize a coalition of supporters in the absence of party cohesion requires protracted negotiations that foster legislative delay. The relative lack of extensive policy initiatives sponsored by the political parties leaves the legislative arena open to the efforts of individual members; hence, the legislative activity of individual legislators largely replaces organized party activity in the formation of public policies.

NOTES

1. Ross Baker (1985) argues that the decision of the Democratic Steering and Policy Committee to deny "Boll Weevil" Phil Gramm (Texas) a second term on the House Budget Committee, effectively stripping him of his seat on the committee, was prompted more by his violation of House norms than his breeches of party discipline. Thus, rather than a successful enforcement of party discipline, the removal of Gramm from the Budget Committee was the result of "something akin to norm-violation and that this behavior—both in terms of his failure to adhere to his pledges and his immoderate manner with colleagues—was an institutional rather than partisan transgression"(p. 334). Baker suggests that "a conspicuous and notorious act of partisan infidelity, in of itself, probably is insufficient to elicit punishment if it is done collegially and atoned for" (p. 334).

2. The expansion in the number of legislators who manage bills on the floor have also made the task of leadership far more difficult today than in the past. "This tends to create competition for scheduling floor business, clog the channels of communication, and generally make life tougher on leaders (of all kinds) in the House" (Deering, 1982, p. 544).

Chapter Ten
COZY TRIANGLES

The term "cozy triangle" captures the essence of the relationship between representatives of executive agencies or bureaus, congressional committees and subcommittees, and outside interest groups. Douglas Cater (1964) was one of the first scholars to call attention to the subgovernment phenomena:

> In one important area of policy after another, substantial efforts to exercise power are waged by alliances cutting across the two branches of government and including key operatives from outside. In effect, they constitute subgovernments of Washington comprising the expert, the interested, and the engaged.... But the subgovernment's tendency is to strive to become self-sustaining in control of power in its own sphere. Each seeks to aggregate the power necessary to its purposes. Each resists being overridden. (p. 17)

Agencies, congressional committees, and groups are brought together for a common goal: Each has a vital interest in the maintenance and growth of a program or a series of programs supported by the federal government. Committee and subcommittee members seek generous appropriations for district projects or federal grants and favorable agency decisions that promote the interests of their constituents. Bureaucrats pursue increased programmatic responsibility and budgetary support for agency programs.

"The typical bureaucrat can be expected to seek to expand his agency in terms of personnel, budget, and mission. One's status in Washington (again, not to mention more tangible things) is roughly proportional to the importance of the operation one oversees. And the sheer size of the operation is taken to be a measure of importance" (Fiorina, 1977, p. 40). Interest groups, in turn, seek favorable treatment for their members in the form of preferred policies and regulations; the "exchange" relationship between committee members and groups within their constituencies involves the provision of electoral resources and support for those congressmen who advance the group's causes in Washington.

Subgovernments (or cozy triangles) are influential because they effectively make the most of routine decisions in a specific policy area. Such "routine" policies change very slowly, largely in response to the efforts of those most interested in them. Since policy making is frequently routine, subgovernments can function for long periods of time without interference from political actors outside the subgovernment. There is a strong incentive for those involved in subgovernment relationships to reach compromises among themselves because failure to do so broadens the number of participants involved in policy decisions thereby increasing uncertainty as to the outcome.

Given the rather blurred lines between private and public institutions (or governmental and nongovernmental institutions) that is implied by the existence of these cozy triangles, it should not be too surprising that there is a rather constant interchange of personnel among executive agencies, interest groups, and even members of Congress and their staffs. Former members of Congress "retire" to jobs representing group interests in Washington (i.e., lobbyists), and committee staff either gravitate to agencies (overseen by committees that previously employed them) or to interest groups.

Randall Ripley and Grace Franklin (1984) make a convincing argument that the impact of subgovernments on the formation of national policy varies by policy area: ". . .each type of policy generates and is therefore surrounded by its own distinctive set of political relationships. These relationships in turn help to determine substantive, concrete outcomes when policy decisions emerge" (Ripley and Franklin, 1984, p. 22). Ripley and Franklin identify six types of policy areas: distributive, protective regulatory, redistributive, structural, strategic, and crisis. Table 10-1 describes the importance of a subgovernment in a particular policy area, and the degree of conflict or cooperation between Congress and the relevant agency in each area. Subgovernments dominate policy making in the areas of distributive and structural policy—areas associated with unusually cooperative relations between Congress and the bureaucracy. In the following pages, six policy areas and the nature of the subgovernment

TABLE 10-1   Subgovernment Importance, Cooperation, and Conflict in Six Policy Areas

Policy Area	Importance of Subgovernment	Degree of Cooperation between Congress and Bureaucacy
Distributive	High.	High.
Protective Regulatory	Low. Major new decision made by Congress	Low. Potentially high degree of conflict when legislators seek exceptions to general policies
Redistributive	Very low. Major decisions are made in executive branch	Low.
Structural	High.	High.
Strategic	Low. Major decisions are made in executive branch.	Some chance for conflict if Congress becomes involved.
Crisis	Very low. Major decisions are presidential	Low. Little chance for either cooperation or conflict to develop during decision making, though it may arise after decision and event have subsided

Source: Compiled from Ripley and Franklin (1984, pp. 100-101).

relationship that persists in each one are described; this discussion relies on the analysis of national policymaking by Ripley and Franklin (1984).

Distributive Policy. These policies tend to provide tangible benefits in the form of subsidies to private individuals or groups. The beneficiaries of these subsidies are really not in competition with one another; rather, each seeks a high level of subsidization for themselves and ignores the efforts of others to do likewise. Cooperation and logrolling characterize the sub-government relationship in this policy area. Subgovernments—groups, agencies, and committees or subcommittees—involved in distributive policy making are relatively stable from year to year. Examples of distributive policies include subsidies for various agricultural commodities, contracts for scientific research to universities and private laboratories, and grants for a wide range of local projects such as airport construction, sewage treatment plants, and mass transportation facilities.

Normally, disagreements within a subgovernment are resolved through a compromise that is satisfying to the bureaucratic and congressional actors involved in the dispute. Since agreement is relatively painless, there is no need to appeal a dispute to a higher level of authority. Further, both parties have an incentive to resolve their differences among themselves since involving a higher level authority runs the risk of exposing existing agreements among subgovernment participants to criticism and change.

Protective Regulatory Policy. Policies in this area are designed to protect the public by establishing the conditions under which private activities can be pursued. While those most vulnerable eschew any sort of regulation, sometimes they have no choice; in these circumstances, they pursue policies that minimize the regulation as much as possible. The subgovernment relations in this policy area are less stable than in the distributive policy area, partially because of the constant shifting of substantive issues. Examples of protective regulatory policies include prohibitions of unfair business and labor practices, strip mining restrictions, control of harmful food additives, and taxation of scarce commodities.

Conflict is more frequent in this policy area than in distributive policy making. Conflicts at the bureau-subcommittee level normally arise from the efforts of subcommittees to gain exemptions or exceptions to regulations for important constituents; conflict emerges when (and if) these efforts meet bureaucratic resistance. When bureaucrats and subcommittees (or committees) are unable to resolve their disagreements among themselves, the conflict is frequently transferred to a higher level of authority, sometimes involving votes in committee or on the floor of the House or Senate. This occurs with some frequency because participants often appeal to higher levels for support or action or because these higher-level officials intervene on their own initiative.

Redistributive Policy. The distinguishing feature of redistributive policies is that they are perceived as shifting wealth to, or as conferring benefits on, a disadvantaged group in society at the expense of other groups in society. Policy making in this area is marked by high levels of visibility and conflict because these policies create winners and losers in terms of who will be indulged by governmental action and who will not. Examples of redistributive policies include affirmative action policies in the hiring of minorities by employers with federal contracts, food stamps, federally subsidized legal services for the poor, and racial discrimination policies applying to housing and public facilities.

There is a high probability of conflict between bureaucratic and congressional actors on redistributive issues because these policies touch sensitive ideological and partisan nerves; sometimes this conflict can be muted by casting the issue in distributive terms. Conflict is unlikely to be resolved at the bureau-subcommittee level; rather, the resolution is usually the result of negotiations between the president, his top appointees and advisors, and leaders of the relevant congressional committees and of the two political parties. Frequently, however, the resolution of the conflict escapes these actors, sometimes for years. In short, the subgovernment relationship is of minimal influence on decisions regarding redistributive policies: It is the relevant strength of competing ideologies in Congress, the ties of those ideologies to the political parties, and the relevant strength of the parties and the ideological factions within them that determines which view will prevail in conflicts over redistributive policies.

Structural Policy. The characteristics of structural policy formation closely resemble those associated with distributive policy making; the basic difference is that structural policy refers to foreign policy, not domestic policy. Structural policies refer to those programs that procure, deploy, or organize military personnel and weapons. Here, as in the distributive policy area, subgovernment relations largely determine policy outcomes: "Subgovernments composed of actors from bureaus, subcommittees, and small units in the private sector (individuals, corporations, small interest groups) dominate policymaking on the basis of mutual noninterference and logrolling" (Ripley and Franklin, 1984, p. 204). Bureaucrats and congressmen are motivated to cooperate and compromise to prevent the intervention of higher authority levels, such as the secretary of defense or party leaders in Congress. Rarely are the decisions reached through subgovernment interactions modified at subsequent stages in the formal legislative process. Examples of structural policies include weapon procurement decisions, expansion and contraction of military bases, and placement of defense installations.

Strategic Policy. These policies deal with the basic tenets of U.S. foreign and defense policy; they involve the use and deployment of military forces. The importance of the subgovernment is greatly reduced in the strategic policy area since the major decisions are made in the executive branch, and legislative involvement usually follows rather than precedes these policy decisions. Examples of strategic policies include trade tariffs and quotas, foreign aid, and arms sales to foreign nations.

Crisis Policy. Subgovernments play no role in the area of crisis policy. Crisis policies represent responses to a serious problem that requires immediate attention. In such situations, the president and his advisors are the only major actors. Examples of crisis policies include decisions in response to the Japanese attack on Pearl Harbor in 1941, the placement of Soviet missiles in Cuba in 1962, and the Iranian seizure of U.S. hostages in 1979.

Therefore, in discussing the significance of subgovernments and the "cozy triangles" they create, I will focus on two policy areas where these relationships are strongest: distributive and structural policies. Subgovernment relations exist to some degree in the other policy areas, but the relationships are considerably weaker. This might leave the impression that the importance of subgovernments is exaggerated because of the limited number of policy areas that they dominate. In the whole range of government policy this might be true, but with respect to Congress, distributive and structural policies command a large amount of attention from committees, subcommittees, and individual legislators. No matter how infrequently such decisions occur, there is little doubt that distributive and structural policies are an important preoccupation of congressmen (Mayhew, 1974a; Fiorina, 1977).

HOW TO SPOT COZY TRIANGLES

Most of the research on cozy triangles takes the form of case studies of a decision (or set of decisions) or the operations of a subgovernment during a precise span of time. Generally, we have found subgovernments flourishing where we have expected them to operate. While "wishful thinking" may have produced "wishful seeing," since researchers are occasionally biased against outcomes contrary to their preconceptions of those outcomes, this does not seem to be the case in the vast majority of case studies. What type of evidence can be cited to demonstrate the existence of subgovernment relations? The symptoms of cozy triangles include: the overrepresentation of congressmen from certain types of constituencies on committees with jurisdiction over benefits important to those constituencies; the preferential legislative treatment that certain agencies that traffic in distributive and structural policy decisions receive in Congress; and the ways in which bureaucrats allocate the benefits that arise from the policies and programs they administer.

Overrepresentation on Committees. One symptom of the cozy triangle phenomenon is the overrepresentation on a committee of congressmen from constituencies that have an explicit interest in the programs and policies in the committee's jurisdiction. Congressmen with similar constituency interests have reason to form a coalition to support those interests, and the greater the number of these congressmen the greater the likelihood that such interests will be served. In some cases, the similarities in constituency interests may be so widespread that unusually large coalitions form on a regular basis within the committee.

Committees are critical elements in the triangular subgovernment relationship that exists among bureaucrats, congressmen, and groups for at least two reasons. First, a committee not only exercises control over an agency's budget, but it also has a virtual monopoly over all policies and programs related to an agency. This often results in the committee's ability to exercise a veto over any legislation relating to an agency that is introduced by committee outsiders. Granted, committees need the approval of the larger institution to uphold their preferences, but a large committee consensus will often overwhelm any opposition to a committee's policy preferences on the floor of the House or Senate. The committee system also represents an implicit trade: Legislators trade their control over a large number of decisions for exclusive control over a smaller set of policies that matter more to them (i.e., those policies and programs falling into their committee's jurisdiction).

Second, committees are populated through a process of self-selection. Members request their committee assignments from their party leaders, and most obtain their preferred assignments within the first few terms of office; hence, there are few obstacles to the self-selection process, although the availability of vacancies on a committee and party ratios still regulate choices. While members may have several goals to satisfy, the committee system creates no barriers to such goal pursuits. Multiple committee assignments enable members to satisfy many goals, perhaps simultaneously. For example, even if serving constituency interests ranks rather low on a member's list of goals, multiple committee assignments and personal staff enable him to satisfy this goal along with others that he values more. Thus, congressmen find few obstacles interfering with their selection of committees on which to serve.

This means that congressmen from similar constituencies can gravitate to committees that serve the interests of their constituents without sacrificing other policy interests (i.e., different committee assignments) and can expect success in obtaining such assignments. The result is an overrepresentation of constituency interests on those committees that deal with legislation (and agencies) vital to the survival and prosperity of those interests. For instance, many members on the Agriculture Committee share an interest in one agricultural commodity or another (Jones, 1961; Parker and Parker, 1985), and the Interior Committee's jurisdiction over public lands and reclamation projects tends to attract congressmen from western states. In the House Armed Services Committee, committee members represent constituencies with higher than the average employment on military bases (Goss, 1972).

This overrepresentation makes it easier to serve constituency interests since many members share the same concerns, and the number is sufficient to control most committee decisions on matters of relevance to these interests. It is unlikely that members follow district interests in selecting committee assignments because they believe they can increase the magnitude or flow of benefits that their constituents already receive from agencies under their committees' jurisdiction; rather, the representative or senator looks upon the existing federal largesse in his constituency as a ready-made opportunity for claiming credit for the federal outlays that enhance prosperity in the district or state. In short, the overrepresentation of certain constituencies on committees makes these committees unusually sensitive to the interests championed by the biased membership. This means that agencies that administer policies desired by constituency interests will find a strong consensus on the committee in support of these policies.

Agency Favoritism. Another symptom of the subgovernment phenomenon is the preferential treatment that certain agencies receive in the legislative process. The benefits that are provided in programs administered by executive agencies give some agencies a position of privilege. For example, agencies that distribute benefits directly to constituents and groups often find themselves courted and "stroked" by congressmen seeking these benefits for their districts and states. These privileged agencies normally encounter fewer obstacles in justifying their programs and budgets than less appreciated agencies. For example, Robert Thomas and Roger Handberg (1974) concluded after studying the budgets of eight agencies between 1947 and 1972 that highly constituency oriented agencies (e.g., Corps, Bureau of Reclamation, and the TVA) received more generous treatment from the Appropriations Committees in both chambers than other agencies (p. 184).

This friendly attitude toward an agency may lead committee members to adamantly defend the agency from its critics, ignore instances of agency misfeasance, and generally promote the well-being of an agency by protecting and expanding programs and budgets. And congressmen are certainly not supportive of attempts to restructure their relationships to these agencies; hence, reorganization and reform efforts aimed at modifying these subgovernment linkages are usually met with strong opposition. For instance, Roger Davidson and Walter Oleszek (1977) consider the jurisdictional reforms of the committee system in the early 1970s as a major reason for the failure of the reform effort to survive legislative action. "Along with executive agencies and clientele groups, many congressional committees and subcommittees are enmeshed in 'subgovernments' that monopolize specific policy through mutually beneficial relationships. When importuned by their congressional allies, these groups, especially elements of organized labor, fought aggressively to protect their established alliances" (p. 263).

Perhaps a better example is the protection that Congress has accorded the Army Corps of Engineers (USED). The Army Corps is responsible for the design, construction, operation, and maintenance of navigation and flood control improvements in districts and states throughout the United States. Such responsibilities are likely to engender considerable congressional support since these functions often result in pork-barrel projects that benefit constituencies and perhaps enhance the reelection of incumbents. Improving rivers and harbors and eliminating flood hazards are just two of the types of projects administered by the Army Corps that ingratiate constituents to their congressman. Therefore, it should not be too surprising to find congressmen vehemently opposing any attempt to rearrange this relationship or to make the Corps less responsive to the demands of congressmen for Corps' projects in their districts or states.

One example of this protective attitude is the effort of Congress to prevent administrative reorganization of the Corps in the 1930s and 1940s:

> From the very first moment that any proposed reorganization legislation was reported by committee to either the Senate or the House, that legislation contained a provision exempting the USED and its rivers and harbors functions from all provisions of the bill, thus insuring that, under his authority to reorganize and consolidate government agencies and functions, the President might not transfer Engineer Corps functions to any other agency, and further insuring that a planning agency would not have authority to assume any Engineer Corps functions. This exemption is noteworthy because with respect to the reorganization bill which passed the Senate in 1938, the Engineer Department was the only "regular" agency of Government so favored and, with respect to the reorganization bill as finally passed in 1939, the Engineer Department was one of the relatively few "regular" agencies exempted. (Maass, 1951, p. 96)

The Reorganization Act of 1939 expired in 1941, and shortly after that period (immediately after World War II) President Truman requested that Congress reenact reorganization legislation that would no longer exempt agencies from its provisions. Although the Reorganization Act of 1945 contained relatively few exceptions—most exemptions involved independent regulatory commissions—the Corps was once again given preferential treatment. "The Act established three categories of exempted agencies, and the Corps of Engineers was the only agency in the most protected category—that for which Congress prohibited any reorganization whatsoever" (Maass, 1951, p. 97).

Favored agencies not only receive "protection" against executive initiatives that might alter their functioning, but they receive preferential treatment in the appropriations process. Congressional committees normally look out for the interests of those agencies that distribute benefits to groups and individuals within their constituencies. Committee members tend to have "biased" views of these favored agencies, extolling their virtues and minimizing their failures. "They talk of their 'pet' and 'sacred cows,' of bureaus that are 'popular' or 'unpopular' with the Committee. They speak of developing 'a college spirit' toward particular agencies. They say that, 'of course, your personal favorites do better' " (Fenno, 1966, p. 371). These perceptions usually translate into budget increases for "favored" agencies during the appropriations process.

Other considerations also figure into the budgetary success of bureaus, such as the noncontroversial nature of the functions performed (e.g., Food and Drug Administration, Federal Bureau of Investigation, Immigration and Naturalization Service, Bureau of Customs) and the extent to which a bureau's workload produces tangible results (Fenno, 1966, pp. 370–371). However, these latter two factors—noncontroversial functions and a well-defined work load—are considerably less relevant to the budgetary success of other bureaus, such as those found in the Department of Agriculture, which perform constituency-oriented functions for a great number of congressmen. Such agencies provide the linch pin of the subgovernment relationship. Thus, the Forest Service and the Soil Conservation Service are generally more successful than other agencies in increasing their base (previous budget allocation) (Fenno, 1966, pp. 367–413) because they administer programs popular with committee and subcommittee members, and they assiduously cultivate the support of committee members.

The significance of having a committee supportive of an agency and its programs is best illustrated by the House and Senate appropriations decisions on funding levels for the Interior Department. Richard Fenno (1966, pp. 370–413) found that between 1947 and 1962, agencies within the Interior Department were among the least successful in having their budget requests accepted by the House Committee on Appropriations but received unusually favorable treatment from the Senate Appropriations Committee. One of the reasons for the greater support in the Senate is due to the overrepresentation of senators from western states on the Appropriations Committee:

> The Interior Department programs are heavily concentrated in the Western area of the country. The Western area sends proportionately more members to the Senate than it does to the House. Western Senators achieve a greater degree of representation on the Appropriations Committee than they have in the Senate. And, since Senate subcommittee assignments are made on the basis of interest, the Interior Subcommittee is almost wholly composed of Westerners.... Conversely, the House Subcommittee on Interior has been led and, for the most part, manned by non-Westerners. (p. 581)

Thus, Fenno found that the Senate Appropriations Committee not only increased Interior Department appropriations more frequently and considerably above the figure approved in the House, but also by larger percentages than it did for other departments.

Allocating Agency Benefits. Bureaucrats can allocate a given supply of benefits in numerous ways. Particularly important is their responsibility for deciding where funds will be spent and how much will be spent in each state and district. Control of these two allocation decisions gives bureaucrats the ability to regulate the flow of federal funds to individual constituencies. Thus, the basis of the exchange between bureaus and committees and bureaucrats and committee members becomes clear. Bureaucrats, as I suggest later, seek budgetary security, discretion, and growth—decisions that require the support of committee members; congressmen seek slices of the federal budget for their districts and states—decisions within the purview of agency officials. Bureaucrats and committee members exchange support on programmatic and budgetary questions for favorable consideration on allocational matters. "Bureaucrats allocate expenditures both in gratitude for past support and in hopes of future congressional support; and congressmen support agencies both because they owe them for past allocations and because they desire future allocations" (Arnold, 1979, p. 36).

Two committees that generally benefit from the allocation decisions of bureaucrats are the legislative committee with jurisdiction over their programs (authorizes funds and sets conditions for expenditures) and the subcommittee of the Appropriations Committee that reviews a program's past expenditures and recommends new budget targets. The members of these committees receive preferential treatment because they have a greater influence on an agency's fortunes than nonmembers. Committee members establish the agenda for all legislative activity relating to a program such as budget authorizations and appropriations. Further, committee members have access to nonstatutory techniques for influencing bureaucratic behavior that are denied nonmembers. For example, committee reports often contain detailed instructions regarding what bureaucrats can and cannot do and how funds should be spent; bureaucrats treat these provisions with the same sanctity that they reserve for legislative statutes.

Finally, committee members are more important to the fortunes of bureaucrats than nonmembers because committee members may become coalition leaders either supporting or opposing an agency's pet projects. By allocating generous shares of a program's benefits to those favorably disposed, bureaucrats hope to persuade them to lead supporting coalitions, and they allocate benefits to potential opponents of the program to dissuade them from leading the opposition. Thus, bureaucrats tend to allocate a disproportionate share of benefits to members of those committees that have jurisdiction over their programs (Arnold, 1979). For example, Charles Plott (1968) found that ". . .50 percent of all states which are represented on these committees receive almost 80 percent of all urban renewal expenditures at the federal level" (p. 307).

WHY COZY TRIANGLES SURVIVE AND THRIVE

Motivations of Congressmen and Bureaucrats. There are a number of rewards that motivate congressmen and bureaucrats to engage in behaviors that promote subgovernment relationships, but some of the most important relate to the benefits bureaucrats associate with an expanding budget and congressional committee support and the satisfaction congressmen associate with achieving reelection. These motivations define the terms of the exchange between legislators and bureaucrats: Bureaucrats cultivate congressmen to gain their support in general, and budgetary growth in particular, and reward legislators who can supply these commodities. The rewards may range from a cooperative attitude toward bureaucratic interventions by congressmen at the behest of their constituents[1] or the explicit distribution of federal monies to the districts and states represented by legislators supportive of the agency.[2] Bureaucrats, then, seek to protect and nurture their agencies, and to do so requires the cooperation of congressmen in committees and on the floor of the House and Senate. Even those who believe in the efficacy of their programs seek to expand them. In short, whether out of self interest or because of loftier goals, bureaucrats seek to expand their budgets, programs, and personnel. Agency expansion necessitates congressional action and yields reciprocal benefits that each agent to the exchange relishes:

> Congress keeps program administrators on a short leash, first with single-year authorizations and then with single-year appropriations. Although in the short run bureaucrats are free to allocate benefits as they see fit, those who seek long term budgetary security and growth must pay careful heed to congressmen's allocational preferences. If they expect Congress to approve their budgetary requests in subsequent years, they have little choice but to allocate benefits in a manner pleasing to at least a majority of congressmen. (Arnold, 1979, pp. 208–209)

In addition, bureaucrats cultivate political support among legislators who can be counted upon to come to the defense of the agency and its career public servants. From the perspective of the career bureaucrat, political appointees who head most federal agencies are not dependable sources of support in times of crisis. Presidents and political appointees are notorious for blaming lower level officials for programs that falter, and they are reluctant to defend career bureaucrats from attack. Thus, career bureaucrats seek to win the favor of those who are best able to provide the type of support these officials desire—congressmen and interest groups:

> Beyond their sheer impermanence, which injects enormous uncertainty into the life of the agency, these heads cannot be counted on for support in times of crisis. They often do not have great power to begin with, and their long-range interests usually lie outside the agency. Hence it may not be worth the political costs for them to defend a lower-level employee against attack from Congress or the press. The employee is left to fend for himself.... The career official knows this and seeks support elsewhere, especially in the sub-

committees with which he has regular dealings. Having the backing of a powerful committee chairman and several senior members is a crucial asset in the unending bureaucratic struggles that face the public employee. (Warwick, 1975, pp. 78–79)

Expenditures in a congressman's district enable the incumbent to generate favorable publicity that can strengthen reelection prospects. Congressmen gain visibility within their constituencies and cultivate a favorable reputation among voters as they pursue benefits for their districts or states. Bringing home the "pork" not only increases a congressman's visibility among constituents but also associates his name with deeds beneficial to the interests of the district or state. Moreover, the economic prosperity of the district (or state) may be influenced by the allocation of federal expenditures, and district prosperity also enhances the congressman's reelection prospects. "Congressmen consider new dams, federal buildings, sewage treatment plants, urban renewal projects, etc. as sweet plums to be plucked. Federal projects are highly visible, their economic impact is easily detected by constituents, and sometimes they even produce something of value to the district" (Fiorina, 1977, p. 41).

Thus, the motives of congressmen and bureaucrats lead to the types of behavior that foster subgovernment politics. Bureaucrats desire larger budgets and political support—commodities easily supplied by committee members. Congressmen, in turn, desire a strong and continuous flow of federal benefits to their constituencies that is of sufficient volume to impress voters. It is easy for congressmen to see the value of exchanging programmatic support for the allocation of benefits to constituents; the "trade" poses few moral dilemmas since most committee members are generally protective of the programs and agencies within their committee's jurisdiction.

Careerism. As already noted, there is a bias in the committee recruitment process since certain constituency interests are overrepresented on committees that oversee programs beneficial to those interests. Since congressmen are gaining their preferred assignments at early points in their careers, they have less incentive to "hop" from committee to committee throughout their terms. This means that members are likely to establish long careers in their committees and to form long-term relationships with the clientele groups that deal with their committees. Biased recruitment patterns, reinforced by long-term relationships between committee members and interest groups, promote a decision-making system that is heavily predisposed toward the very interests that the committee is expected to regulate.

Career patterns among federal executives also provide fertile conditions for subgovernments: Careerism among bureaucrats is characterized by long service and little mobility. Simply put, many bureaucrats stay in the same agency and the same job for long periods. "In the early 1960s, for example, the higher civil servants had an average length of service of 23 years. Almost three quarters of these individuals had served for more than 20 years. Over 86 percent of them had spent their entire careers in no more than two departments...." (Ripley, 1984, pp. 45–46). The stability in the career patterns of bureaucrats means that they will have long-term associations with the same committee members and clientele interests. Such familiarity breeds cooperative relations rather than contemptuous ones.

In addition, there is an interchangeability of personnel among these subgovernment institutions. Members of Congress and their staff, as well as bureaucrats, frequently move into jobs in the private sector, often taking positions with the very clientele interests that they previously regulated; similarly, interest group representatives assume jobs in the agencies they "lobbied." One example of this interchangeability is the infamous "beltway bandit." The term is used to describe the large number of research firms doing business with the federal government, mostly the Defense Department, that have offices surrounding Washington, D.C. Many of these research firms employ former agency specialists, which apparently aids the firms' efforts to obtain large government contracts. In sum, the career patterns of congressmen, committee staff, bureaucrats, and interest group personnel promote the type of friendly, cooperative relations that foster subgovernments.

Philosophy of Government. Subgovernments also survive and thrive because they have become an essential component of the American philosophy of government. Theodore Lowi (1969) argues that the role of nongovernmental groups in governmental decisionmaking is a recognized philosophy of American politics. Lowi contends that this philosophy accords legitimacy to the efforts of groups to influence national policy: "...it sees as both necessary and good that the policy agenda and the public interest be defined in terms of the organized interests in society" (p. 71). Indeed, Joel Aberbach and Bert Rockman (1978) present data on the attitudes of congressmen that support Lowi's argument. Aberbach and Rockman found a large consensus among congressmen that interest groups should have an important role in government decisions and access to those who make and implement these decisions. Thus, subgovernment relations persist not only because of the acquiescence of the immediate participants but also because they have become etched into our philosophy of government.

POLICY CONSEQUENCES

Cozy triangles are one of the most highly criticized features of legislative policy making. For example, Roger Davidson and Walter Oleszek (1977) provide convincing evidence that the mutually beneficial relationship between committee members and the interest groups with a stake in a committee's decisions hindered efforts at structural reform (i.e., realignment of committee jurisdictions). Some of these relationships, like those between the Merchant Marine and Fisheries Committee and its clientele groups, would have been destroyed through the jurisdictional changes proposed, but the strong reaction from these clientele groups provided the support necessary to defeat the proposed reform.

Another criticism is that these subgovernment relationships prevent thorough oversight of an agency. Because of the mutually beneficial exchanges between agencies and committee members, committees cannot be expected to exercise critical surveillance over their pet agencies; rather, agency programs and personnel are protected, not scrutinized. When oversight does occur, it is apt to be friendly. That is, committee members will do everything they can to make an agency "look good." Even if such oversight should turn up some errors or failures, the treatment at the hands of a friendly committee will be far less severe than that applied by a neutral or critical group. "Far better to let your friends rather than your enemies shoot at you," might be an unwritten rule of agency behavior; however, if a committee is unable to convince its parent body that the oversight was indeed thorough, a far more critical review by another committee (for example, a select committee) might occur.

Even the inefficient expansion of the federal budget can be blamed on subgovernments. William Niskanan (1971) argues that committees are overrepresented by congressmen representing areas with the highest demand for the goods and benefits that the committee controls legislatively. Since these decisions are rarely overturned by the parent body, committee decisions are of paramount importance in determining the distribution of these benefits. As a consequence, committee members expand programs that will benefit their constituents. Since the costs of the programs are shared by all states and districts but the benefits are not, even inefficient programs (e.g., dams) will leave constituencies favored by these programs with a net gain.

Finally, subgovernments promote policies that favor certain societal groups. It should be clear from the preceding discussion that certain constituency interests are indulged in agency programs and committee legislation. As Harold Seidman (1970) notes, "each of the agencies dispensing federal largesse has its personal lobby: the Corps of Engineers has the Rivers and Harbors Congress; the Bureau of Reclamation, the National Reclamation Association; the Soil Conservation Service, the National Association of Soil and Water Conservation Districts" (p.127). Agencies and committees act in concert, therefore, to promote the interests of clientele groups in the constituencies of committee members.

SUMMARY

Agencies, congressional committees, and interest groups form mutually benefical relationships (cozy triangles): Bureaucrats receive favorable treatment at the hands of the committee that oversees their programs; committee members receive generous allocations of the "pork" distributed through an agency's programs, and preferential treatment in resolving constituency complaints—electorally useful resources; and interest groups receive preferred policies and regulations. Some of the symptoms of cozy triangles include: the overrepresentation on a committee of congressmen from constituencies that have an explicit interest in the programs and policies in the committee's jurisdiction; the preferential treatment that certain agencies receive in the legislative process; and the preferential treatment that committee members who have influence over an agency's budgets and programs receive in agency decisions.

Congressmen and bureaucrats harbor motives that foster subgovernments: Bureaucrats desire larger budgets and political support, and congressmen want a strong and continuous flow of federal benefits to their constituents that is sufficient to impress voters. Hence, congressmen and bureaucrats exchange favors for mutual benefit. Subgovernments are also fostered by stability in the career patterns of bureaucrats and congressmen, which breed cooperative relationships. Finally, subgovernments prosper because our philosophy of government—that private groups should be involved in the formation of public policy—legitimizes the efforts of groups to gain beneficial treatment.

These subgovernments are difficult, if not impossible, to dismantle, as evident by the futile attempts at committee reform. Subgovernments also reduce the incentives for congressional oversight since committees cannot be expected to exercise critical oversight over "pet" agencies. Finally, cozy triangles promote budgetary expansion and the indulgence of certain societal groups because committee members expand programs benefical to their constituents and act in concert with government bureaucrats to promote policies favorable to groups within their districts and states.

NOTES

1. Abraham Holtzman (1970) reports that congressional liaison officers in a number of agencies "agreed that members of their substantive committees or appropriations subcommittees took precedence in time and attention as well as services and favors over other members of the legislative system" (p. 183). Thomas Murphy (1972) makes a similar point: Members of committees with jurisdiction over NASA received marginally better treatment than other legislators.
2. Gerald Strom (1975) found that states represented on the House Public Works committee received more funds from the Environmental Protection Agency's waste treatment

construction grant program relative to the demand than did states that had no membership on the committee. John Ferejohn (1975) reached a similar conclusion on the basis of his study of the distribution of rivers and harbors projects administered by the Corps of Engineers: Committee and subcommittee members of the public works committees get more new projects than nonmembers, and the leaders of these committees receive more favorable treatment for their state's budget requests than do nonleaders.

Chapter Eleven
PUTTING THE PIECES TOGETHER

I have now dissected Congress and its members into 10 characteristics. In this final chapter I suggest how these characteristics fit together. This is accomplished by describing hypothetical interrelationships among these characteristics and by demonstrating how they can be simulated in a game-like environment. In the first part of this chapter I describe the various relationships among the 10 characteristics of Congress; in the second part, I describe how a simulation of Congress might be constructed to exhibit these characteristics. I have tried to demonstrate that the characteristics of Congress are important tools for understanding congressional behavior. Each characteristic represents a collection of diverse empirical findings; the greater the heterogeneity of facts represented by a single characteristic, the more useful it (the characteristic) is in explaining a wide range of congressional behavior. Individually, then, these characteristics of Congress can shed light on numerous aspects of legislative behavior and policy making. There are, in addition, some interesting interrelationships among these characteristics that help to explain still other patterns in congressional behavior.

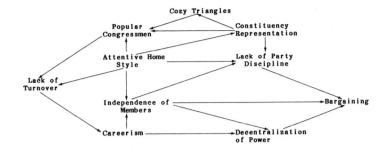

FIGURE 11–1 Hypothesized Interrelationships among Characteristics of Congress

INTERRELATIONSHIPS AMONG CHARACTERISTICS

The relationships among the characteristics of Congress are illustrated in Figure 11-1. The linkages drawn between and among the characteristics of Congress should be viewed as hypotheses that I hope will stimulate further study and investigation. In the following paragraphs I describe the logical relationships between and among these 10 characteristics of Congress.

Lack of turnover in congressional membership can be viewed as promoting the desire among incumbents for some payoff to their longevity; such circumstances triggered the evolution of the seniority system (Price, 1975). The seniority system rewarded members for "staying around" and established patterns of succession to positions of power. Another benefit of the seniority system is that it offers members protection against the discretionary actions of their leaders, which in turn promotes the independence of congressmen and senators. Perhaps more important, the seniority system has enhanced the independence of committees since members cannot be removed by party leaders except under unusual conditions.

A committee's membership, secure in knowing that party leaders cannot easily reorganize the committee or alter its membership, can exercise considerable power both by serving as voting cues (if there is a consensus of opinion within the committee) for the less informed and by supplying policy leadership because of the committee's substantive jurisdiction and specialization. Both conditions serve to decentralize power within Congress. This decentralization is reinforced by the desire of legislators to exercise power—a motivation associated with the independence of congressmen. The decentralized structure of Congress creates multiple decision points (or veto groups) in the legislative process which necessitate the bargaining processes that are so characteristic of Congress. Again, the independent nature of congressmen promotes this characteristic: Independent legislators cannot be commanded; they must be persuaded or convinced.

A final characteristic promoting bargaining is the lack of party discipline and cohesion: The relative inability or unwillingness of party leaders to discipline recalcitrant colleagues denies them a powerful sanction to command obedience. Without such sanctions, leaders find it necessary to bargain with their members for legislative support. While bargaining has always and will always mark Congress, the extent to which leaders have emphasized bargaining rather than discipline serves to reinforce the expectations of members that bargaining is an established mode of legislative leadership. Here again, the independence of congressmen fosters this characteristic. Since independent congressmen are neither beholden to their parties nor necessarily committed to their party's legislative efforts, there is little incentive for them to follow the dictates of their leaders. The result is a general lack of party discipline and voting cohesion.

An important factor sustaining the independence of congressmen is the adoption of attentive home styles. Attentive home styles promote constituent trust, which enables members to exercise freedom in their behavior in Washington. This political maneuverability, in turn, enhances the independence of congressmen. The persistence of attentive home styles, like the independence of congressmen, reduces party cohesion: Attentive home styles promote constituent trust and political freedom in Washington, enabling incumbents to exercise voting leeway—legislators are not forced to follow either the preferences of their constituents or those of their party leaders. Political maneuverability reduces the incentives to follow party leaders and thereby weakens party cohesion.

Attentive home styles also sustain two other characteristics of Congress: the popularity of congressmen and the representation of constituency interests. Attentive home styles foster favorable impressions of the incumbent and his performance in office. These images are tinged with a positive valence that, when taken together, enhance the popularity of congressmen. Since attentive home styles are predicated on serving the interests of constituents, such behavior promotes constituency representation. The desire to serve constituency interests can create cross-pressures on members, countering partisan appeals and arguments, and reducing the compulsion to follow the party's position on legislative matters—obstacles to party cohesion. Finally, attentive home styles reduce turnover in Congress by promoting images especially beneficial to electoral support and by helping marginal members expand their electoral coalitions through nonprogrammatic behavior.

Constituency representation sustains two other characteristics: the existence of cozy triangles and the popularity of congressmen. Congressmen can enhance their popularity by demonstrating that they are serving the interests of their constituents. This may mean the favorable resolution of a constituent's complaint or the diversion of federal funds for district or state projects. Whatever the service provided, the preoccupation with the representation of the interests of constituents enhances the popularity of incumbents, and the pursuit of constituency benefits promotes the mutually beneficial relationships that we associate with cozy triangles. By serving organized groups in a member's constituency and granting them favorable treatment, an agency earns a congressman's gratitude for making him popular among his constituents. Popularity, in turn, promotes electoral safety and reduces membership turnover by discouraging strong opposition candidates from challenging incumbents.

These interrelationships account for a significant amount of the behavior we associate with the activities of legislators, but they do not represent an overarching theory of legislative behavior. Rather, these interrelationships should be viewed as hypotheses that link together diverse generalizations. Hopefully, future theoretical developments can build upon these generalizations and their interrelationships in constructing broad-gauged theories about Congress.

SIMULATING MAJOR CHARACTERISTICS OF CONGRESS

I have tried to demonstrate that the characteristics of congressmen and the institution in which they serve are important forces in shaping legislative policy making. These characteristics can serve, therefore, as a basis for constructing a simulation of the legislative process. In this section, I describe the principles involved in organizing a simulation of the legislative process that exhibits many of the characteristics of Congress discussed in this book. Since most scholars who use simulations (participant as contrasted with computer simulations) in their research or teaching find it necessary to modify their simulations to meet certain contingencies or experimental conditions, I describe only the basic features that such a legislative simulation might incorporate. This should ease the task of adapting the simulation to the specific needs of the instructor, the students, or situational constraints.

Many of the parameters of the simulation can be modified to simulate the composition of past congresses or hypothetical ones or to expand or contract the number of leadership positions within the simulation to accommodate large classes or experimental situations. For example, although the simulation makes no provision for a subcommittee system, this additional layer of legislative structure could be added to the simulation with little alteration in the overall organization and operation of the simulation. I also describe my own experiences in supervising a simulation of Congress and how I address some of the more technical questions that arise in using it for teaching purposes; hopefully, my own experiences will aid instructors in directing their own simulations of the legislative process.

Assumptions. There are three basic assumptions in the operation of the simulation. First, the simulation is restricted to modeling the U.S. House of Representatives. A number of features of the House recommend it for simulation. For example, the House has a greater hierarchical organization than the Senate, which permits a more objective identification of positions of influence and therefore a more elaborate power structure. The varying levels of power within the simulation sharpen bargaining skills among the participants by equipping some with greater leverage in striking bargains, and hierarchical power structures tend to stimulate the interest of students in holding and exercising power. The regular two-year electoral cycle in the House fosters more consistent attention to constituent opinion and interests than the six-year Senate term and accompanying staggered electoral cycle. Thus, all participants labor under the same electoral exigencies and approach their representational obligations with the same degree of immediacy. Finally, the more limited size of congressional districts, as compared to Senate constituencies (states), limits the students' concerns and makes the job of representing constituent interests far more manageable. It also promotes the type of particularism that is one of the most fascinating and identifiable features of the legislative process—pork-barreling.

While I have found this assumption useful in my own simulations for the reasons already mentioned, there is no reason why the simulation could not be adapted to model the U.S. Senate. Changes in rules (for example, the introduction of some form of filibuster) are probably warranted in modeling the behavior of senators and the Senate. The instructor will also want to give attention to how the characteristics of the Senate differ from that of the House and what effect these differences might have on the organization of the simulation.

The second assumption is that the Senate will affirm the decision of the House without altering it in any way. In short, there is no need for a conference between the House and Senate once legislation is passed because "both" houses are assumed to have passed identical versions of the same bill. This assumption is necessary in organizing a simulation of Congress that only incorporates the actions of one of the two legislative branches. Therefore, we must assume that the actions of the "other" branch confirm the decisions of the simulated institution. While there are very few issues of major importance that the House and Senate will agree upon without hashing out their differences in a conference committee, attempting to simulate both branches of Congress is an immensely difficult task of coordination. Further, ignoring the existence of a second house (assuming a unicameral legislature) diminishes some of the reality of the simulation of Congress.

Finally, the simulation assumes committee government. This is a pretty accurate assumption of the loci of power within the House and Senate, though subcommittees have gradually gained influence as decision-making arenas. With a large number of students it might be useful to add a subcommittee layer of organization to each committee to permit individuals more influence within the simulation than might occur with only a committee system; some committees in the House have expanded their subcommittee structure in order to create such additional positions of legislative leadership (Parker, 1986a). However, such a further dispersion of authority tends to slow the simulation, and makes meetings outside of class (subcommittee meetings) a necessity. Subcommittees not only slow the operations of the simulation, but they may also reduce the value that students associate with positions of legislative power. The addition of another set of leaders (subcommittee leaders) tends to deflate the worth of leadership positions since most individuals can boast of holding one. While it is true that positions of legislative power have increased to the point that most members indeed can claim a position of institutional influence, equipping participants in the simulation with the same opportunities obscures the delineations of power and influence that mark Congress.

These three assumptions—the simulation is restricted to the House, the Senate will concur with decisions reached in the House, and the major organizational unit for making legislative decisions is the committee— serve as the foundation for organizing a simulation of Congress. Five categories of legislative actors assume roles in the simulation: congressmen, the White House, party leaders, committee leaders, and leaders of informal groups or voting blocs. The roles and responsibilities of these five legislative actors are described in the following pages.

LEGISLATIVE ACTORS

A variety of individuals are involved in the legislative process, some playing direct roles in the passage or defeat of legislation while others exercise indirect influence; similarly, some actors may be important in a dramatic way on some legislative measures but ineffective on others. Five legislative actors with direct influence over the course of most legislation are congressmen, executive branch officials, party leaders, committee leaders, and the leaders of organized voting blocs. While few of these officials are likely to influence the course of each and every piece of legislation, collectively they profoundly affect the nature of policy making within the House.

Congressmen. The central actors in the simulation are the individual congressmen. Each participant in the simulation is assigned (or selects) a given set of political characteristics: political party, region of the country in which the district is located, and the degree of urbanization of the district. Instructors can modify the distributions of these characteristics among the participants to simulate different political conditions (e.g., divided control of Congress and the White House, large or small legislative majorities, over-representation of areas gaining or losing population) by altering the preferences or assignments of the participants. In addition to these characteristics, each participant selects a district to represent within a given range of electoral security: marginal (previous electoral vote was less than 55%) or safe (previous electoral margin was equal to or greater than 60%). Of course, the exact levels of electoral security can be adjusted to suit the designs of the instructor in the same way that other political characteristics can be altered to simulate different political conditions within Congress.

Acting as a representative of a district the participant or student evaluates the interests of the district and arrives at a political solution as how to best represent the interests of the district and those within the district that provide the basis of his electoral support. The student is expected to be knowledgeable about the following aspects of the congressional district that he represents: (1) the interests that are economically and politically important within the district; (2) the past voting behavior of the congressman who actually represents that district in the House of Representatives, as well as his reelection margins; and (3) the predictable distribution of constituent opinion on various policy issues.

Information concerning incumbent legislators and their political fortunes can be obtained from numerous sources. Good overviews can be found in *Politics in America* and *The Almanac of American Politics*, which contain biographical information concerning present members of Congress, committee assignments, ratings by important lobby groups, tabulations of recent key votes in Congress, and previous election results. Other sources of biographical information include the *Congressional Directory* (with material supplied by the incumbents themselves); *Who's Who in America*; *Who's Who in American Politics*; the profiles of members of Congress developed by Ralph Nader; the indices to the *Congressional Record*, *Congressional Quarterly* publications, *National Journal*, *New York Times*, *Washington Post*, and other journals and periodicals. Statistical information for each congressional district has been compiled by the Bureau of the Census: *Congressional District Data Book*. Additional information about congressional districts can be obtained from *Politics in America, Almanac of American Politics* and, occasionally, *Congressional Quarterly Weekly Report*.

As the participant examines his own objectives in light of the need to maintain a coalition capable of ensuring reelection, he makes certain decisions concerning the kind of legislator he wants to be. Put another way, the student decides upon the roles to be performed within the simulation. The participant will need to allocate his time between legislative interests, bargaining and negotiation among colleagues, and "running errands" for one's constituents. The student will need to decide to what extent, and on what particular issues, to follow the dictates of the constituents, party leadership, or conscience. As a legislator, the student will also have to develop a stance toward the president, the political party to which he is affiliated, and relevant interest groups.

In addition to decisions relating to these roles, it is necessary for each student to establish personal goals and to pursue them. Unfortunately, the pursuit of individual goals often conflicts with constituency demands, forcing members to try to balance the two—keeping home fences mended while attaining more personal legislative goals. This dilemma confronts most members of Congress, and its resolution is apt to vary from member to member since there is no "ideal" solution to the problem and each member tackles it with some degree of individuality.

This dilemma is simulated by requiring students to rank three salient legislative goals—power, influence over specific policies, and reelection—and to hypothetically allocate their personal time to legislative and constituency affairs. These goals should be ordered in ways that are consistent with the proportion of time devoted to legislative and constituency work. For instance, the goal ranked highest by a participant should receive the majority of his time and considerably more time than goals ranked below it. Forcing participants to consider the expenditure of their personal time at the same point at which they order their personal goals highlights the classic dilemma for congressmen: the need to balance personal aspirations against electoral and representational responsibilities within rigid limits of personal time and energy.

The rankings of goals and the allocation of time help to define the "home" and "hill" styles of congressmen. Because of the uniqueness of home styles and the individuality that they exhibit, even members who rank their goals in an identical way and allocate the same amounts of time to personal and constituency pursuits can be expected to approach the representation of their constituencies differently. Not only might the districts of these members differ, thereby requiring contrasting home styles, but the strategies that the individuals pursue in realizing these goals may also depart rather radically. This occurs because home styles reflect a fit between goals and personality. That is, some members would not follow the strategies of others because of the constraints imposed by their own personality. For example, some members could not assume a flamboyant attitude, like former congressman Adam Clayton Powell (D-N.Y.), even if it would win votes; others may find it difficult to maintain a "good old boy" image no matter how electorally successful such a posture might be. Congressmen weigh the costs and benefits involved in adopting a certain type of home style, and the patterns of behavior they choose reflect their personalities, aspirations, and electoral necessities. For these reasons, each participant can be expected to exhibit some individuality in the design of an effective home style.

In order to force participants to consider how they intend to represent their districts within the range of available time, and consistent with their own personalities and aspirations, each student is asked to write a paper that describes the type of home-style behaviors and images that he intends to pursue while at home. The student is expected to adequately justify the selection of whatever complexion of behaviors he proposes to pursue at home in terms of their effectiveness in enhancing electoral support and political leeway. One final point: The extent to which the student should follow the behavior of the actual congressman from the district is entirely up to the individual student. In no sense is the student expected to perform the role of the real-life incumbent who presently serves the district. On the other hand, the incumbent's statements and voting record provide an instructive model of how to deal with a given constituency.

In addition, each student is asked to look out for the interests of some element of society (e.g., environmentalists, citizens in western states, poor, unemployed, small businesses, farmers). This assures that all segments of society receive some representation. This is a necessary facet of the simulation since the selection of congressional districts often leaves some areas of societal interest unrepresented. The ability of the student to advance the causes of that segment of society assigned to him provides an indicator of his effectiveness in the legislative assembly. Students demonstrate how they have served their assigned interest by writing a brief paper describing the actions taken to advance those interests.

Executive Branch. One of the major sources of policy initiative is the White House. Through a variety of mechanisms, and with an arsenal of resources, presidents set the legislative agenda for Congress and seek to have their legislative preferences become law. In the simulation, a group of three to five participants exercises collective responsibility for the president's performance during the simulation. The most important responsibility is to formulate and work for the passage of the president's legislative program, which is initially presented in the State of the Union address at the first general session of Congress and describes the major elements of the president's program. Throughout the simulation, the president will endeavor to have his program enacted by lobbying, giving testimony before committees, and presenting special messages to Congress. To accomplish these tasks, the White House is expected to make full use of the resources of the office, which include awarding a limited number of federal contracts to congressional districts, threatening presidential vetos, pleading for party support or bipartisanship, exploiting personal friendships and contacts, and helping members to get their "pet" bills passed by Congress and signed into law.

The instructor must decide whether the Democrats or the Republicans will control the White House. Often this decision will reflect the interests of the instructor in simulating different types of congresses and institutional arrangements. For example, the instructor might want to explore the effects of unified party control of government by the Republican Party, an institutionalized minority, or to experiment with the effects of majority party control of the White House *and* Congress.

My own preference is to split control of government, either by having the minority party in the electorate control the White House or the Congress. The rationale for divided control of government is that it helps to reduce the frustration that goes along with being a member of the minority party. Since the majority party in the simulation controls the flow of legislation to and from committees, minority party congressmen exercise little influence over the substance of legislation, especially legislation favored by the majority party. My experience has been that by dividing control of government between the Republican and Democratic Parties, minority party congressmen gain influence over legislation. This not only reduces their frustration but also maintains their interest in the simulation. The literature on Congress is replete with examples of the frustrations encountered by minority party congressmen due to their minimal involvement in policy making. Divided control of government, however, tends to strengthen the hand of the minority party in influencing legislation, even legislation that has the backing of the majority party.

Party Leaders. The responsibility for mobilizing partisan majorities to defeat or pass legislation falls primarily to the elected leaders of the individual parties. The formal leadership of the parties is involved in formulating legislation, "pushing" bills through committees, and managing voting patterns on the floor of the House. These leaders are elected by their colleagues to serve as the party's leadership: The minority party elects a minority leader while the majority party elects the Speaker *and* the majority leader. These leaders are assisted by "whips"—one for each party—who are appointed by each party's highest ranking leader. That is, the Speaker of the House selects the majority whip while the minority leader appoints the minority whip. These leaders may be assigned committee responsibilities, but my own experience has been that the assignment of leaders to individual committees confuses power distributions in the simulation, elevating the influence of party leaders and reducing the influence of committee leaders.

Leaders cannot function without resources for enticing members to follow them. Most congressional leaders exploit their personal charm and charisma in generating support for their legislative measures, and leaders in the simulation will also have to place heavy reliance upon their personal relations with their colleagues in inducing cooperation and support. In addition to their personal appeal, party leaders in the simulation are also equipped with certain legislative resources similar to those possessed by past and present leaders in the House of Representatives. The Speaker possesses the following powers:

1. assigning members of the majority party to specific committees
2. appointing the leaders of each of the committees (committee chairperson)
3. assigning legislative measures to individual committees (unless the ruling is appealed by a majority vote)
4. scheduling legislative business

These powers provide party leaders with resources for inducing support and influencing the outcome of legislative deliberations. For instance, the majority leadership can use the assignment of members to preferred committees as a means of eliciting future support from their party colleagues; the appointment power also ensures that party leaders will have the cooperation of the leaders of the committees. The assignment of bills to committees and the establishment of the legislative schedule (the order of bills considered by the House) also enable majority leaders to influence legislative outcomes. At times, the majority and its leaders may want to withhold certain bills from floor consideration in order to extract some desired compromise on the part of individual congressmen, the minority party, or the White House; or bills may be assigned to certain committees that are more likely than others to support the preferences of the majority leadership. While party leaders are expected to use their own interpersonal skills to elicit party support, these formal powers ensure that party leaders also possess some real sanctions and rewards to encourage support.

The minority party is far more impoverished in terms of legislative resources than the majority party; assigning control over the White House to the minority party helps to equalize the resources between the minority and majority parties. The minority leader possesses the same powers as the majority leadership: appointing committee leaders (ranking minority member on each committee) that lead the minority's opposition to legislation within committees and assigning minority party members to specific committees. All powers to assign bills to committees or to schedule legislation, however, fall entirely to the Speaker.

My experience has been that there is a tendency for the majority party to exploit their control over legislative scheduling to punish the minority party for their opposition to certain legislative initiatives sponsored by the majority party or to use the scheduling of legislation to extort minority party support. While one of the informal rules of the simulation is that

preference is given to the legislative program of the president in scheduling legislation, partisan acrimony leads at times to the avoidance of this
informal principle. For this reason, I introduce the rule that the minority
party, speaking on behalf of the president (assuming a minority party
president), may request that a single legislative measure receive priority
treatment, which makes it the first piece of legislative business at the next
floor session. This ensures that the president's program gets the type of
attention on the floor of the simulation that it receives in the House of Representatives.

Other Leaders.   Committee leaders and leaders of informal voting blocs
also exercise considerable legislative influence. Committee leaders preside
over deliberations within their committees, exercise discretion in the conduct of committee debate, and schedule legislation for committee consideration. Committee leaders, although initially appointed by the
majority leadership, are an independent lot: They are primarily concerned
with running their committees and enhancing their committees' prestige
within the chamber; the latter is related to the success of committees in
having their legislation approved without damaging amendments on the
floor of the House. These goals often put committee leaders at odds with
their party leaders, encouraging bargaining and persuasion. The same is
true for the ranking minority member of each committee: Their loyalties
are normally divided between the party and their committees. Committee
leaders, whether they be the leader or ranking minority member, exercise
some degree of discretion as they approach their responsibilities, even
though they owe their initial appointment to the party's leadership. Part
of the basis for the independence of these leaders stems from the fact that
once appointed, they cannot be removed. For this reason, party leaders
need to exercise care in selecting committee leaders to ensure their loyalty to the party since the course of the simulation tends to enhance the independence of these leaders.

Informal voting blocs are also an important determinant of legislative outcomes in the House. Many of these voting blocs are organized
around the geographical location of congressional districts or ideological
identifications. In the House such informal groups as the Democratic
Study Group, the Wednesday Group, or individual state caucuses provide
members with cues as how to vote, information about pending legislation,
and influence beyond that exercised by a single individual. The influence
of informal groups stems from their ability to organize as a reliable voting
bloc. That is, the cohesion of informal groups, as well as their "numbers,"
make them valuable allies in forming successful legislative coalitions.

Informal groups tend to emerge rather idiosyncratically within the
simulation as events and legislation dictate. For instance, ideological
voting blocs appear when particular ideological issues are being hotly

debated within the simulation, and geographically centered voting factions often arise when constituency interests are at stake. At times, some of these informal groups organize by electing leaders and devising a legislative agenda. When informal groups organize, and not with respect to just a single issue or set of issues, the bloc can exercise unusual influence within the simulation as both the minority and majority parties court their support. The existence of informal groups or voting blocs introduces another set of important legislative leaders into the simulation and disperses power even further within the game. These informal groups may have a partisan or bipartisan membership base, but the key to their legislative success depends upon the ability of their leaders to consistently "deliver" blocs of votes in support of, or opposition to, legislative measures.

CONGRESSIONAL COMMITTEES

One of the critical junctures in legislative decision making occurs in House committees, since major legislation rarely reaches the floor of the House of Representatives for a vote without first surviving committee scrutiny. A distinctive attribute of House committees is that some are more "attractive" to incumbents than others. This is evident by the patterns in committee transfers (members giving up an assignment on one committee for an assignment to another committee): Few members leave prestigious committees to go elsewhere, and the least prestigious committees can rarely hold on to their members for any length of time. Members frequently take the first available opportunity to transfer from a committee low in prestige to one of greater prestige. Prestigious committees appear to share two characteristics: They have government-wide responsibilities that are institutionalized into legislative jurisdictions, and appointment to them is limited.

Since committees in the simulation are designed to approximate those in the House, they are also hierarchically ordered to reflect their importance and prestige in the same way as in the House of Representatives. This is accomplished by varying the *opportunities* for members to obtain assignment to certain committees. This makes some committee assignments scarce, and therefore more "valuable," than others. The power of party leaders to decide the committee assignments of their members ensures them control over a currency of variable value that can be used to elicit present or future support: The committee assignments that are the most difficult to obtain will "cost" the most, and the recipients of choice assignments are expected to pay dearly to obtain them.

Committee Assignments. There are a number of ways to structure participant perceptions of the significance (prestige and influence) of individual committees. The instructor or experimenter can alert the participants to the most and least important committees, or certain committees can be assigned broader legislative responsibilities (wide versus narrow committee jurisdictions). Perhaps the simplest way is to vary the size of the committees; this defines some committee assignments as more difficult to obtain than others. My own experience is that using all three methods to influence perceptions of the importance of individual committees strengthens the notion of a prestige hierarchy within the committee system.

Clearly, some committee assignments that might seem less valuable because of the narrow confines of their legislative jurisdictions and the size of the committee are nevertheless quite attractive to some members. This is one result of the multiple goals pursued by members and the wide range of strategies available to them for realizing these goals. That is, not all members may desire assignment to the most important and powerful committee if power is ranked below other goals. Interest in particular policy questions, the existence of a vacant committee leadership position, or the reelection benefits derived from assignment to certain committees contrive to promote preferences for committee assignments that depart from what one might predict on the basis of committee prestige. For example, southern Democrats in my simulation always end up dominating the Defense Committee, despite its narrow jurisdiction and the large size of the committee. Thus, participants gravitate to those committees where they feel they can best realize their personal goals.

The number of party members on each committee reflects the proportion of Democrats and Republicans in the simulation, but the membership of each committee is determined by each party's leaders. Each participant indicates his committee preferences, although the assignment the individual receives depends upon a number of factors such as loyalty to party leaders and the composition of the requested committee. Favorable committee assignments and committee leadership positions will be both implicitly and explicitly part of the bargaining through which candidates for leadership positions mobilize support.

Since a member cannot be removed from a committee once he is assigned to it, party leaders gain their greatest leverage with their colleagues during the initial assignment process. After that point, leaders must depend upon the "good faith" of their colleagues to uphold their end of bargains. This is not normally a problem in Congress, but the limited duration of most simulations makes some participants less willing to adhere to the letter of their agreements. If failure to adhere to bargains occurs, instructors can remind participants of the necessity of fulfilling obligations, but my experience has been that party leaders can devise more effective ways of reprimanding members who renege on deals. For instance, withholding a bill from floor consideration or mobilizing party opposition to a recalcitrant member's pet bill are just two potent means for punishing those who fail to "keep their word." Party leaders cannot use their resources indiscriminately for fear of a mass uprising among the party faithful and because they recognize that they may need the cooperation of yesterday's or today's enemies in the future. In short, there are incentives for members to cooperate with their party's leaders and for party leaders to accede to the demands of their members, but the relationship between leader and follower is largely negotiable.

Committee Decision Making. The chair controls the scheduling of legislation for committee consideration and presides over these deliberations. Committees meet to decide the content of legislation that reaches the floor for a vote. These meetings are typically hard bargaining sessions where members seek policy, partisan, and personal advantage. Some members take the lead in offering and supporting specific legislative proposals or seek to modify the proposals of others through amendments; others may remain relatively silent but will be objects of pleas from the various contending interests. There is no proxy voting.

PREFLOOR CONGRESSIONAL PROCEDURES

Introduction of Legislation. Bills are introduced in the simulation by giving them to the Speaker of the House. (I require each student to submit three pieces of legislation prior to the first legislative session in order to facilitate the organization of the legislative schedule and floor debate; additional legislation can be submitted at any time.) The Speaker, in turn, will refer them to *one* of the committees. Bills may originate in the committee with appropriate jurisdiction, or they may be written by individuals outside of the committee and referred by the Speaker to the relevant committee. All bills must be referred to a committee but the committee is under no obligation to take action. Bills may be either public or private in nature, and the committee may process as many as it can. Most of the work in passing or thwarting the passage of legislation starts long before the measure reaches the floor of the House. The following activities should be performed by each legislative actor prior to every scheduled floor session.

Committee Members. Minority and majority committee members meet separately to determine how bills will be managed on the floor. Committee leaders decide on the legislator who will "bring the bill to the floor" by being recognized by the Speaker, start the debate, and "yield" time to other colleagues to speak on the issue. The committee chair communicates this "advice" to the Speaker and Majority Leader, and they make the decision as to the management of the legislation. The ranking minority member makes the same decisions and also decides on amendments to the bill and who will make those amendments (the ranking minority committee member will usually manage the legislation on the floor). The ranking minority committee member conveys this information to the minority leader, who makes the final decision as to amendments to the bill and who will manage opposition or support for the bill on the House floor.

Party Leaders. The leaders of each party meet with their respective committee leaders (committee chair, ranking minority member) to decide who will manage the bill on the floor. Party leaders (with the exception of the Speaker) are expected to take a vigorous role in the debate. Party leaders should conduct "whip" counts prior to a vote to determine party support on the bill and the proposed amendments. Since amendments must circulate prior to the bill's emergence on the floor, both parties should be aware of the amendments to be offered. In any case, there should not be any "surprise" amendments—i.e., party leaders should share information regarding the nature and substance of amendments. The party leaders *collectively* draft and distribute whip notices describing the legislative schedule and the amendments that will be offered.

Members of Congress. Members of Congress are expected to study the proposed legislation and attached amendments prior to their consideration on the floor. Most of the information should be gathered from friends or party colleagues serving on the committee reporting the legislation. Members should examine the legislation to determine its impact on reelection, constituency, and personal goals and values. Party members are surveyed through whip counts regarding their position on pending legislation and amendments, and they are asked to respond in one of several ways:

1. favor legislation or amendment
2. oppose legislation or amendment
3. undecided
4. available support, *if needed*; otherwise, opposition

It does not "help" an individual (in the long run) to lie or mislead their party leaders.

White House. The White House should be in constant communication with its party leaders regarding party support of pending legislation and amendments and sentiment (as far as can be determined) within the parties. They should be prepared to supply information to those supporting their position on the legislation, and they are expected to "lobby" (the *term* is illegal, not the act) for action favorable to their position.

Simplified Parliamentary Procedure.   Business may be brought before the floor of the House by a motion. The formality of a motion may, in some cases, be dispensed with, but should any member object, the question must be stated in the form of a motion. Before any question may be debated, it should be stated in the form of a motion by a member who has obtained the floor, and the motion must be seconded. The Speaker must then rule the motion out of order or state the *pending question.*

When a debatable question is pending, the mover is automatically entitled to speak first in the debate. The debate then proceeds as the Speaker recognizes members wishing to speak. No member who has obtained the floor may speak again in the debate until all who desire the floor and have not spoken are recognized. As far as is possible, the Speaker should allow the floor to alternate between opposing sides if he has some knowledge of the friends and enemies of a measure.

When a member has the floor, he may be interrupted only by (1) a point of order or (2) a parliamentary inquiry. These interruptions do not take the floor away from the speaker; as soon as they are dealt with, he must be recognized by the Speaker again. None of these motions require a second. If a member desires to end debate, he may call for or move the previous question. This type of motion requires a majority vote to pass. When debate ceases, the question, bill, or amendment is then put to a vote. A motion may be made to table any question on the floor, either for a definite period or indefinitely, by a majority vote.

An appeal from any decision of the Speaker may be made by a member rising immediately after the decision is made to challenge it. Recognition by the Speaker is not necessary in this case. If seconded, the Speaker should state the question and, if he so desires, his reasons for his decision. An appeal may not be debated. The Speaker puts the question to a vote by asking if his decision shall be sustained. In this case, a majority "no" vote is required to reverse the decision.

Most floor business reflects the following basic actions:

Making Motions	The member stands when recognized by the presiding officer. He then states his motion: "I move that...."
Discussion	After the presiding officer hears a second, he will announce that the motion is open for discussion.
Amending a Motion	A motion may be amended at any time during a discussion; when it is seconded, the presiding officer will call for debate. This debate can only deal with the amendment, not with the main motion.
Voting	If during discussion, you wish to have the motion or amendment voted on, you gain recognition and "call for the question" or "move the question." The assembly will

then vote on whether the motion should be voted on. It is not a vote on the motion. A vote on the motion follows a vote on calling the question only if the latter vote is affirmative. If you doubt the decision of the presiding officer, you may call for a division of the House. You may interrupt the next speaker to do this, but only immediately after the vote. *An amendment to an amendment, the amendment,* and *the main motion* are voted on separately, and *in that order.*

Interrupting the Speaker	1. If you desire parliamentary information, rise and say, "I rise to a point of parliamentary inquiry."
	2. If you doubt a decision of the Speaker on anything you may say, "I appeal the decision of the chair."
	3. If you notice some of these rules being broken or anything unjust being done, just say "point of order." Then state what is wrong.

It is useful to have a student skilled in parliamentary procedure to act as parliamentarian for the simulation and to assist students in making procedural inquires and motions. Instructors can introduce additional parliamentary rules (and rulings) to expedite or complicate the process.

Floor Action. Bills reported by the committees are taken up in the legislative session in the order determined by the Speaker—unless the legislature should decide by a majority vote to overrule him. There are four actions that the legislature is permitted to take with respect to a bill: (1) return the bill to the committee that reported it, which in most cases means to kill it, though in a less public way (this vote for "reconsideration" precedes final vote on legislation); (2) amend the bill—but only *two* major amendments will be permitted to a single bill; (3) vote the bill down; or (4) approve the bill by a majority vote. This is the *order* of legislative action.

Debate on any legislative measure should be limited (e.g., 10 minutes) and divided equally between the proponents and opponents of the bill. The leader of the proponents of the bill—i.e., the floor manager— will be in charge of allocating ("yielding") time to those wishing to speak in favor of the bill, and the leader of the opposition forces has a similar responsibility. Debate on amendments should also be limited and equally divided between proponents and opponents of the bill. Time for debate can be extended by a two-thirds vote. Roll calls are taken upon the demand of 20 percent of the members present: otherwise, a *standing* vote. Presidential vetoes must be returned to Congress by a certain period of time after the bill has been approved, or the bill automatically becomes law.

EVALUATING LEGISLATIVE SUCCESS
IN THE SIMULATION

There is always the problem of how to evaluate a student's performance in a simulation. It is perhaps more difficult in this legislative simulation because of the existence of multiple goals and the variety of alternative legislative styles. For instance, students who rank reelection as a personal goal below that of power and policy cannot be expected to roll-up huge reelection margins since their interest lies elsewhere. In this simulation, the student is evaluated on the basis of the extent to which legislative goals have been realized. This can be accomplished in the following manner:

1. *Legislative Influence.* Students are surveyed at the conclusion of the simulation and asked to rate the effectiveness of each member in the simulation. Those who have earned the esteem of their colleagues are considered to be successful in attaining legislative influence.
2. *Public Policy.* Students are asked to chart the progress of their legislation from its initial introduction to final legislative action, noting changes (amendments) and bargains made during the bill's course through the House. Students who are able to move their legislation quickly through the House, with few damaging amendments, are considered to have effectively achieved their policy goals.
3. *Reelection.* Students are expected to create policies and agency programs that further the interests of their constituents. This can be accomplished by initiating new legislative programs or broadening the range of benefits provided by existing federal programs that benefit a segment of society that is important to reelection constituencies.

Success in each of these three areas is then weighted by the student's ranking of each of the goals. This enables students to express their individuality in their goal pursuits, and to be evaluated on the basis of goals that they themselves have established.

ADDITIONAL SUGGESTIONS

In addition to the basic structure of the simulation, I have introduced two refinements: a biographical directory of the districts represented in the simulation and a simulation newspaper that represents the external and internal political environment. The biographical directory alerts participants to those members of the simulation with similar constituency interests and therefore potential coalition partners. These biographical directories contain information on the geographical nature of constituencies, past reelection margins, presidential electoral performance in the district, and the voting behavior of congressmen as evaluated by various political groups (e.g., ratings by the Americans for Democratic Action). The existence of such a document facilitates coalition building among participants.

Every simulation that I have participated in has had a "newspaper." Often these papers provide experimenters with opportunities to introduce "treatment effects" into the simulation or to inject a measure of external reality into the simulation. The newspaper in my simulation—called *Whispers in the Halls*—is designed to serve these purposes as well as to keep students adequately informed about what's going on in the simulation. I use the paper to inform the participants of astute political maneuvers (*after* they have occurred), to keep students aware of similarities between their behavior and the behavior of congressmen, and to call attention to real-life external conditions that might impinge upon the behavior of the participants (e.g., declines in the unemployment rate, rise in federal deficit). At times, the newspaper can stimulate behavior, such as the formation of particular voting blocs, but the paper exists primarily to make sure that all participants are kept well informed about the politics of the simulation. One result is that most students are fairly well informed about political maneuverings and few feel "left out" of the action.

CHARACTERISTICS OF A SIMULATED CONGRESS

In the previous sections I have tried to describe how a simulation of Congress could be structured to exhibit many of the characteristics examined in this book. I conclude by describing how these characteristics are exhibited in such a simulation. *Bargaining* is ubiquitous to Congress, and so it is in the simulation. Bargaining occurs over a wide range of matters. Early in the simulation, participants construct coalitions to support candidates for leadership positions within the parties. In building these coalitions, members bargain with one another, often trading support for a position of leadership or a good committee assignment. Participants quickly gain an appreciation of the major bargaining strategies—partisan discussion, compensation, and reciprocity—in these negotiations. As the game moves on, participants also engage in these same bargaining tactics as they seek to pass legislation. This involves bargaining with other members, party leaders, and the president and his staff.

Decentralization of influence in the simulation occurs in much the same way as it does in Congress: committees and voting blocs. The committee system decentralizes influence in the simulation in two ways. First, committee leaders and members cannot be removed from their committees once they are assigned to them. This creates a set of committees that are largely immune from leadership sanctions and interference. Second, because of the volume of legislation and the specialization of committees, committee members serve as experts on particular legislative issues; hence, committee members supply voting cues that compete with those supplied by party leaders. In addition, informal groups—comprised of those with similar ideological or constituency interests—often emerge to exercise power and to counter centralized leadership.

Constituency representation occurs in a variety of ways. Participants pursue the interests of their constituents as they seek to pry federal contracts and projects from the federal budget either by passing legislation favorable to their constituents or by trading support on legislation for the promise of federal dollars for the district; such "promises" are usually negotiated with the president, who has a limited supply of federal projects (e.g., water treatment and sewage plants) and contracts (e.g., defense weapons systems) to distribute. Voting on the floor and in committee is often responsive to constituency interests, and participants gain a quick appreciation of logrolling when these votes involve district benefits (e.g., public works projects, education programs).

Lack of party discipline is most evident in the simulated Congress in mobilizing coalitions behind legislation. Legislative leaders, as well as the members themselves, quickly realize that membership in a party is insufficient reason to support party policies. Members must be persuaded or compensated in many instances. Unable to "crack the whip," party leaders cannot generate high levels of partisanship (or party cohesion) on all but a handful of votes. The ideological divisions that fragment the parties in the U.S. Congress and weaken party discipline play the same role in the simulation. For instance, southern Democrats frequently oppose party policies on ideological grounds in both the U.S. Congress and the simulated one.

Cozy triangles exist between executive branch departments (as represented by individual White House staff members) and committees in the simulation. Each staff member is assigned to "work with" a specific committee, and he is instructed to build and maintain cordial relations with committee members in order to secure support for the administration's legislation. Staff members cultivate committee members and leaders by consulting with them about legislative initiatives, addressing their questions, negotiating with them over legislation, and promising them a slice of the federal budget for their districts. The result is that a large number of committee members are supportive of increased budgets (i.e., new programs or expansion of existing programs) for those agencies that can deliver benefits to their constituents, such as the departments of Defense and Agriculture. And these members do in fact receive generous helpings of the federal pork barrel!

Institutional characteristics of Congress are much easier to simulate than those associated with congressmen. Specifically, the *lack of turnover* of congressmen, the *popularity of incumbents*, and the pursuit of *congres-*

sional careers are attributes that are not easily translated into simulation rules or procedures. In fact, these three characteristics are best determined artificially by the qualitative judgments of the instructor. That is, the instructor's evaluation of the behavior of the participants is probably the best way to incorporate these attributes into the simulation. For instance, the ability of the participant to realize his goals might be construed as the failure or success of career pursuits, and the number of constituency benefits delivered might be indicative of the participants popularity within the district. Finally, the lack of turnover might be demonstrated by "defeating" at election time (i.e., conclusion of the class) only those who show no interest in "getting reelected"—those who have done little for their constituents and those who have poor attendance records.

Two other characteristics of congressmen are better simulated: independence and attentive home styles. The *independence of congressmen* is exhibited in the voting leeway that the participants exercise and their pursuit of goals within the simulation. Most participants find themselves pulled by their personal convictions, no matter the issue or the countervailing forces. Intensity of belief, rather than the intensity of constituent opinion, often dictates vote decisions on controversial issues. Moreover, the lack of meaningful sanctions leaves most participants free to oppose party policy or the will of the president. Finally, the difficult decisions associated with maintaining an *attentive home style* confronts the participants as they formulate their resource allocations. Here, participants must decide how to allocate their personal time (and that of their hypothetical staffs) between legislative interests and district affairs. Participants who allocate too little time to constituency matters experience a loss of popularity—a damaging blow near election time in the simulation.

This should not be constructed to mean that any adaptation of the simulation will exhibit these characteristics. Clearly, the types of students recruited to the class, the structural features of the simulated Congress, and the instructor's involvement can influence the emergence or submergence of these characteristics of Congress. In short, there is no assurance that these characteristics will evolve spontaneously from the play of the game. Some no doubt will, but others will require the intervention of the instructor in shaping conditions to foster these characteristics. In the preceding chapters I have described some of the conditions necessary for sustaining these characteristics of Congress. This information can be used to introduce rules and incentives into the simulation to increase the saliency of specific characteristics.

Appendix
TRUST/DISTRUST ITEMS

CODE NUMBER	ITEM CONTENT
213	Dependable, trustworthy, reliable; a man you can trust with the responsibilities of government (23)
214	Undependable, untrustworthy, unreliable; a man you can't trust with the responsibilities of government (6)
224	Has fulfilled/kept (campaign) promises (12)
225	Has not fulfilled/kept (campaign) promises (11)
307	People have confidence in him (7)
308	People don't have confidence in him (1)
313	A politician/political-person; (too) much in politics; a good politician; politically motivated, part of Washington crowd; just wants to be reelected (45)
314	Not a politician; not in politics; above politics; a bad politician; not part of Washington crowd (9)
315	Independent; no one runs him; his own boss (16)
316	Not independent; run by others; not his own man/boss (7)
401	Honest, sincere; keeps promises; man of integrity; means what he says; not tricky, open/candid; straightforward; fair (391)
402	Dishonest, insincere; breaks promises; no integrity; doesn't mean what he says; tricky; not open/candid; not straightforward (74)

403	Man of high principles/ideals; high moral purpose (12)
404	Lacks principles/ideals (3)
409	Doesn't use office for personal benefit; not in office to maximize personal benefit (3)
410	In office (uses office) for personal benefits (junket trips, big salary, other perks) (23)
421	Intelligent/smart (57)
422	Unintelligent, stupid, dumb (7)
502	Controlled by party regulars/bosses, machine (14)
503	Not controlled by party regulars/bosses (3)
709	Good for country; has country's interests at heart; not just out for self/own best interests (60)
710	Bad for country; don't have country's interests at heart; only looking out for their own interests (4)
831	Generous, compassionate, believes in helping others (23)
832	Selfish, only help themselves (1)

The figures in parentheses are the number of respondents mentioning that response.

Source: American National Election Study, 1978, University of Michigan (1979), pp. 615–635.

REFERENCES

ABERBACH, JOEL, D. "Changes in Congressional Oversight." *American Behavioral Scientist* (May–June 1979): 495–498.

ABERBACH, JOEL D., AND BERT A. ROCKMAN. "Bureaucrats and Clientele Groups: A View from Capitol Hill." *American Journal of Political Science* (November, 1978):818–832.

ABRAMS, MICHAEL, AND JOSEPH COOPER. "The Rise of Seniority in the House of Representatives." *Polity* (Fall 1968): 52–85.

AMERICAN INSTITUTE FOR PUBLIC OPINION, omnibus national surveys, 1947–1965.

ARNOLD, R. DOUGLAS. *Congress and the Bureaucracy: A Theory of Influence*. New Haven, Conn.: Yale University Press, 1979.

ASHER, HERBERT B. "The Changing Status of the Freshman Representative." In *Congress in Change*, edited by Norman J. Ornstein, pp. 216–239. New York: Praeger, 1975.

———. "The Learning of Legislative Norms." *American Political Science Review* (June 1973): 499–513.

ASHER, HERBERT B., AND HERBERT F. WEISBERG. "Voting Change in Congress: Some Dynamic Perspectives on an Evolutionary Process." *American Journal of Political Science* (May 1978): 391–425.

BAKER, ROSS K. "Party and Institutional Sanctions in the U.S. House: The Case of Congressman Gramm." *Legislative Studies Quarterly* (August 1985):315–338.

BOND, JON R., CARY COVINGTON, AND RICHARD FLEISHER. "Explaining Challenger Quality in Congressional Elections." *Journal of Politics* (May 1985):510–529.

BORN, RICHARD. "Strategic Politicians and Unresponsive Voters." *American Political Science Review* (June 1986):599–612.

———. "Perquisite Employment in the U.S. House of Representatives." *American Politics Quarterly* (July 1982):347–362.

BRADY, DAVID W. "Critical Elections, Congressional Parties and Clusters of Policy Changes." *British Journal of Political Science* (January 1978): 79–99.

BRADY, DAVID W., AND CHARLES S. BULLOCK III. "Is There a Conservative Coalition in the House?" *Journal of Politics* (May 1980): 549–559.

BRADY, DAVID W., AND NAOMI B. LYNN. "Switched-Seat Congressional Districts: Their Effect on Party Voting and Public Policy." *American Journal of Political Science* (August 1973): 528–543.

BRADY, DAVID W., JOSEPH COOPER, AND PATRICIA HURLEY. "The Decline of Party in the U.S. House of Representatives, 1887–1968." *Legislative Studies Quarterly* (August 1979):381–406.

BROOKSHIRE, ROBERT G., AND DEAN F. DUNCAN, III. "Congressional Career Patterns and Party Systems." *Legislative Studies Quarterly* (February 1983a):65–78.

———. "Changes in Senate Careers Over Time." Paper delivered at the annual meeting of the American Political Science Association, Chicago, Illinois, September 1–4, 1983b.

BUCKLEY, JAMES L. "On Becoming a United States Senator." *National Review* (February 2, 1973): 147–148.

BULLOCK, CHARLES S., III. "U.S. Senate Committee Assignments: Preferences, Motivations, and Success." *American Journal of Political Science* (November 1985):789–808.

———. "Motivations for U.S. Congressional Committee Preferences: Freshmen of the 92nd Congress." *Legislative Studies Quarterly* (May 1976):201–212.

———. "Committee Transfers in the United States House of Representatives." *Journal of Politics* (February 1973): 85–120.

———. "House Careerists: Changing Patterns of Longevity and Attrition." *American Political Science Review* (December 1972a):1295–1300.

———. "Freshman Committee Assignments and Re-Election in the U.S. House." *American Political Science Review* (September 1972b):996–1007.

———. "Influence of State Party Delegations on House Committee Assignments." *Midwest Journal of Political Science* (August 1971):525–546.

BULLOCK, CHARLES S. III, AND DAVID W. BRADY. "Party, Constituency, and Roll-Call Voting in the U.S. Senate." *Legislative Studies Quarterly* (February 1983): 29–44.

BULLOCK, CHARLES S. III, AND MICHAEL J. SCICCHITANO. "Partisan Defections and Senate Incumbent Elections." In *Studies of Congress*, ed. Glenn R. Parker, pp. 35–43. Washington, D.C.: Congressional Quarterly, 1985.

BULLOCK, CHARLES S. III, AND JOHN SPRAGUE. "A Research Note on the Committee Reassignments of Southern Democratic Congressmen." *Journal of Politics* (May 1969):493–512.

BURNHAM, WALTER DEAN. "Insulation and Responsiveness in Congressional Elections." *Political Science Quarterly* (Fall 1974): 411–435.

CAIN, BRUCE E., JOHN A. FEREJOHN, AND MORRIS P. FIORINA. "The Constituency Service Basis of the Personal Vote for U.S. Representatives and British Members of Parliament." *American Political Science Review* (March 1984):110–125.

CALVERT, RANDALL B., AND JOHN A. FEREJOHN. "Coattail Voting in Recent Presidential Elections." *American Political Science Review* (June 1983):407–419.

CAMPBELL, ANGUS, PHILIP E. CONVERSE, WARREN E. MILLER, AND DONALD E. STOKES, (eds.). *Elections and the Political Order*. New York: John Wiley, 1966.

CATER, DOUGLASS. *Power in Washington*. New York: Random House, 1964.

CAVANAGH, THOMAS E. "The Two Arenas of Congress." In *The House at Work*, edited by Joseph Cooper and G. Calvin Mackenzie, pp. 56–77. Austin: University of Texas Press, 1981.

CLAPP, CHARLES L. *The Congressman: His Job As He See It*. Washington, D. C.: The Brookings Institution, 1963.

CLEM, ALAN L. "Do Representatives Increase in Conservatism as They Increase in Seniority?" *Journal of Politics* (February 1977): 193–200.

CLAUSEN, AAGE. *How Congressmen Decide*. New York: St. Martin's Press, 1973.

COMMITTEE ON POLITICAL PARTIES. *Toward a More Responsible Two-Party System*. New York: Rinehart, 1950.

Congressional Directory. Washington, D. C.: U.S. Government Printing Office, 1963–1987.

Congressional Quarterly Alamanac. Vols. 2–42. Washington, D. C.: Congressional Quarterly, 1946–1986.

Congressional Quarterly Weekly Report, August 1, 1987: 1699–1705.

COOPER, JOSEPH. "Organization and Innovation in the House of Representatives." In *The House at Work*, edited by Joseph Cooper and G. Calvin Mackenzie, pp. 319–355. Austin: University of Texas Press, 1981.

———. *The Origins of the Standing Committees and the Development of the Modern House.* Houston: Rice University Studies, 1971.

COOPER, JOSEPH, AND DAVID W. BRADY. "Institutional Context and Leadership Style: The House from Cannon to Rayburn." *American Political Science Review* (June 1981):411–425.

COOPER, JOSEPH, AND WILLIAM WEST. "The Congressional Career in the 1970s." In *Congress Reconsidered*, 2d ed., edited by Lawrence C. Dodd and Bruce I. Oppenheimer, pp. 83–106. Washington, D.C.: Congressional Quarterly, 1981.

COPELAND, GARY W. "Seniority and Committee Transfers: Career Planning in the Contemporary House of Representatives." *Journal of Politics* (May 1987):553–564.

COVER, ALBERT D. "Contacting Congressional Constituents: Some Patterns of Perquisite Use." *American Journal of Political Science* (February 1980): 125–135.

———. "One Good Term Deserves Another: The Advantage of Incumbency in Congressional Elections." *American Journal of Political Science* (August 1977): 523–542.

COVER, ALBERT D., AND BRUCE S. BRUMBERG. "Baby Books and Ballots: The Impact of Congressional Mail on Constituent Opinion." *American Political Science Review* (June 1982): 347–359.

COVER, ALBERT D., AND DAVID R. MAYHEW. "Congressional Dynamics and the Decline of Competitive Congressional Elections." In *Congress Reconsidered*, 2d ed., edited by Lawrence C. Dodd and Bruce I. Oppenheimer, 62–82. Washington, D.C.: Congressional Quarterly, 1981.

DAVIDSON, ROGER H. "Subcommittee Government: New Channels for Policy Making." In *The New Congress*, edited by Thomas E. Mann and Norman J. Ornstein, pp. 99–133. Washington, D.C.: American Enterprise Institute, 1981.

———. *The Role of the Congressman.* New York: Pegasus, 1969.

DAVIDSON, ROGER H., AND WALTER J. OLESZEK. *Congress and Its Members.* Washington, D.C.: Congressional Quarterly, 1981.

DAVIDSON, ROGER H., AND WALTER J. OLESZEK. *Congress Against Itself.* Bloomington, Ind.: Indiana University Press, 1977.

DEERING, CHRISTOPHER J. "Subcommittee Government in the U.S. House: An Analysis of Bill Management." *Legislative Studies Quarterly.* (November 1982):533–546.

DODD, LAWRENCE C. "Congress and the Quest for Power." In *Studies of Congress*, edited by Glenn R. Parker, pp. 489–520. Washington, D. C.: Congressional Quarterly, 1985.

DODD, LAWRENCE C., AND RICHARD L. SCHOTT. *Congress and the Administrative State.* New York: John Wiley, 1979.

DOWNS, ANTHONY. *An Economic Theory of Democracy.* New York: Harper and Row, 1957.

DYSON, JAMES, AND JOHN SOULE. "Congressional Committee Behavior on Roll Call Votes: The U.S. House of Representatives, 1955–1964." *Midwest Journal of Political Science* (November 1970): 626–647.

EDWARDS, GEORGE C., III. *Presidential Influence in Congress.* San Francisco: W. H. Freeman, 1980.

ELDERSVELD, SAMUEL J. *Political Parties in American Society.* New York: Basic Books, 1982.

ENGLAND, DAVID E., AND CHARLES S. BULLOCK, III. "Prescriptive Seats Revisited". *American Journal of Political Science* (May 1986):496–502.

ERIKSON, ROBERT S. "The Electoral Impact of Congressional Roll Call Voting". *American Political Science Review* (December 1971):1018–1032.

EVANS, ROWLAND, AND ROBERT NOVAK. "The Absentees of Congress." *The Washington Post.* (February 19, 1976): A19.

FENNO, RICHARD F., JR. *The United States Senate: A Bicameral Perspective.* Washington, D.C.: American Enterprise Institute, 1982.

———. *Home Style.* Boston: Little, Brown, 1978.

———. "If, as Ralph Nader Says, Congress Is 'the Broken Branch', How Come We Love Our Congressmen So Much?" In *Congress in Change*, edited by Norman J. Ornstein, pp. 277–287. New York: Praeger, 1975.

———. *Congressmen in Committees.* Boston: Little, Brown, 1973.

——. *The Power of the Purse*. Boston: Little, Brown, 1966.

——. "The Internal Distribution of Influence: The House." In *Congress and America's Future*, edited by David B. Truman, pp. 52–76. Englewood Cliffs, N.J.: Prentice-Hall, 1965.

FEREJOHN, JOHN A. "On the Decline of Competition in Congressional Elections." *American Political Science Review* (March 1977): 166–176.

——. *Pork Barrel Politics: Rivers and Harbors Legislation, 1947–1968*. Sanford, Calif.: Stanford University Press, 1974.

FEREJOHN, JOHN A., AND RANDALL L. CALVERT. "Presidential Coattails in Historical Perspective". *American Journal of Political Science* (February 1984):127–146.

FIORINA, MORRIS P. *Congress: Keystone of the Washington Establishment*. New Haven, Conn.: Yale University Press, 1977.

——. *Representatives, Roll Calls, and Constituencies*. Lexington, Mass.: Lexington Books, 1974.

——. "Electoral Margins, Constituency Influence, and Policy Moderation: A Critical Assessment." *American Politics Quarterly* (October 1973):479–498.

FIORINA, MORRIS P., DAVID W. ROHDE, AND PETER WISSEL. "Historical Change in House Turnover." In *Congress in Change*, edited by Norman J. Ornstein, pp. 24–57. New York: Praeger, 1975.

FITZGERALD, RANDALL, AND GERALD LIPSON. *Porkbarrel*. Washington, D.C.: CATO Institute, 1984.

FOLEY, MICHAEL. *The New Senate*. New Haven, Conn.: Yale University Press, 1980.

FOWLER, LINDA L., SCOTT R. DOUGLASS, AND WESLEY D. CLARKE, JR. "The Electoral Effects of House Committee Assignments." *Journal of Politics* (February 1980): 307–319.

FOX, HARRISON W., AND SUSAN W. HAMMOND. *Congressional Staffs*. New York: Free Press, 1977.

FROMAN, LEWIS A., JR. "The Importance of Individuality in Voting in Congress." *Journal of Politics* (May 1963):324–332.

FROMAN, LEWIS A., JR., AND RANDALL B. RIPLEY. "Conditions for Party Leadership." *American Political Science Review* (March 1965):52–63.

GALLOWAY, GEORGE B. *History of the United States House of Representatives*, H. Doc. 87–246, 87th Cong., 1st session, 1962.

GARAND, JAMES C., AND DONALD A. GROSS. "Changes in the Vote Margins for Congressional Candidates: A Specification of Historical Trends." *American Political Science Review* (March 1984):17–30.

GAWTHROP, LOUIS C. *Bureaucratic Behavior in the Executive Branch*. New York: Free Press, 1969.

——. "Changing Membership Patterns in House Committees." *American Political Science Review* (June 1966): 366–373.

GELLHORN, WALTER. *When Americans Complain*. Cambridge, Mass.: Harvard University Press, 1966.

GERTZOG, IRWIN N. "The Routinization of Committee Assignments in the U.S. House of Representatives." *American Journal of Political Science* (November 1976): 693–712.

GLAZER, AMIHAI, AND MARC ROBBINS. "Congressional Responsiveness to Constituency Change." *American Journal of Political Science* (May 1985):259–273.

GOLDENBERG, EDIE N., AND MICHAEL W. TRAUGOTT. *Campaigning for Congress*. Washington, D. C.: Congressional Quarterly, 1984.

GOLDSTONE, JACK A. "Subcommittee Chairmanships in the House of Representatives." *American Political Science Review* (September 1975):970–971.

GOSS, CAROL F. "Military Committee Membership and Defense-Related Benefits in the House of Representatives." *Western Political Quarterly* (June 1972):215–233.

HIBBING, JOHN R. "Voluntary Retirements from the U.S. House of Representatives." *American Journal of Political Science* (August 1982):467–484.

HINCKLEY, BARBARA. *Stability and Change In Congress*, 3d ed. New York: Harper and Row, 1983.

——. *Congressional Elections*. Washington, D.C.: Congressional Quarterly, 1981.

——. *The Seniority System in Congress*. Bloomington, Ind.: Indiana University Press, 1971.

HOLTZMAN, ABRAHAM. *Legislative Liaison: Executive Leadership in Congress.* Chicago: Rand McNally, 1970.

How Congress Works. Washington, D.C.: Congressional Quarterly, 1983.

HUITT, RALPH K. "The Internal Distribution of Influence: The Senate." In *Congress and America's Future,* edited by David B. Truman, pp. 77–101. Englewood Cliffs, N.J.: Prentice-Hall, 1965.

———. "The Outsider In The Senate." *American Political Science Review* (September, 1961a): 566–575.

———. "Democratic Party Leadership in the Senate." *American Political Science Review* (June, 1961b): 334–344.

HUNTINGTON, SAMUEL P. "Congressional Responses to the Twentieth Century." In *Congress and America's Future,* edited by David B. Truman, pp. 5–31. Englewood Cliffs, N.J.: Prentice-Hall, 1965.

HURLEY, PATRICIA, DAVID BRADY, AND JOSEPH COOPER. "Measuring Legislative Potential for Policy Change." *Legislative Studies Quarterly* (November 1977): 385–398.

Inside Congress. Washington, D.C.: Congressional Quarterly, 1983.

IPPOLITO, DENNIS S. *The Budget and National Politics.* San Francisco, Calif.: W. H. Freeman, 1978.

JACOBS, ANDY. *The Powell Affair.* Indianapolis: Bobbs-Merrill, 1973.

JACOBSON, GARY C. "The Marginals Never Vanished: Incumbency and Competition in Elections for the U.S. House of Representatives, 1952–1982." *American Journal of Political Science* (February 1987): 126–141.

———. *The Politics of Congressional Elections.* Boston: Little, Brown, 1983.

———. *Money in Congressional Elections.* New Haven: Yale University Press, 1980.

JACOBSON, GARY C., AND SAMUEL KERNELL. *Strategy and Choice in Congressional Elections.* New Haven, Conn.: Yale University Press, 1981.

JEWELL, MALCOLM E., AND CHU CHI-HUNG. "Membership Movement and Committee Attractiveness in the U.S. House of Representatives, 1963–1971." *American Journal of Political Science* (May 1974): 433–441.

JEWELL, MALCOLM E., AND SAMUEL C. PATTERSON. *The Legislative Process in the United States,* 3d ed. New York: Random House, 1977.

JOHANNES, JOHN R. "Casework in the House." In *The House at Work,* edited by Joseph Cooper and G. Calvin Mackenzie, pp. 78–96. Austin, Tex.: University of Texas Press, 1981.

———. "The Distribution of Casework in the U.S. Congress: An Uneven Burden." *Legislative Studies Quarterly* (November 1980): 517–544.

———. "Casework as a Technique of U.S. Congressional Oversight of the Executive." *Legislative Studies Quarterly* (August 1979):325–351.

JONES, CHARLES O. *The United States Congress: People, Place, and Policy.* Homewood, Ill.: Dorsey, 1982.

———. "Representation in Congress: The Case of the House Agriculture Committee." *American Political Science Review* (June 1961):358–367.

KEEFE, WILLIAM J., AND MORRIS S. OGUL. *The American Legislative Process,* 6th ed. Englewood Cliffs, N.J.: Prentice-Hall, 1985.

KERNELL, SAMUEL. "Toward Understanding 19th Century Congressional Careers: Ambition, Competition, and Rotation." *American Journal of Political Science* (November 1977):669–694.

KINGDON, JOHN W. *Congressmen's Voting Decisions.* New York: Harper and Row, 1973.

KRITZER, HERBERT. "Ideology and American Political Elites." *Public Opinion Quarterly* (Winter 1978): 484–502.

KRITZER, HERBERT M., AND ROBERT B. EUBANK. "Presidential Coattails Revisited: Partisanship and Incumbency Effects." *American Journal of Political Science* (August 1979):615–626.

KUKLINSKI, JAMES H., AND DARRELL WEST. "Economic Expectations and Voting Behavior in United States House and Senate Elections." *American Political Science Review* (June 1981):436–447.

LIGHT, LARRY. "Pressing the Flesh: For Many Incumbents, Running for Reelection is Now a Full-Time Job." *Congressional Quarterly Weekly Report* (July 7, 1979): 1350–1357.

LINDBLOM, CHARLES E. *The Intelligence of Democracy.* New York: Free Press, 1965.

LIPSET, SEYMOUR M., AND WILLIAM SCHNEIDER. *The Confidence Gap.* New York: Free Press, 1983.

LOOMIS, BURDETT A. "Congressional Careers and Party Leadership in the Contemporary House of Representatives." *American Journal of Political Science* (February 1984):180–202.

LOWI, THEODORE J. *The End of Liberalism: Ideology, Policy, and the Crisis of Public Authority.* New York: Norton, 1969.

MAASS, ARTHUR A. *Muddy Waters.* Cambridge, Mass.: Harvard University Press, 1951.

MANLEY, JOHN F. *The Politics of Finance: The House Committee on Ways and Means.* Boston: Little, Brown, 1970.

MATTHEWS, DONALD R. "Can The 'Outsider's' Role Be Legitimate?" *American Political Science Review* (December 1961): 882–883.

―――. *U.S. Senators and Their World.* New York: Vintage Books, 1960.

MATTHEWS, DONALD R., AND JAMES A. STIMSON. *Yeas and Nays.* New York: John Wiley, 1975.

MAYHEW, DAVID R. *Congress: The Electoral Connection.* New Haven, Conn.: Yale University Press, 1974a.

―――. "Congressional Elections: The Case of the Vanishing Marginals." *Polity* (Spring, 1974b): 295–317.

MCCUBBINS, MATHEW, AND THOMAS SCHWARTZ. "Congressional Oversight Overlooked: Police Patrols Versus Fire Alarms." *American Journal of Political Science* (February 1984): 165–179.

MILLER, WARREN E. "Majority Rule and The Representative System of Government." In *Cleavages, Ideologies and Party System,* edited by E. Allardt and Y. Littmen, pp. 343–376. Helsinki: Transactions of the Westermarck Society, 1964.

MILLER, WARREN E., AND JOHN P. KATOSH. "Design and Core Data for the 1978 Election Study." In *Congressional Elections,* eds. Louis Sandy Maisel and Joseph Cooper, pp. 11–130. Beverly Hills, Calif.: Sage Publications, 1981.

MILLER, WARREN E., AND DONALD E. STOKES. "Constituency Influence in Congress." In *Elections and the Political Order,* edited by Angus Campbell et al., 351–372. New York: John Wiley, 1966.

MITCHELL, WILLIAM C. "The Ambivalent Social Status of the American Politician." *Western Political Quarterly* (September 1959): 683–698.

MUELLER, JOHN E. *War, Presidents and Public Opinion.* New York: Wiley, 1973.

MURPHY, JAMES T. "Political Parties and the Porkbarrel: Party Conflict and Cooperation in House Public Works Committee Decision Making." In *Studies of Congress,* edited by Glenn R. Parker, pp. 234–260. Washington, D. C.: Congressional Quarterly, 1985.

MURPHY, THOMAS P. "Congressional Liaison: The NASA Case." *Western Political Quarterly* (June 1972):192–214.

NELSON, GARRISON. "Partisan Patterns of House Leadership Change, 1789–1977." *American Political Science Review* (September 1977):918–939.

NISKANAN, WILLIAM A. *Bureaucracy and Representative Government.* Chicago: Aldine-Atherton, 1971.

OLESZEK, WALTER J. *Congressional Procedures and the Policy Process,* 2d ed. Washington, D. C.: Congressional Quarterly, 1978.

ORNSTEIN, NORMAN J. "Causes and Consequences of Congressional Change: Subcommittee Reforms in the House of Representatives." In *Congress in Change,* edited by Norman J. Ornstein, pp. 88–114. New York: Praeger, 1975.

ORNSTEIN, NORMAN J., THOMAS E. MANN, MICHAEL J. MALBIN, AND JOHN F. BIBBY. *Vital Statistics on Congress, 1982.* Washington, D.C.: American Enterprise Institute, 1982.

PACKWOOD, ROBERT W. "The Senate Seniority System." In *Congress in Change,* edited by Norman J. Ornstein, pp. 60–71. New York: Praeger, 1975.

PARKER, GLENN R. "The Role of Constituent Trust in Congressional Elections." Paper delivered at the annual meeting of the American Political Science Association. Chicago, Illinois, September 2–6, 1987.

―――. "Is There A Political Life Cycle in the House of Representatives?" *Legislative Studies Quarterly* (August 1986a):375–392.

―――. *Homeward Bound: Explaining Changes in Congressional Behavior.* Pittsburgh, Pa.: University of Pittsburgh Press, 1986b.

———. "Incumbent Popularity and Electoral Success." In *Congressional Elections*, edited by Louis Sandy Maisel and Joseph Cooper, pp. 249–279. Beverly Hills: Sage Publications, 1981a.

———. "Can Congress Ever Be a Popular Institution?" In *The House at Work*, edited by Joseph Cooper and G. Calvin Mackenzie, pp. 31–55. Austin: University of Texas Press, 1981b.

———. "The Selection of Committee Leaders in the House of Representatives." *American Politics Quarterly* (January 1979):71–93.

———. "Some Themes in Congressional Unpopularity." *American Journal of Political Science* (February 1977): 93–109.

PARKER, GLENN R., AND SUZANNE L. PARKER. *Factions In House Committees*. Knoxville, Tenn.: University of Tennessee Press, 1985.

PARKER, GLENN R., AND ROGER H. DAVIDSON. "Why Do Americans Love Their Congressmen So Much More Than Their Congress?" *Legislative Studies Quarterly* (February 1979): 52–61.

PAYNE, JAMES L. "The Personal Advantage of House Incumbents, 1936–1976." *American Politics Quarterly* (October 1980): 465–482.

PEABODY, ROBERT L. *Leadership in Congress*. Boston: Little, Brown, 1976.

———. "Party Leadership Change in the United States House of Representatives." *American Political Science Review* (September 1967):675–693.

———. "The Enlarged Rules Committee." In *New Perspectives on the House of Representatives*, eds. Robert L. Peabody and Nelson W. Polsby, pp. 129–164. Chicago: Rand McNally, 1963.

PLOTT, CHARLES R. "Some Organizational Influences on Urban Renewal Decisions." *American Economic Review* (May 1968):306–311.

POLSBY, NELSON W. "Good-bye to the Inner Club." In *Congressional Behavior*, edited by Nelson W. Polsby, pp. 105–110. New York: Random House, 1971.

———. "The Institutionalization of the U.S. House of Representatives." *American Political Science Review* (March 1968):144–168.

POLSBY, NELSON W., MIRIAM GALLAGHER, AND BARRY S. RUNDQUIST. "The Growth of the Seniority System in the U.S. House of Representatives." *American Political Science Review* (September 1969): 787–807.

POOLE, KEITH, AND R. STEVEN DANIELS. "Ideology, Party, and Voting in the U. S. Congress, 1959–1980." *American Political Science Review* (June 1985): 373–399.

POWELL, LYNDA W. "Issue Representation in Congress." *Journal of Politics* (August 1982): 658–678.

PRESSMAN, JEFFREY. *House vs. Senate*. New Haven, Conn.: Yale University Press, 1966.

PRICE, H. DOUGLAS. "Congress and the Evolution of Legislative 'Professionalism'." In *Congress in Change*, edited by Norman J. Ornstein, pp. 2–23. New York: Praeger, 1975.

———. "The Congressional Career-Then and Now." In *Congressional Behavior*, edited by Nelson W. Polsby, 14–27. New York: Random House, 1971.

RAGSDALE, LYN, AND TIMOTHY E. COOK. "Representatives' Actions and Challengers' Reactions: Limits to Candidate Connections in the House." *American Journal of Political Science* (February 1987):45–81.

RAY, BRUCE A. "Committee Attractiveness in the U. S. House, 1963–1981." *American Journal of Political Science* (August 1982):609–613.

———. "Federal Spending and the Selection of Committee Assignments in the U. S. House of Representatives." *American Journal of Political Science* (August 1980):494–510.

RIED, T. R. *Congressional Odyssey*. San Francisco: W. H. Freeman, 1980.

RIPLEY, RANDALL B. *Congress: Process and Policy*, 3d ed. New York: W. W. Norton, 1983.

———. *Power in the Senate*. New York: St. Martin's Press, 1969.

———. *Party Leaders in the House of Representatives*. Washington, D. C.: Brookings Institution, 1967.

RIPLEY, RANDALL B., AND GRACE A. FRANKLIN. *Congress, The Bureaucracy, and Public Policy*, 3d ed. Homewood, Ill.: Dorsey, 1984.

ROBINSON, MICHAEL J. "Three Faces of Congressional Media." In *The New Congress*, edited by Thomas E. Mann and Norman J. Ornstein, pp. 55–98. Washington, D.C.: American Enterprise Institute, 1981.

ROHDE, DAVID W., AND KENNETH A. SHEPSLE. "Democratic Committee Assignments in the House of Representatives: Strategic Aspects of a Social Choice Process." *American Political Science Review* (September 1973):889–905.

ROHDE, DAVID W., NORMAN J. ORNSTEIN, AND ROBERT L. PEABODY. "Political Change and Legislative Norms in the U. S. Senate, 1957–1974." In *Studies of Congress*, ed. Glenn R. Parker, pp. 147–188. Washington, D. C.: Congressional Quarterly, 1985.

ROPER, omnibus national surveys, 1973–1984.

SALISBURY, ROBERT H., AND KENNETH SHEPSLE. "U.S. Congressmen as Enterprise." *Legislative Studies Quarterly* (November 1981): 559–576.

SALOMA, JOHN S., III. *Congress and the New Politics*. Boston: Little, Brown, 1969.

SCHELLING, THOMAS C. *The Strategy of Conflict*. London: Oxford University Press, 1960.

SCHICK, ALLEN. *Congress and Money*. Washington, D. C.: The Urban Institute, 1980.

SEIDMAN, HAROLD. *Politics, Position, and Power: The Dynamics of Federal Organization*. New York: Oxford University Press, 1970.

SHEPSLE, KENNETH, AND BARRY WEINGAST. "The Institutional Foundations of Committee Power." *American Political Science Review* (March 1987): 85–104.

SILVERMAN, CORINNE. "The Legislators' View of the Legislative Process." *Public Opinion Quarterly* (Summer 1954): 184–188.

SINCLAIR, BARBARA. "The Transformation of the U. S. Senate—Institutional Consequences of Behavioral Change." Paper delivered at the annual meeting of the Midwest Political Science Association, April 9–11, 1987, Chicago, Ill.

———. "Senate Norms, Senate Styles and Senate Influence." Paper delivered at the annual meeting of the American Political Science Association, August 23–31, 1986, Washington, D. C.

———. *Majority Leadership in the U. S. House*. Baltimore, Md.: Johns Hopkins University Press, 1983.

———. *Congressional Realignment 1925–1978*. Austin, Tx.: University of Texas Press, 1982.

SMITH, STEVEN S. "Decision Making On the House Floor." Paper delivered at the annual meeting of the American Political Science Association, August 28–31, 1986, Washington, D. C.

SMITH, STEVEN S., AND CHRISTOPHER J. DEERING. *Committees In Congress*. Washington, D. C.: Congressional Quarterly, 1984.

———. "Changing Motives for Committee Preferences of New Members of the U. S. House." *Legislative Studies Quarterly* (May 1983):271–281.

STEINER, GILBERT Y. *The Congressional Conference Committee*. Urbana, Ill.: University of Illinois Press, 1951.

STEVENS, ARTHUR G., DANIEL P. MULHOLLAN, AND PAUL S. RUNDQUIST. "U. S. Congressional Structure and Representation: The Role of Informal Groups". *Legislative Studies Quarterly* (August 1981):415–438.

STEWART, JOHN G. "Two Strategies of Leadership: Johnson and Mansfield." In *Congressional Behavior*, edited by Nelson W. Polsby, pp. 61–92. New York: Random House, 1971.

STOKES, DONALD E., AND WARREN E. MILLER. "Party Government and the Saliency of Congress." In *Elections and the Political Order*, edited by Angus Campbell et al., pp. 194–211. New York: John Wiley, 1966.

STROM, GERALD S. "Congressional Policy Making: A Test of a Theory." *Journal of Politics* (August 1975):711–734.

SULLIVAN, JOHN L., AND ERIC M. USLANER. "Congressional Behavior and Electoral Marginality." *American Journal of Political Science* (August 1978):536–553.

SULLIVAN, JOHN L., AND ROBERT E. O'CONNOR. "Electoral Choice and Popular Control of Public Policy: The Case of the 1966 House Elections." *American Political Science Review* (December 1972):1256–1268.

SURREY, STANLEY S. "How Special Tax Provisions Get Enacted." In *Legislative Politics U.S.A.*, edited by Theodore J. Lowi and Randall B. Ripley, pp. 203–213. Boston: Little, Brown, 1973.

SWANSBOROUGH, ROBERT. "Southern Images of President Reagan, Congress, and Southern Congressmen." Paper delivered at the annual meeting of the Southern Political Science Association, October 23–30, 1982, Atlanta, Ga.

TAGGART, WILLIAM A., AND ROBERT F. DURANT. "Home Style of a U.S. Senator: A Longitudinal Analysis." *Legislative Studies Quarterly* (November 1985): 489–504.

THOMAS, MARTIN. "Election Proximity and Senatorial Roll Call Voting." *American Journal of Political Science* (February 1985): 96–111.

THOMAS, ROBERT D., AND ROGER B. HANDBERG. "Congressional Budgeting for Eight Agencies, 1947–1972." *American Journal of Political Science* (February 1974): 179–187.

TRUMAN, DAVID B. *The Congressional Party.* New York: Wiley, 1959.

———. *The Governmental Process.* New York: Alfred A. Knopf, 1951).

TUFTE, EDWARD R. "Determinants of the Outcomes of Midterm Congressional Elections." *American Political Science Review* (September 1975):812–826.

TURNER, JULIUS. *Party and Constituency: Pressures on Congress.* Baltimore, Md.: John Hopkins Press, 1951.

USLANER, ERIC M., AND M. MARGARET CONWAY. "The Responsible Congressional Electorate: Watergate, the Economy, and Vote Choice in 1974." *American Political Science Review* (September 1985):788–803.

UNIVERSITY OF MICHIGAN, American National Election Studies, 1964–1984. Ann Arbor, Mich.

U. S. CONGRESS, HOUSE. *Final Report of The Commission on Administrative Review.* H. Doc. 95–276, 95th Congress, second session, 1977.

———. Senate, Commission on the Operation of the Senate. *Toward a Modern Senate,* S. Doc. 94–278, 94th Cong., 2d. session, 1976.

———. Senate, Committee on Government Operations: *Confidence and Concern: Citizens View American Government.* 93d Cong. lst session, part 1, December 3, 1973 (a survey of public attitudes).

———. Senate, Committee on Rules and Administration. *Hearing Before Ad Hoc Subcommittee to Consider the Reimbursement of Actual Travel Expense of Senators.* 92d Cong., 2d session, June 20, 1972.

VOGLER, DAVID J. *The Third House.* Evanston, Illinois: Northwestern University Press, 1971.

WARWICK, DONALD P. *A Theory of Public Bureaucracy.* Cambridge, Mass.: Harvard University Press, 1975.

WEISSBERG, ROBERT. "Collective vs. Dyadic Representation in Congress." *American Political Science Review* (June 1978):535–547.

WESTEFIELD, LOUIS P. "Majority Party Leadership and the Committee System in the House of Representatives." *American Political Science Review* (December 1974): 1593–1604.

WILDAVSKY, AARON. *The Politics of the Budgetary Process,* 4th ed. Boston: Little, Brown, 1984.

WILSON, WOODROW. *Congressional Government.* New York: Meridian Books, 1956.

WITMER, T. RICHARD. "The Aging of the House." *Political Science Quarterly* (December 1984):526–541.

WOLANIN, THOMAS R. "Committee Seniority and the Choice of House Subcommittee Chairmen: 80th–91st Congresses." *Journal of Politics* (August 1974):687–702.

WOLL, PETER. *Congress.* Boston: Little, Brown, 1985.

WRIGHT, GERALD C., AND MICHAEL B. BERKMAN. "Candidates and Policy in United States Senate Elections." *American Political Science Review* (June 1986):567–588.

YIANNAKIS, DIANA EVANS. "House Members' Communication Styles: Newsletters and Press Releases." *Journal of Politics* (November 1982):1049–1071.

INDEX

Aberbach, J.D., 41, 181, 212
Abourezk, James (D–S.D.), 77
Abrams, M., 111
Absenteeism, strategic use of, 62, 64n10
Abzug, Bella (D–N.Y.), 3
Administration cleavages, 145–46
Advertising, 25–26
  enhancing reelection by, 84
Agencies, federal. *See also* Cozy triangles
  allocations to, 208–9
  authority of, 180–81
  budgetary politics and, 120–21
  expansion of, 210
  favoritism for, 206–8
  oversight of, 41, 92, 213
Agenda, legislative, 62
Agreements, unanimous consent, 43n5,
  125
Agriculture Committee, 105, 205
Agriculture, Department of, 208
Aldrich, Nelson (R–R.I.), 185
Allison, W.B. (R–Io.), 185
Allocation decisions of bureaucrats, 209
Allowance
  clerk-hire, 30–31, 36, 37, 43n3
  expense, 31, 35–38, 43n3
Almanac of American Politics, The, 222
Amendments, floor, 20n6
Appointment system for subcommittee
  leadership, 101

Apprenticeship norm, decline of, 2–3
Appropriations, budget, 141
Appropriations Committees, 97, 103, 104,
  122–23, 208, 209
Appropriations subcommittees, 141–42
Army Corps of Engineers (USED), 206–7
Arnold, R.D., 40, 209, 210
Asher, H.B., 2, 6, 90, 103
Assignments. *See* Committee assignments
At-large whips, 113
Attentive home styles. *See* Home styles,
  attentive
Attitudes
  conducive to constituency representation,
  173–76
  influence of individual, 6–7
Authorization, 141
Automatic decision rules, lack of party
  discipline and, 195

"Backdoor spending," 141–42
"Backscratching," senatorial, 121–22
Baker, R.K., 198n1
Banking Committee, 105
"Bargained compensation," 124
Bargaining, 117–36, 217–18, 235
  in budgetary politics, 119–22
  in committees, 127–29
  in conference committees, 122–24
  effect on federal budget, 134–35
  effect on legislative process, 134–35

Bargaining (*con't.*)
  factors promoting, 129–33
    decentralization of Congress, 17, 131–32
    lack of party discipline and, 218
    norms supportive of bargaining, 132–33
    weakness of party leaders, 129–31
  in leader–follower relations, 124–27, 130, 131–32
  logrolling, 117–18
  policy consequences of, 133–35
Berkman, M.B., 24
Bias in information reaching congressional offices, 177
Bibby, J.F., 13, 14, 66, 78, 113
Bill of rights, subcommittee, 157
Biographical directory, 234–35
Blocs, voting, 152, 156
  influence of, 160
  leadership of, 227
"Boll Weevils," 154
Bond, J.R., 87, 94n6
Born, R., 94nn5, 7, 106
Brademas, John (D–Ind.), 2
Brady, D.W., 6, 91, 124, 130, 173, 186, 195, 196
Brookshire, R.G., 68, 69–70
Brumberg, B.S., 12, 94n5
Buckley, W., 3
Budget Committees, 142, 143
Budget resolutions, 142–43
Budgets
  bargaining and, 119–22
  decentralization and, 141–43
  effect of bargaining on, 134–35
  expansion of, cozy triangles and, 210, 213
Bull Moose Progressive Movement, 67
Bullock, C.S., III, 6, 9, 83, 103, 105, 169–70, 173, 183n2
Bureaucracy, federal
  constituency representation and, 26–29, 165–68
  partisan discussion and strategies of, 120
Bureaucrats, federal
  allocation decisions of, 209
  career, 210–11
  cultivation of congressmen, 210
  desire to expand budget, 210
  motivation to join cozy triangles, 200, 209–11
Burnham, W.D., 80, 81
Byrd, Robert C. (D–W.Va.), 167
Cain, B.E., 87
Calvert, R.B., 80, 81
Campaign funds, 85, 86–87
  "war chests," 87
Campbell, A., 24
Cannon, Joseph G. (R–Ill.), 12, 97, 98, 111, 138
Career bureaucrat, 210–11
Careerism, 236–37
  cozy triangles and, 211–12
Careers, 95–116
  constituency, stages of, 88–89
  goals sought during, 95–96
  institutionalization of, 109–12
  patterns, 96–109

  in committee system, 96–97, 99–106
  in leadership, 99
  party leadership opportunities in House and Senate and, 96, 97–98, 113
  political life cycle and, 106–9
  policy consequences of, 112–15
  professionalization of Congress and, 95
Carter, Jimmy, 14
Carverse, P.E., 24
Casework, 26–29
  growth of, 28–29
  oversight hearings and, 180
  oversight of agencies and, 41
Cater, D., 199
Cavanagh, T.E., 40, 174–75
Chairmen, committee, 147
Challengers, weak, 86–87, 94n6
Chi–Hung, C., 103
"Chits," 131, 152
Civil rights issues, 172
Civil War party system, 67
Clapp, C.L., 2
Clarke, W.D.Jr., 9
Clausen, A., 5, 20n3, 172, 176
Cleavages in House committee system, 145–46
Clem, A.L., 89
Clerk-hire allowance, 30–31, 36, 37, 43n3
Cliques, 152
Cloture rule, 157
Clubs, 152, 153
Coalitions, 152, 153. *See also* Groups; Cozy triangles
  personal electoral, 7–8, 82–83
  resistance to negative sanctions and building of, 188
Coattails, presidential, 79–81, 93n1
  decline of, 196
Cohesion, lack of. *See* Party discipline, lack of
Committee assignments, 228–30
  biased, decision making and, 211–12
  constituency and, 9
  independence of congressmen and, 8–10
  multiple, 114–15
  overrepresentation of constituency interests and, 204–6
  party leaders and, 12
  self-selection for, 168–69, 205
  seniority system and, 11–12, 116n2
Committee hearings held in subcommittees, 147–48
Committees, congressional, 228–30. *See also* Cozy triangles; Senate committees
  attractiveness to incumbents, 228
  bargaining in, 127–29
  budget, 142, 143
  career patterns in, 96–97, 99–106
  cleavages in, 145–46
  compensation in bargaining between, 121
  conference, 122–24
  constituency representation in, 168–70
  decentralization and, 138–51
    budgetary process and, 141–43
    factionalism and, 143–46

staff involvement and, 146
subcommittees and, 146–51
vote cuing and, 140–41, 217
weakened party leadership and, 138–39
decision-making environment of, 144, 230
decline in prescriptive seats, 183n2
ex post veto power of, 163n1
institutionalization of career patterns and, 109–10
leadership of, 100, 113, 227
legislative jurisdictions of, 146
Legislative Reorganization Act (1946) and, 139–40
norms of reciprocity in, 132
party, 150
power of, 163n1
prestigious, 103–5
revenue, 143
specialization of members of, 140–41
state delegations' control of, 169–70, 183n2
transfers between, 103–6, 116n1
Communication, committee factionalism and, 144–45
Compensation, 118, 119. *See also* Bargaining
  "bargained," 124
  in between-committee bargaining, 121
  in budgetary interactions between agencies and committee members, 120–21
  in conference committees, 123
  effect on federal budget, 135
  in leader-follower relations, 126
  during legislative process, 128
Competition
  decline in, 86–87, 93n2
  political moderation and, 179
Complaints, constituent's, 168. *See also* Constituency representation
  attention to, 179–81
Comprehensive party programs, independence of congressmen and improbability of, 17–18
Compromise, norm of, 132
Conference committees, 122–24
Confidence, public
  in congressmen vs. Congress, 46–49
  in reform, 46
Conflicts
  avoidance of, 134
  on bureau-subcommittee level, 202–3
Congress, relationships among characteristics of, 217–19
Congressional Budget and Impoundment Control Act (PL 93–344), 142
Congressional Budget Office, 4, 142
Congressional Directory, 222
Congressional District Data Book, 222
Congressional Quarterly, 222
Congressional Quarterly Weekly Report, 222
Congressional Record, 13, 222
Congressional Research Service, 4

Congressmen. *See also* Home styles, attentive; Incumbents; Representatives
bureaucratic intercessions made by, 165–66
bureaucrats' cultivation of, 210
change in type of, 16
freshman
  committee assignments, 9
  decline of apprenticeship norm for, 2–3
goals of, 95–96
  adaptation of attentive home styles and, 35
  conflicts with constituency demands, 223
  decentralization and, 157, 159–60
  party leadership and, 189
as "home-town boys," 175
image of politician in contrast to, 45
independence of, 1–20, 237
  accounting for, 10–17
  committee assignments and, 8–10
  decline of apprenticeship norm and, 2–3
  elections and, 7–8, 13–16
  home styles and, 10–11, 16, 24, 218
  individuality and, 3–4
  institutional conditions and, 11–13
  membership turnover and, 16
  policy consequences of, 17–18
  policy making and, 4–7
  waning of constraints on, 1–2
interest in federal projects, 211
internalization of constituency attitudes and values, 174–76
longevity in office, 178–79
motivation to join cozy triangles, 209–11
percentage of electorate writing to (1947–1984), 28
perception of constituent opinion, 172, 173
popularity of, 45–64
  attentive home styles and, 218
  constituency representation and, 57–60, 87–89, 218–19
  denigration of Congress and, 54, 59–60, 61
  media treatment and, 55, 60–61
  perceptions of responsiveness and, 51–54
  performance evaluations and, 49–51
  policy consequences of, 61–62
  public confidence and, 46–49
  public expectations and, 54, 55–58
  reasons for, 54–61
self-selection into committees, 168–69, 205
specialization from committee membership, 140–41
Consent agreements, unanimous, 43n5, 125
Conservative Democratic Forum ("Boll Weevils"), 154
Constituency
  careers, stages of, 88–89
  cleavages in, 145–46
  committee assignments and, 9
  congressmen's goals conflicting with interests of, 223

Constituency (*con't.*)
  expectations of, 34
  importance in legislative voting of, 5
  informal groups and, 154
  perception of congressmen, 32, 33–34, 51–54
  trust of, 24, 25, 48–49, 63*nn*3, 4
Constituency representation, 165–83, 236
  allocation of time to, 22, 29–30
    seniority and, 106–9
  arenas of, 166–73
    bureaucracy, 26–29, 165–68
    committees, 168–70
    floor voting, 170–73
  attentive home styles and, 218
  complaint handling, 168
  costs associated with, 34–39
  cozy triangles and, 218–19
  emphasis on, 40–41
  factors promoting, 173–79
    attitudes conducive to representation, 174–76
    elections, 176–79
  growing burden of, 76
  "justifiable" policy voting and, 181
  measurement of, 165
  overrepresentation in committees, 204–6
  policy consequences of, 179–83
  popularity of congressmen and, 57–60, 87–89, 218–19
  protection of industries, 170–71
  protective legislation and, 166–68
Controversial issues, avoiding taking stands on, 61–62
Conway, M.M., 94*n*7
Cook, T., 94*n*6
Cooper, J., 71–76, 111, 124, 130, 186, 195, 196
Cooperation, 201
Coordination of decision making, 134, 136*n*1
Copeland, G.W., 103, 105
Cover, A.D., 12, 94*n*5, 106–7
Covington, C., 87, 94*n*6
Cozy triangles, 167, 199–215, 236
  agency oversight and, 213
  budget expansion and, 210, 213
  careerism and, 211–12
  congressional and bureaucratic motivations for, 200, 209–11
  constituency representation and, 218–19
  crisis policy and, 203–4
  defined, 199
  distributive policy and, 201–2
  identifying, 204–9
    agency favoritism and, 206–8
    allocating agency benefits and, 208–9
    overrepresentation on committees and, 204–6
  impact of, 200–201
  philosophy of government and, 212
  policy consequences of, 212–13
  protective regulatory policy and, 202
  redistributive policy and, 202–3
  reform attempts and, 213
  strategic policy and, 203

structural policy and, 203
Credit claiming, 25–26, 84
Crisis policy, cozy triangles and, 203–4
Cues, voting, 20*n*3, 140–41, 145
  based on expertise, 159
  from committee members, 217
  incumbency and, 83–84
  from state party delegations, 156
Czar rule, 129–30

Daniels, R.S., 6
Davidson, R.H., 8, 33, 50, 55, 98, 147, 152, 153, 155, 176, 206, 212–13
Debate on legislative measures, 233
Decentralization of Congress, 137–64, 217, 235–36
  bargaining and, 17, 131–32
  committees and, 138–51
    budgetary process and, 141–43
    factions in, 143–46
    staff involvement and, 146
    subcommittees and, 146–51
    voting cued by, 140–41, 217
    weakened party leadership and, 138–39
  defined, 137
  expansion of leadership positions and committee assignments and, 114–15
  forces promoting, 157–60
    congressional reforms, 157–58
    member goals, 157, 159–60
    specialization norm, 157, 158–59, 163*n*3
  lack of party discipline and, 194–95
  party leaders' adaptation to, 194
  policy consequences of, 160–62
  political parties and, 151–57
    informal groups, 152–56
    party organization, 151–52
    state party delegations, 156
Decision making. *See also* Policy outcomes
  in committees, 144, 230
    biased recruitment and, 211–12
  on congressional spending, 141
  coordination of, 134, 136*n*1
  on floor of House and Senate, 163*n*1
  power motive and, 160
  subcommittee involvement in, 147
Decision rules, lack of party discipline and automatic, 195
Deering, C.J., 9, 113, 149, 198*n*2
Defections, partisan, 83–84
Defense policy, 203
Delay, legislative, 161–62, 196–97
Delegations, state, 156
  control of committee seats by, 169–70, 183*n*2
  role of, 7
Democratic Caucus, 130–32
Democratic Party, weakness during Civil War party system era, 67
Democratic Study Group (DSG), 154
Democratization of congressional rules and procedures, 130–31
Democrats, southern, 193
Demonstration Cities conference (1966), 123
Directory, biographical, 234–35

Discipline, party. *See* Party discipline, lack of
Discussion, partisan. *See* Partisan discussion
Distributive policy, cozy triangles and, 201–2
Districts, marginal, 77–79, 94n4
Dodd, L.C., 23, 115, 116n1, 160
Dodd, L.W., 147, 148
Douglass, S.R., 9
Downs, A., 60, 61
Duncan, 68, 69–70
Durant, R.F., 15
Dyson, J., 127
Education Committee, 97
89th Congress, citizen satisfaction with performance of, 51
Eldersveld, S.J., 185
Elections
    constituency representation and, 174
    independence of congressmen and, 7–8, 13–16
    as mechanisms of constituency influence, 176–79
    realigning, 196
    turnover and structural changes in, 69
Electoral coalitions, personal, 7–8, 82–83
Electoral safety of congressional candidates, 14–16, 93n1
England, D.E., 183n2
Enterprises, member, 37–38
Entitlements, "mandatory," 141–42
Entrepreneurship, policy, 196–97
Environment, congressional, unpopularity of Congress and, 56
"Errand boy" activities, 180
Esteem, public. *See* Popularity of congressmen
Evans, R., 64n10
Executive agencies. *See* Agencies, federal; Cozy triangles
Expansionist stage of constituency career, 88
Expectations
    of Congress vs. congressmen, 54, 55–58
    constituent, 34
Expense allowance, 31, 35–38, 43n3
Expertise, voting cues based on, 159
Experts, committee members as, 140
Explanation of Washington activities to constituents, 23–25
Ex post veto power of committees, 163n1
Factionalism, 143–46
Favoritism, agency, 206–8
Federalist Party, 67
Fenno, R.F., 2, 16, 22–26, 37, 43n1, 46, 49, 56, 59, 60, 84, 85, 88, 95–97, 106, 122, 122–24, 127, 132, 133, 135, 140, 146–47, 156, 159, 181, 207, 208
Ferejohn, J.A., 14, 80, 81, 87
Filibusters, 3, 157
Fiorina, M.P., 26, 27, 40, 66, 67, 70, 87, 94n3, 121, 179, 200, 204, 211
Fire-alarm oversight system, 180–81

First Concurrent Budget Resolution, 142–43
1st Congress, 65
Fitzgerald, R., 128, 166–67
Fleisher, R., 87, 94n6
Floor
    actions on, 232–33
    number of legislators managing bills on, 198n2
    order of legislative action, 233
Floor amendments, 20n6
Floor leader, 98, 226
Floor manager, 233
Floor voting, 5–6
    constituency representation in, 170–73
    explanations of, 23, 181
Foley, M., 89–90
Foreign Affairs Committee, 97
Foreign policy, 203
Forest Service, 208
Fowler, L.L., 9
Fox, H.W., 146
Fragmentation, regional, 191–94
Franking privilege, 31, 35–36, 43n
Franklin, G., 200, 201, 203
Freshman congressmen
    committee assignments, 9
    decline of apprenticeship norm for, 2–3
Froman, L.A., Jr., 6, 195
Funds, campaign, 85, 86–87
Gallagher, M., 12, 65, 111, 112, 126
Galloway, G.B., 137
Gallup Poll survey of institutional confidence, 47–48
Garand, J.C., 93n1
Gawthrop, L.C., 114
Gellhorn, W., 168, 175
General Accounting Office (GAO), 4, 180
Geographic constituency, 172–73
Gertzog, I.N., 12, 103
Glazer, A., 183n3
Goals of congressmen, 95–96
    adaptation of attentive home styles and, 35
    conflicts with constituency demands, 223
    decentralization and, 157, 159–60
    multiple, 35
    party leadership and, 189
Goldenberg, E.N., 87, 189
Goldstone, J.A., 101
Goldwater, Barry (R), 101
Goss, C.F., 205
Government
    party, 191
    philosophy of, 212
Government Operations Committee, 105
Gramm, Phil (D.–Tex.), 198n1
Gramm-Rudman-Hollings balanced-budget measure, 64n9
Great Depression, 67
Gross, D.A., 93n1
Groups. *See also* Cozy triangles
    informal, 152–56, 227–28
    interest, 153, 200
"Gypsy Moths," 154

Hammond, S.W., 146
Handberg, R.B., 206
Hansen plan (1974), 158
Harris, L., 55
Hatfield, Mark (R–Oreg.), 38
Health Subcommittee, 102
Hearings
    on legislation, 127–28
    oversight, casework and, 180
Hebert, Edward, 102
Hibbing, J.R., 76, 77
Hill styles, 223–24
Hinckley, B., 99, 102
Holtzman, A., 214n1
Home styles, attentive, 21–44, 223–24, 237
    advertising, credit claiming, and position taking to transmit, 25–26
    constituency representation and, 218
    evidence of, 26–34
        casework, 26–29
        office resource exploitation, 30–32
        perceptions of congressmen and, 32, 33–34
        personal time of congressmen, 29–30
    explanation of Washington activities to constituents and, 23–25
    independence of congressmen and, 10–11, 16, 24, 218
    individuality in, 26
    policy consequences of, 40–41
    political life cycle and, 107–9
    popularity of congressmen and, 218
    presentation of self and, 23
    reasons for adopting, 34–39
        cost subsidization and shifting, 35–36
        legislative scheduling, 30, 35, 38–39
        satisfying multiple goals, 35
    resource allocation and, 21–22
    of senator vs. representative, 24–25
    stability in membership of Congress and, 82, 87–89
House Armed Services Committee, 205
House Budget Committee (HBC), 121
House of Representatives
    attractiveness of, as decision-making body, 68–69
    average amount of service in, 66
    challengers to incumbents in, 86
    cleavages in committees, 145–46
    committee assignments of freshmen in, 9
    committee leadership positions in, 100
    committee prestige and corresponding rank, index of, 103–5
    conference committees and, 124
    decision making on floor of, 163n1
    decline of marginal districts and turnover in, 77–78
    electoral safety of incumbents in, 14, 15
    ideology and voting in, 6–7
    informal groups in, 155
    interpositional change in leadership offices in, 99
    leadership structure of, 96
    learning legislative norms in, 2–3

    office resource increases in (1945–1975), 36, 37
    party leadership opportunities in, 96, 97–98, 113
    reforms, 113
    role of party in, 187
    schedule of legislative business, 38
    seniority system in, 111–12, 137
    specialization in, 158–59
    subcommittee chairs in, 101–2
    survivability of members of, 70–77
    turnover trends in, 66–68
    voluntary retirements in, 71–77
    votes on reciprocal trade issues between 1948–1958, 6
    whips, 98
House party committees, 150
House Public Works committee, 214n2
House Rules Committee, 139
Huitt, R.K., 3, 19n1, 59
Huntington, S.M., 41, 135
Hurley, P., 195, 196
Identification
    committee factionalism and subjective, 144–45
    with party, 82
Ideological cleavages, 145–46
Ideological voting, 20n3
Ideology, influence on House and Senate voting, 6–7
Incumbency as replacement for party cue voting, 83–84
Incumbents. *See also* Congressmen; Home styles, attentive; Stability in congressional membership
    atypical for their constituencies, 88–89
    campaign resources of, 85
    electoral safety of, 14–16
    freedom from constraints, 1
    information on, 222
    personal electoral coalitions of, 7–8
    popularity of, 236–37
Independent congressmen. *See* Congressmen
Individuality, 3–4
    in home style, 26
    in policy making behavior, 4–7
Industries, congressmen's protection of constituency, 170–71
Informal groups, 152–56, 227–28
Innovations, membership stability and policy, 91
Institutional conditions promoting independence of congressmen, 11–13
Institutional confidence, 46–48
Institutionalization
    characteristics associated with, 109
    of congressional career, 109–12
Interest groups, 200
    sponsorship of informal legislative groups, 153
Interests, committee factionalism and, 144–45
Interior Committee, 97, 205
Interior Department, funding levels for, 208

Ippolito, D.S., 143
Issue(s)
  saliency of
    constituency influence and, 172
    party cohesion and, 195
  unilateral promotion of, 4–5
Jacobson, G.C., 86, 87, 93n3
Jewell, M.E., 103
Johannes, J.R., 27, 29, 41, 183n1
Johnson, Lyndon (D–Tex.), 126
Jones, C.O., 84, 205
Katosh, J.P., 63n2
Keefe, W.J., 90–91
Kernell, S., 69, 70, 86, 87
Kingdon, J.W., 23, 170–72, 175–79, 181
Korean War, 50
Kritzer, H.M., 6
Kuklinski, J.H., 24

Labor Committee, 97
Leadership, congressional
  career patterns in, 99
  committee, 100, 113, 227
  of informal voting blocs, 227
  layers of, 151–52
  partisan discussion among, 125–26
  reforms strengthening, 157
  subcommittee, 101–2, 113
  succession patterns in, 109
  time spent in district and, 108, 109
Leadership, party, 113–14, 225–27
  adaptation to decentralization, 194
  bargaining and, 124–27, 130, 131–32
  committee assignments and, 12
  dependence on personal persuasion, 186–
    87
  influence of, 12, 13, 115
  layers of, 151–52
  majority and minority, 226
  member's personal goals and, 189
  opportunities in House and Senate for,
    96, 97–98, 113
  patterns of change in, 99
  pressure from, 187
  relationships with newer members, 189
  resources available to, 188–89
  Senate, 96, 97–98, 113, 138–39, 190
  toleration of individualistic policy pur-
    suits of members, 5
  weakness of, 129–31, 185–90
  committees and, 138–39
Legislation
  actors involved in, 221–28
    congressmen, 222–24
    executive branch, 224–25
    other leaders, 227–28
    party leaders, 225–27
  agency favoritism in, 206–8
  authorization of, 141
  committee jurisdictions on, 146
  debate on, 233
  delays in, 161–62, 196–97
  effect of bargaining on, 134–35
  introduction of, 230
  perceived importance and time spent on,
    57–58

pork barrel, 40, 61, 119
  to protect constituency, 166–68
  reciprocal trade, 6
  subcommittee involvement in, 149
  tax, logrolling associated with, 128
  unilateral promotion of issues, 4–5
  unpopularity of Congress and, 56
Legislative action, order of, 233
Legislative agenda, 62
Legislative goals, 159–60
Legislative hearings, 127–28
Legislative influence, evaluation of, 234
Legislative interests, coordination by in-
    formal groups, 153–54
Legislative Reorganization Act
  of 1946, 139–40
  of 1970, 39
Legislative schedule, 112
  attentive home style and, 30, 35, 38–39
Life cycle, political, 106–9
Light, L., 29
Lindblom, C.E., 118, 119, 124, 134,
    136n1, 161
Lipset, S.M., 47, 48
Lipson, G., 128, 166–67
Logrolling, 117–18, 135, 201
  associated with tax legislation, 128
  in conference committees, 123–24
Long, Russel (D–La.), 126
Loomis, B.A., 102, 113, 115, 116n5
Louis Harris surveys of institutional con-
    fidence, 46–47
Lowi, T.J., 133, 212
Lynn, N.B., 6

Maass, A., 207
McCubbins, M., 41, 180–81
Mailing, seniority effects on, 106–7. *See
    also* Resources
Majority leader (floor leader), 98, 226
Malbin, M.J., 13, 14, 66, 78, 113
"Mandatory entitlements," 141–42
Manley, F., 135
Mann, T.E., 13, 14, 66, 78, 113
Marginal districts and states, decline of,
    77–79, 94n4
Marginality hypothesis, 179
Mark-up sessions, 127
Matthews, D.R., 1–2, 19n1, 20n3, 127,
    132, 140–41, 187
Mattingly, Mack (D–Ga.), 166
Maverick, role of, 19n1
Mayhew, D.R., 25, 77–78, 112, 135, 180,
    204
Media treatment of Congress vs. con-
    gressmen, 55, 60–61
"Member enterprises," 37–38
Metcalf, Lee (D–Mont.), 166
Miller, W.E., 6, 24, 63n2, 172, 176–77,
    178
Minority leader, 98, 226
Mitchell, W.C., 45
Mobile offices, 28–29
Moderation, political, electoral competi-
    tiveness and, 179
Moss, Frank (D–Utah.), 166

Mueller, J.E., 51
Multiple goals of congressmen, 35
Murphy, T.P., 214*n*1
Nader, Ralph, 222
National Journal, 222
National tides
  favoring one party, quality of challengers
    and, 87
  susceptibility of congressional elections
    to, 91
Nelson, G., 99
Newsletters, 84. *See also* Resources
New York Times, 222
94th Congress, 113
92nd Congress, 66, 113
Niskanen, W.A., 213
Nomination for congressional seat, rota-
    tion of, 69
Norm(s)
  apprenticeship, decline of, 2–3
  of compromise and reciprocity, 132–33
  declining adherence to, 131
  in House of Representatives, 2–3
  rotation, 69
  supportive of bargaining, 132–33
Northeast-Midwest Coalition, 153
Northern states, safe Democratic and
    Republican Senate seats in (1946–
    1980), 78–79
Novak, R., 64*n*10

O'Connor, R.E., 178
Offices, mobile, 28–29
Office Technology Assessment, 4
Ogul, M.S., 90–91
Oleszek, W.J., 39, 43*n*5, 50, 98, 125, 152,
    153, 155, 206, 212–13
O'Neill, Thomas P. ("Tip"), 113, 188–89
Opinion, constituency, 172–73
Opposition party, costs of voting with, 1
Organization, party, 151–52
Ornstein, N.J., 2–3, 13, 14, 66, 78, 100,
    113, 132, 159, 164*n*3
Oversight
  of agencies, 41, 92, 213
  fire-alarm system of, 180–81
  hearings, casework and, 180
Packwood, R.W., 110, 111
Parker, G.R., 6–9, 12, 23, 26, 28–30, 33–
    35, 37, 43*nn*1, 2, 48, 50, 51, 55, 85,
    87–89, 91, 94*n*3, 102, 104, 113, 114,
    116*n*3, 133, 145, 205, 221
Parker, S.L., 6, 91, 104, 133, 145, 205
Particularism in distribution of federal
    projects, 179
Parties, political
  committee prestige and, 105
  decentralization and, 151–57
    informal groups and, 152–56
    party organization and, 151–52
    state party delegations and, 156
  decline of, 195–96
  decline of influence, 14, 15–16
  decline of partisanship, 81, 82–84
  identification with, 82
  importance in legislative voting of, 5

leadership. *See* Leadership, party
system of
  five periods in development of,
    67–68
  operation of, 184–85
  realignments in, 91
  voter likes and dislikes of their repre-
    sentatives by, 32
Partisan cleavages, 145–46
Partisan composition of Congress, change
    in, 91
Partisan defections, 83–84
Partisan discussion, 118–19. *See also* Bar-
    gaining
  bureaucratic strategies entailing, 120
  in conference committees, 123
  among congressional leaders, 125–26
  during legislative hearings, 127–28
Partisanship, decline of, 81, 82–84
Party discipline, lack of, 184–98, 236
  automatic decision rules and, 195
  bargaining and, 218
  decentralization and, 194–95
  evidence of, 185–94
    lack of party voting, 190–93
    regional fragmentation, 191–94
    weakened party leaders, 185–90
  policy effects of, 196–97
  reasons for, 194–96
Party government, notion of, 191
Party programs, lack of, 196–97
Party voting, lack of, 190–93
Patman, Wright, 102
Payne, J.L., 10, 16
Peabody, R.L., 2–3, 99, 132, 159, 163*n*2,
    164*n*3
Perceptions of congressmen and Congress
  about responsiveness, 51–54
  about time spent on legislative activities,
    57
  attentive home style and, 32, 33–34
Performance evaluation of Congress vs.
    congressmen, 49–51
Perquisites ("perks"), office. *See* Resources
Personal problems, people viewed as sour-
    ces of assistance for, 52, 53
PL 93–344, 142
Plott, C.R., 209
Poage, W.R., 102
Policy
  avoiding association with unpopular, 61
  bargaining and, 133–35
  careers in Congress and, 112–15
  constituency influence over, 178–83
  cozy triangles and, 201–4, 212–13
  decentralization and, 160–62
  defense, 203
  disjointed, 161
  evaluation of, 234
  foreign, 203
  incremental nature of, 161
  independence of congressmen and, 4–7,
    17–18
  lack of party discipline, 196–97
  popular congressmen and unpopular
    Congress and, 56, 61–62

stability in membership of Congress and, 89–92
subgovernment and, 200
Policy entrepreneurship, 196–97
Policy outcomes, 144, 230
Political issues, unpopularity of Congress and, 56
Politician, image of, 45
Politics in America, 222
Polsby, N.W., 12, 16, 65, 66, 97, 109, 111, 112, 126, 165
Polsby, Nelson, 111
Poole, K., 6
Popularity of congressmen, 45–64
  constituency service and, 57–60, 87–89, 218–19
  denigration of Congress and, 54, 59–60, 61
  media treatment and, 55, 60–61
  perceptions of responsiveness and, 51–54
  performance evaluations and, 49–51
  policy consequences of, 56, 61–62
  public confidence and, 46–49
  public expectations and, 54, 55–58
  reasons for, 54–61
Pork barrel legislation, 40, 61
  reciprocity and, 119
Position taking, 25–26
Postage allowance, 36, 37
Post Office Committee, 97, 105
Powell, Adam Clayton (D–N.Y.), 3, 223
Powell, L.W., 171
Power. *See also* Decentralization of Congress
  of committees, 163n1
  decision making and, 160
  of Speaker of the House, 97–98, 129–30, 186
Prefloor congressional procedures, 230–34
  committee members and, 230–31
  congressional members and, 231
  floor action, 233
  introduction of legislation, 230
  parliamentary procedures, 232–33
  party leaders and, 231
  White House and, 231
Prescriptive committee seats, decline in, 183n2
Presentation of self, 23, 59
Presidential coattails, 79–81, 93n1
Presidential elections (1900–1980), ticket splitting in, 13, 14
Press, treatment of Congress vs. congressmen by, 60–61
Pressman, J., 123
Pressure from leadership, 187
Price, H.D., 20n4, 65, 68, 69, 95, 109, 110, 111–12, 165, 217
Procedures, democratization of, 130–31
Professionalization of Congress, 95
Projects, federal
  congressmen's interest in, 211
  particularism in distribution of, 179
Protectionist stage of constituency career, 88

Protective regulatory policy, cozy triangles and, 202
Proxmire, William, 3, 19nn1, 2
Publications, use of government, 31
Public Works Committee, 105

Ragsdale, L., 94n6
Ray, B.A., 106, 169
Reagan, Ronald R., 14
Realigning elections, 196
Realignments in party system, 91
Recess periods, 39, 44n6
Reciprocal trade legislation, 6
Reciprocity, 118, 119. *See also* Bargaining
  in budgetary decisions, 121–22
  in conference committees, 124
  effect on federal budget, 135
  in leader-follower relations, 126–27
  during legislative process, 128
  norm of, 132–33
Redistributive policy, cozy triangles and, 202–3
Reelection
  advertising to enhance changes of, 84
  evaluation on basis of, 234
Reelection constituency, 172–73
Reform, congressional
  cozy triangles and, 213
  decentralization and, 157–58
  House, 113
  public confidence in, 46
  subcommittees and, 113, 157–58
Regional fragmentation, 191–94
Reorganization Act (1939 & 1945), 207
Representation, constituency. *See* Constituency representation
Representational obligations, delegate vs. trustee role required in, 7
Representatives. *See also* Congressmen
  attentive home style of, 24–25
  constituent perception of, 33–34
  expectations of, 56
  perception of voters, 177
  style of representation, 176
  survivorship rate of, 70–77
  view of functions expected of them, 174–75
  voter likes and dislikes of (1978–1984), 32, 33
Republican Party
  in early development of party system, 67
  improved electoral position in South of, 78
Republicans, northeastern, 193–94
Resolutions, budget, 142–43
Resources
  available to party leadership, 188–89
  office, 35–38, 112
    automatic allocation of, 11–13
    exploitation to maintain attentive home style, 30–32
    increases in House (1945–1975), 36, 37
    intertwining of electoral and representational purposes in use of, 84, 94nn4, 5, 6
    stability in membership of Congress and, 81–82, 84–85

Resources (*con't.*)
  used for campaigning, 85
  personal, 21–22
Retirements, voluntary, 71–77
Revenue committees, 143
Ripley, R.B., 118, 122, 125–27, 156, 185–
    87, 187, 188, 190, 195, 197, 200,
    201, 203, 212
Robbins, M., 183n3
Rockman, B.A., 181, 212
Rohde, D.W., 2–3, 12, 66, 67, 70, 116n2,
    132, 159, 164n3
Roll calls, 6, 233
Roll-call voting. *See* Floor voting
Roosevelt, Franklin D., 67, 119
Roosevelt, Theodore, 67
Roper, 28
Rotation, norm of, 69
Rules, democratization of, 130–31
Rules Committee, 103, 104, 139
Rundquist, B.S., 12, 65, 111, 112, 124, 126

Safety, electoral, 93n1
Saliency of issues
  constituency influence and, 172
  party cohesion and, 195
Salisbury, R.H., 31, 37
Saloma, J., 25, 29
Schedule, legislative schedule, 112
  attentive home style and, 30, 35, 38–39
Schick, A., 121
Schneider, 47, 48
Schott, R.L., 147, 148
Schwartz, T., 41, 180–81
Scicchitano, M.J., 83
Second Budget Resolution, 143
Seidman, H., 213
Self, presentation of, 23, 59
Senate
  ambition within, 16
  attractiveness of, as decision-making
    body, 68
  challengers to incumbents in, 86
  class of 1958, changes in policies due to,
    89–90
  congressional reforms' impact on, 158
  decision making on floor of, 163n1
  decline of apprenticeship norm in, 2–3
  electoral safety of incumbents, 15
  filibuster, 3
  individualistic pursuits in, 3–4
  influence of ideology on voting in, 6–7
  informal groups in, 155
  leadership change in, 99
  leadership structure of, 96
  party leadership in, 96, 97–98, 113, 138–
    39, 190
  president *pro tempore*, 96
  schedule of legislative business, 38–39
  seniority system in, 110–11, 137
  specialization in, 159
  unanimous consent agreements in, 43n5,
    125
  voluntary retirements in, 71–77
  whips, 98
Senate Budget Committee (SBC), 121
Senate committees

conference committees, 124
declining autonomy of, 164n4
leadership positions, 100
party, 150
reforms streamlining system of, 157
reliance on subcommittees, 147
Senate majority leader, 138–39
Senate subcommittees, 149–51
Senators
  attentive home style of, 24–25
  "backscratching" among, 121–22
  constituent perception of, 33–34
  expectations of, 56
  exploitation of office resources, 85
  turnover trend among, 68
Seniority system, 137, 138, 195, 217
  challenges to, 102–3
  committee assignments and, 11–12,
    116n1
  committee leadership and, 100–103
  evolution of, 12, 20n4
  in House, 111–12
    voluntary retirements and demise of,
      76–77
  independence of congressmen and, 11
  institutionalization of, 109–12
  in Senate, 110–11, 137
  subcommittee leadership and, 101–2
  time spent on constituent affairs and,
    106–9
  transfer among committee and, 105
Shepsle, K.A., 12, 31, 37, 116n2, 163n1
Silverman, C., 158
Simulation of Congress, 219–37
  characteristics of, 235–37
  committees, 228–30
  legislative actors, 221–28
  prefloor congressional procedures, 230–34
Sinclair, B., 3, 5, 20n4, 113, 125, 131,
    132, 164n4, 188–89, 193–95
Smith, S.S., 9, 20n4, 113, 149, 164n3
Soil Conservation Service, 208
Soule, J., 127
Speaker of the House, 96, 138–39, 185–86
  powers of, 97–98, 129–30, 186
Specialization of committee members,
    140–41
  decentralization and, 157, 158–59, 163n3
Spending, congressional
  "backdoor," 141–42
  decisions on, 141
Split-ticket voting, 13, 14, 196
Sponsorship of informal groups, 153
Sprague, J., 105
Stability in congressional membership,
    65–94
  conditions promoting, 81–89
    attentive home styles, 82, 87–89
    decline of partisanship, 81, 82–84
    office resources, 81–82, 84–85
    weak challengers, 86–87
  legislative oversight of agencies and, 92
  policy consequences of, 89–92
  turnover and, 65, 66–81
    in contemporary Congress, 66–68,
      70–81

decline of marginal districts and states
and, 77–79
historical trends in, 66–70
survivorship rate of representatives and,
70–77
weakness of presidential coattails and,
79–81
Stability in voting records of congressmen, 90–91
Staff
committee, 146
personal, 20n5, 112
allowance for hiring, 30–31
casework done by, 27–29
constituency service activities of, 22, 37
independence of congressmen and, 12–13
"small business" operations of, 37–38
use of, as function of seniority, 106
Standing vote, 233
State party delegations, 156
control of committee seats, 169–70, 183n2
States, marginal, decline of, 77–79, 94n4
Steering and Policy Committee, 113–14
Stewart, J.G., 126
Stimson, J.A., 20n3, 140–41
Stokes, D.E., 6, 24, 172, 176–77
Strategic policy, cozy triangles and, 203
Strom, G., 124, 214n2
Structural policy, cozy triangles and, 203
Styles of congressmen, 223–24. *See also*
Home styles, attentive
Subcommittees, 146–51. *See also* Cozy tri-
angles
"bill of rights," 157
congressional reform and, 113, 157–58
expansion of, 148
leadership, 101–2, 113
as leading drafters of legislative
measures and reports, 149
norms of reciprocity in, 132–33
Senate, 149–51
Subgovernments. *See* Cozy triangles
Subsidization, attentive home style and,
35–36. *See also* Resources
Sullivan, J.L., 178
Sun Belt Caucus, 153
Supreme Court, Roosevelt's attempt to
pack, 119
Surrey, S.S., 135
Survivorship rate of representatives, 70–
77
Swansborough, R., 34, 56

Taggart, W.A., 15
Tax legislation, logrolling associated
with, 128
Telephone and telegraph allowance, 36
Thomas, Albert (D–Tx.), 2
Thomas, M., 15
Thomas, R.D., 206
Time allocation
attentive home style and, 29–30
for constituent affairs, 22, 29–30
seniority and, 106–9
for legislative activities, 30
constituent perception of, 57

legislative scheduling, 30, 35, 38–39
as resource, 21–22
Toward a More Responsible Two-Party
System (report), 184
Tower, John (R–Tex.), 128
Trade legislation, reciprocal, 6
Trading, vote, 118. *See also* Bargaining
Traugott, M.W., 87, 189
Travel allowance, 36, 37
Triangles, cozy. *See* Cozy triangles
Truman, D.B., 5, 129
Truman, Harry S., 207
Trust, constituent, 24, 25, 48–49, 63nn3,
4. *See also* Confidence, public
Trustee role, 7
Turner, J., 5
Turnover, 65, 66–81. *See also* Stability in
congressional membership
in contemporary Congress, 66–68, 70–81
decline of marginal districts and states
and, 77–79
essential for policy change, 90
historical trends in, 66–70
in House, establishment of seniority system and, 111–12
independence of congressmen and, 16
lack of, 217, 236–37
survivorship rate of representatives and,
70–77

**Unanimous consent agreements,
43n5, 125**
Universalism, 135
Unpopularity of Congress, 45–64
denigration by congressmen and, 54, 59–
60, 61
media treatment and, 55, 60–61
perceptions of responsiveness and, 51–54
performance evaluations and, 49–51
policy consequences of, 56, 61–62
public confidence and, 46–49
public expectations and, 54, 55–58
reasons for, 54–61
trend in (1939–1984), 50
Uslaner, E.M., 94n7

Veteran Affairs Committee, 105
Veto power, ex post, 163n1
Vice president of United States, 96, 110
Vogler, D.J., 123, 124
Vote, standing, 233
Voters, representatives' perceptions of,
177
Vote trading, 118. *See also* Bargaining
Voting
coattail, 79–81
constituency representation and "justifiable," 181
floor. *See* Floor voting
ideological, 20n3
importance of party and constituency in, 5
with opposition party, costs of, 1
party, lack of, 190–93
split-ticket, 13, 14, 196
Voting bloc, 152, 156
influence of, 160
leadership of, 227

Voting cues, 20n3, 140–41, 145
  based on expertise, 159
  from committee memb…   7
  incumbency and, 83
  from state party del
Voting histories, 90
War chests, 87
Warwick, D.P.,
Washington Po
Watkins, Wes
Watson, Alber
Waxman, Her
Ways and Mea
Weingast, B., 1
Weisberg, H.F., 6, 90
Weissberg, R., 173

West, D., 24
West, W., 71–76
Westefield, L.P., 114
Whips, 98, 113, 225
White House, 224–25
  control by different party than Congress,
    80
Who's Who in America, 222
Who's Who in American Politics, 222
Wildavsky, A.,   0, 124
Williams, John   1 (D), 101
Wilson, Woodro   7, 117–18
  issel,   ., 66, 6
    me   .R., 70– 5
Wolanin, T.R., 101
Woll, P., 3